F818/218

JONATHAN CAPE
PAPERBACK
JCP 18

THE YOGI
AND THE COMMISSAR

D1027529

ARTHUR KOESTLER

The Yogi
and the Commissar

and other Essays

JONATHAN CAPE

THIRTY BEDFORD SQUARE LONDON

FIRST PUBLISHED 1945
THIS PAPERBACK EDITION FIRST PUBLISHED 1964

Condition of Sale

For copyright reasons, this
book may not be issued on
loan or otherwise except in
its original soft cover

*Printed in Great Britain by
Fletcher & Son Ltd, Norwich
and bound by
Richard Clay and Company Ltd, Bungay, Suffolk*

CONTENTS

To
Professor Michael Polanyi

PREFACE

I

SOME of the essays in this volume were originally written for American magazines where, one is told, each point has to be driven home with the sledgehammer; others for the polished columns of *Horizon* where the correct instrument to use is a nail-file. The disadvantage of collecting pieces of such different purpose and weight in one volume is the resulting patchiness; the advantage, variety.

This, however, refers only to the first two parts. Part Three, 'Explorations', containing a survey of the Soviet experiment and certain conclusions deriving from it, was written specially for this volume and has not been published before.

II

Some of these essays deal with rather complicated processes in politics and psychology, and are accordingly arduous and involved. I admire simplicity of style, but not if it leads to over-simplification or that kind of linguistic asceticism of the Ogden school which actually obscures the content. The far-fetched is often nearer to the truth than the short-cut of common sense. My comfort is what Einstein said when somebody reproached him with the suggestion that his formula of gravitation was longer and more cumbersome than Newton's formula in its elegant simplicity: 'If you are out to describe the truth, leave elegance to the tailor.'

III

Since my school-days I have not ceased to marvel each year at the fool I had been the year before. Each year brought its own revelation, and each time I could only think with shame and

PREFACE

rage of the opinions I had held and vented before the last initiation. This is still true to-day, but in a modified form. I am still unable to understand how I was able to bear last year's state of profound ignorance; but lately the new revelations, instead of shattering and destroying all that went before, seem to combine into a pattern sufficiently elastic to absorb the new material and yet with a certain consistency in its basic features. My justification for publishing this volume is the hope that an outline of this pattern may become recognizable through the variety of subjects treated and across the three-year span between the first essay and the last.

London
October 1944

ACKNOWLEDGMENTS

My grateful thanks are due to Mrs. Margaret Dewar for research work made on the essay *Soviet Myth and Reality*, and also to the editors of the following newspapers, magazines and periodicals for permission to include in this book essays which first appeared in their pages: *Horizon, Tribune*, the *Observer*, the *Evening Standard*, and the *New York Times Magazine*.

PART ONE

MEANDERINGS

I

THE YOGI AND THE COMMISSAR [1]

I. THE STATIC SPECTRUM

I LIKE to imagine an instrument which would enable us to break up patterns of social behaviour as the physicist breaks up a beam of rays. Looking through this sociological spectroscope we would see spread out under the diffraction-grating the rainbow-coloured spectrum of all possible human attitudes to life. The whole distressing muddle would become neat, clear and comprehensive.

On one end of the spectrum, obviously on the infra-red end, we would see the Commissar. The Commissar believes in Change from Without. He believes that all the pests of humanity, including constipation and the Oedipus complex, can and will be cured by Revolution; that is, by a radical reorganization of the system of production and distribution of goods; that this end justifies the use of all means. including violence, ruse, treachery and poison; that logical reasoning is an unfailing compass and the universe a kind of very large clockwork in which a very large number of electrons once set into motion will for ever revolve in their pre-dictable orbits; and that whosoever believes in anything else is an escapist. This end of the spectrum has the lowest frequency of vibrations and is, in a way, the coarsest component of the beam; but it conveys the maximum amount of heat.

On the other end of the spectrum, where the waves become so short and of such high-frequency that the eye no longer sees them, colourless, warmthless but all-penetrating, crouches the Yogi, melting away in the ultra-violet. He has no objection to calling the universe a clockwork, but he thinks that it could be

---

[1] First published in *Horizon*, June 1942.

called, with about the same amount of truth, a musical-box or a fishpond. He believes that the End is unpredictable and that the Means alone count. He rejects violence under any circumstances. He believes that logical reasoning gradually loses its compass value as the mind approaches the magnetic pole of Truth or the Absolute, which alone matters. He believes that nothing can be improved by exterior organization and everything by the individual effort from within; and that whosoever believes in anything else is an escapist. He believes that the debt-servitude imposed upon the peasants of India by the moneylenders should not be abolished by financial legislation but by spiritual means. He believes that each individual is alone but attached to the all-one by an invisible umbilical cord; that his creative forces, his goodness, trueness and usefulness can alone be nourished by the sap which reaches him through this cord; and that his only task during his earthly life is to avoid any action, emotion or thought which might lead to a breaking of the cord. This avoidance has to be maintained by a difficult, elaborate technique, the only kind of technique which he accepts.

Between these two extremes are spread out in a continuous sequence the spectral lines of the more sedate human attitudes. The more we approach its centre, the more does the spectrum become blurred and woolly. On the other hand, this increase of wool on the naked spectral bodies makes them look more decent, and intercourse with them more civilized. You cannot argue with a naked Commissar — he starts at once to beat his chest and next he strangles you, whether you be friend or foe, in his deadly embrace. You cannot argue with the ultra-violet skeleton either, because words mean nothing to him. You can argue with post-war planners, Fabians, Quakers, Liberals and Philanthropists. But the argument will lead nowhere, for the real issue remains between the Yogi and the Commissar, between the fundamental conceptions of Change from Without and Change from Within.

It is easy to say that all that is wanted is a synthesis — the synthesis between saint and revolutionary; but so far this has never been achieved. What has been achieved are various motley forms of compromise — the blurred intermediary bands of the spectrum: compromise but not synthesis. Apparently the two elements do not mix, and this may be one of the reasons why we have made such a mess of our History. The Commissar's emotional energies are fixed on the relation between individual and society, the Yogi's on the relation between the individual and the universe. Again it is easy to say that all that is wanted is a little mutual effort. One might as well ask a homosexual to make a little effort towards the opposite sex, and vice versa.

The Commissar's Dilemma

All attempts to change the nature of man by Commissar methods have so far failed, from Spartacus' Sun State through Inquisition and Reformation to Soviet Russia. This failure seems to be rooted in two disturbing phenomena which Kant could have called the Antinomies of Applied Reasoning. The first is the Antinomy of the Serpentine; the second the Antinomy of the Slopes.

The peak of Utopia is steep; the serpentine-road which leads up to it has many tortuous curves. While you are moving up the road you never face the peak, your direction is the tangent, leading nowhere. If a great mass of people are pushing forward along the serpentine they will, according to the fatal laws of inertia, push their leader off the road and then follow him, the whole movement flying off at a tangent into the nowhere. That is what happened to most revolutionary movements, where the mass-impulse is strong and the inertia of the mass is converted into a violent centrifugal force. In the more cautious reformist movements, on the other hand, the momentum soon fades out and the ascending spiral first becomes a weary circling round and round the peak without gaining in height until it finally degenerates into a descending spiral; e.g. the Trade Unionist movement.

The second root of failure is the Antinomy of the Slopes, or of Ends and Means. Either the Means are subordinated to the End, or vice versa. Theoretically you may build up elaborate liberal or religious half-way houses; but if burdened with responsibility, and confronted with a practical decision to be taken, you have to choose one way or the other. Once you have chosen you are on the slope. If you have chosen to subordinate the Means to the End, the slope makes you slide down deeper and deeper on a moving carpet of common-sense propositions; for instance: the right of self-defence — the best defence is attack — increase of ruthlessness shortens the struggle, etc. Another well-known slope-pattern starts with the 'Healer's Knife' and ends with the Moscow Purges. The fatal mechanism of this slope was already known to Pascal:

> Man is neither angel nor brute, and his misery is that he who would act the angel acts the brute.

The Yogi's Dilemma

The attempts to produce Change from Within on a mass-scale were equally unsuccessful. Whenever an attempt was made to organize saintliness by exterior means, the organizers were caught in the same dilemmas. The Inquisition flew off at a tangent; the Churches in the liberal era circle round and round the peak without gaining height. To subordinate the End to the Means leads to a slope as fatal as the inverse one. Gandhi's slope started with non-violence and made him gradually slide down to his present position of non-resistance to Japanese conquest: the Japanese might kill a few million Indians but some day they would get tired of it and thus the moral integrity of India would be saved.

Obviously the prospects for the masses of common people are not brighter under this inverted Machiavellianism than under the leadership of the Commissars. One slope leads to the Inquisition and the Purges; the other to passive submission to bayoneting and raping; to villages without sewage, septic childbeds and trachoma. The Yogi and the Commissar may call it quits.

II. THE SPECTRUM IN MOTION

But they don't. Unable to form a synthesis and unsatisfied by the patched-up compromises in the medium bands of the spectrum, they attract and repel each other in rhythmical intervals. This strange minuet is one of the more exciting aspects of History which Marxism, otherwise the most serviceable guide, falls short of explaining.

Under certain historic climates mass-migrations start from one end of the spectrum to the other, general displacements from infra-red to ultra-violet or vice versa, like mighty trade winds travelling over the seas. The nineteenth century brought such a general displacement towards the Commissar or infra-red end. The present climate favours the opposite direction. Since the early 'thirties we are all travelling, more or less consciously, more or less willingly, towards the ultra-violet end.

The less consciously we drift with the wind the more willingly we do it; the more consciously the less willingly. Personally I belong to the latter type; I wish one could still write an honest infra-red novel without an ultra-violet ending. But one can't, just as no honest scientist can now publish a book on physics without a metaphysical epilogue, no honest Socialist can write a survey of the Left's defeats without accounting for the irrational factor in mass-psychology. He who clings blindly to the past will be left behind; but he who abandons himself too readily will be carried away like a dry leaf; all one can do is to travel even more consciously and even less willingly.

But again, is such intentional readaptation possible? Are those who survive the great spectral displacements the fittest or merely the glibbest? Thinking of some fellow-writers who achieved the journey from the pink decade to the yogi decade with such monkey-like agility one is tempted to say: 'Let the dead bury their dead'. They answer: 'But we mean it' — and there is no doubt that, at least, they believe that they mean it. Yet what writer has ever written a line without at least meaning to mean it? Hence one first feels disgust with them; then one finds out that one was disgusted for the wrong reasons; and after that one is still disgusted because they were so quick to find the right reasons for their expatriation from the infra-red to the ultra-violet. In these matters clumsiness is respectable and glibness abject. They never seriously attempted to sail against the wind; they abandoned themselves to its first breeze, which broke them gently from their stems, and whirled them round and dropped them gently at the other end; that is perhaps why, when you hear their whisper, it sounds so much like the rattling of dead leaves.

For the political Commissars the spectral displacement has more tragic results than for the arty Commissars. I don't mean that they necessarily feel deeper about it; perhaps it is rather the other way round. In ages of distress when values crumble and survival has an ever so slight but still perceptible touch of glibness and betrayal, artists are often tempted by suicide but rarely commit it, whereas the revolutionary is rarely tempted by suicide, but when it happens it is because he has no other choice. In a sense spiritual life can be defined as the training for the acceptance of death; the Commissar is the human type least advanced in this training and yet by force of circumstances most advanced towards its aim.

Thus the artist shows the least resistance against being carried away; the revolutionary the greatest. Indeed the Commissar can be defined as the human type which has completely severed relations with the subconscious. This is the more remarkable as the constant danger under which he lives — I think Lenin used the phrase 'We are dead men on furlough' — is a constant temptation to communicate with those forbidden zones. In fact he is condemned to live in a permanent state of repressed puberty. While in a normal curriculum the great crisis of adolescence, the confrontation with the tragic and insoluble problems of existence occurs only once — a limited process, like teething — the revolutionary spends all his life in this tropical climate, and those tragic problems remain his daily bread and butter. The ordinary citizen, once the transcendental teething is over, evolves a smooth *modus vivendi* towards the absolute; the best the Commissar can hope is to find a smooth *modus moriendi*.

Yet though living in a climate of perpetual adolescence, his behaviour is as unadolescent, unecstatic and unromantic as can be imagined. One has the feeling that his subconscious has been dealt with not on the analyst's sofa but on the surgeon's table by the amputating knife. In fact one of his often recurring problems is not to give himself away by sleep-talking or other subconscious automatisms; and if he is a good Commissar he succeeds. He is a marvel of unneurotic repression: one of the most admirable achievements of the human species.

Now if life becomes impossible without pity, it is perhaps equally impossible without a grain of self-pity. The Commissar is not immune against suffering, but what he experiences is more the echo of pain than pain itself, like the aching of an amputated limb. He compels admiration, but also pity, that tender pity which the weak sometimes feel for the strong. Faced with giant figures like Blanqui, Luxemburg, Vera Figner, we can do nothing but shut up and realize what futile, frivolous dwarfs we are; yet pity remains.

That this instinct is justified becomes apparent when the Commissar faces the crisis of his life. This is a tragic and complicated process, often misunderstood. The forms it may take vary individually, but basically it is always the same: it is the revenge of the amputated organ. In a story of Gérard de Nerval's, which I remember only vaguely, a judge sentences a thief to have his hand cut off; the amputated hand then pursues the judge and finally strangles him. In the Commissar's case judge and victim are one person and the cut-off organ is not a hand; it is, if we examine it closer, the Yogi's umbilical cord, his means of communication with the Absolute, with the 'Oceanic Feeling', to use Freud's sober term. The Commissar lived in the conviction that it was a luxury-organ, but when the crisis comes he realizes that it is not. The Man-Society connection suddenly proves to be not enough to procure psychic metabolism; the Man-Universe connection has to be re-established.

At this point one of two things might happen. Either the cut connection is re-established, and as an act of atonement the Man-Society connection broken off; this is the classical case of the Revolutionary turning into a Mystic, the total jump from Commissar to Yogi. Or the connection is *not* re-established — then the dead cord coils up and strangles its owner. This is the equally classical case of the ex-revolutionaries whose souls died of suffocation. They might appear as cadaverous as Sinowjew at the Moscow trials; or satanic and cynical like Laval and Doriot; or as impotent and desiccated as the Left party-bureaucracy. Since Rosa Luxemburg there has arisen no man or woman endowed with both the Oceanic feeling and the momentum of action.

Unfortunately we have as yet no scientific terminology to describe these processes, which are of vital importance for the understanding of the 'subjective factor' in History. Hence the more soberly one tries to describe them the more vague imagery one has, *faute de mieux*, to use. The enormous literature of the three main contemporary schools in psychology contains not a single case-history of this conversion, the revolutionary's transformation into a cynic or mystic, whereas history, past and present, abounds in examples. Jung comes nearest to the question: his interpretation of the subconscious bears most resemblance to the 'umbilical cord', but he prefers to study its effects on the most unsuitable human type, the wealthy middle-aged Babbitts. And this for good reason: were he to choose his patients among the type which inhabits the German or Russian concentration camps, not only would his therapy prove to be inadequate but he would have to introduce so many new determining factors into his system that both his terminology and his *Weltanschauung* would go to blazes. The Commissar's spectral displacements are *terra nova* for the psychologist.

Turning to the more muddled, intermediary bands of the spectrum we find that their reactions to the mystic current are of a revealing nature. In the pink regions the reaction first manifests itself by an intense consciousness of the Left's serial defeats, of disgust with the old parties, disgust with their worn-out leaders, with plans and promises, ideas and ideals, and most of all with one's own foolish and frustrated hopes. This pink hangover is the emotional starting point. Next comes the realization that 'there must have been something basically wrong in our approach to the Masses'. Next to this the discovery that on the very point where they failed — activation of the masses — Fascism was horribly successful. Now the feeling which success inspires in the unsuccessful is envy. If we look at things closely we find indeed that the pink attitude to Fascism is envy rather than hatred.

There is one definite profiteer of the spectral displacement: the Scientist. In a certain sense it was he who started the movement; then its momentum carried him further than he probably liked. One should remember that the irrational or ultra-violet element which so strongly taints present-day physics, biology and psychology, was not a philosophical fashion smuggled into the laboratories, but grew out of the laboratories themselves and created the new philosophical climate. The most striking example is the development of physics which was an enormously successful rational Commissar-science up to the closing years of the last century and has since become more and more of a Yogi-science. Matter, substance, time, space, causality, precision of measurement and the belief in the predictability of behaviour of the Measured, have run like sand through the physicist's fingers until nothing remained but a group of formal statements of this type: 'If a small poker-dice is so constructed that we have no reason to assume a preference on its part for falling on the ace-side, then we are entitled to expect that, in the course of a great number of casts, it will show no preference for falling on the ace-side.' This is undeniably a precise statement, but a rather modest one in relation to our hunger for the mysteries of the Universe to be explained to us. The modern physicist of course denies that his task should be to 'explain' anything, and he takes a masochistic delight in producing formulae which establish with precision the degree of imprecision in his statements, i.e. the inadequacy of physics not only to explain, but even to describe what exactly is going on in the physical world. Some time ago Laplace thought that if a superior intelligence counted all atoms and their velocities at a given moment he could predict all future events to the end of the world, including the brand of Mr. Churchill's cigars. Physicists and Philosophers of the last Commissar period tried to jolly around the fatalistic trap of physical determinism, but there was no escape from it. In nineteenth-century physics the world was running down like a clockwork without any freedom, except the arbitrariness of the initial state and of the initial choice of a certain set of 'Natural Laws' which governed the mechanism. In twentieth-century physics this initial arbitrariness or freedom is evenly distributed in minute quantities over all possible cross-sections in time and space; the initial creation has become a *creatio continua*. 'Freedom' or 'arbitrariness' are of course merely terms to indicate the presence of factors which cannot be described or accounted for in the physicist's terminology. Nineteenth-century physics describes a sharply defined world with a blurred initial stage; contemporary physics describes an evenly blurred world, like a film with coarse granulation. (The granulation being indicated by the Quantum of Action 'h' and defined in Heisenberg's Uncertainty Principle.) Whether we describe this world as 'Pantheistic', 'Free', 'Undetermined', 'Statistical', 'Spiritual' or 'Voluntaristic' is more or less a matter of taste. What really matters is that the physicist's instruments of measurement indicate the presence of physically immeasurable factors. And this is the reason why the physicist travels perhaps more consciously than anybody else towards the ultra-violet.[1]

[1] I am talking of the Scientist, not of the Charlatan. If Commissar-journalese of the Communist pamphlet type is bad, Yogi-journalese of the Gerald Heard type is worse. Both discredit the idea they stand for; but while in the first case the defendant may plead that according to his convictions efficient propaganda always includes a certain amount of charlatanism, in the second case this defence cannot be made. Here are a few examples of Yogi-journalese:

'Elijah also acts as a telepathic secret-service agent for the king of Israel' (Gerald Heard, *Pain, Sex and Time*, p. 129). 'Moses we know was married. He could not, therefore, have used complete sex sublimation as a technique for enlarging consciousness.' (Ibid., p. 123.) 'Though, therefore, Vaijroli may seem to offer a secondary path to those who say they cannot sublimate, if "Right Contemplation", Samadhi (the words are the same in Pali) non-personal consciousness (ecstasis: ἐποπτεία) is not only possible but the actual getting into the next evolutionary stage of consciousness, then surely we must aim at nothing else, and the problem of sex, by this and by this only, finds at last its solution.' (Ibid., p. 229.) So much for the form; an analysis of the contents would require more space but lead to equally discouraging results.

MEANDERINGS

III. THE PENDULUM

The Commissar, the Artist, the vague Man of Goodwill, the Scientist, not only seem to react in different ways to the great spectral displacement, but their motives for participating in it seem also different in nature. Is there a common reason for this pilgrimage? To a certain extent the revolution in physics has certainly affected the artist, the revolution in psychology has influenced political outlook, and similar cross-influences are easy to discover. They form a pattern of diagonal lines of forces, but this pattern is that of a network, not of a causal chain. There is no causal chain running from Quantum Mechanics to the self-accusations of Bucharin, but in an indirect way they are all linked together by diagonals. We cannot ask for a common reason, we can only ask for a common denominator in the variety of reasons.

In the critical years of the Weimar Republic, when a Communist or Fascist Revolution seemed equally possible and the only im-possibility the continuation of the worn-out regime, a certain Ernst Juenger coined the phrase of the 'anti-capitalistic nostalgia of the masses'. This vague but violent longing was indeed shared by groups of people of otherwise very different tendencies. Per-haps the common denominator we are looking for can best be described as an 'anti-materialistic nostalgia'. It is allergic to the rationalism, the shallow optimism, the ruthless logic, the arrogant self-assurance, the Promethean attitude of the nineteenth century; it is attracted by mysticism, romanticism, the irrational ethical values, by medieval twilight. In short it is moving towards the very things from which the last-but-one great spectral displace-ment towards the infra-red has moved away. Apparently these movements have a pendular rhythm.

The swinging of this pendulum from rationalistic to romantic periods and back is not contradictory to the conception of a basic dialectic movement of History. It is like the tidal waves on a river which yet flows into the sea. One of the fatal lacunae in the Marxist interpretation of history is that it was only concerned with the course of the river, not with the waves. The mass-psychological aspect of Nazism is not describable in Marxist terms, in terms of the river's course; we need the tidal waves to account for it. On the other hand our pendulum alone is no guide to history. We must know about the river before we talk of the waves.

Perhaps it is not too hazardous to assume that these pendular changes in the mass-psychological spectrum are a process analogous to the rhythmical change of waking and sleep in the individual. The irrational or romantic periods of mass-psychology are periods of sleep and dream. The dreams are not necessarily peaceful; more often they are nightmares; but without these periodic plunges into the subconscious the vital juices would not be provided for the next wideawake Promethean or Commissar period. Perhaps every Gothic period is followed by a Renaissance period and they are but the succession of yoga-nights and commissar-days in the curriculum of the race. And perhaps this, our present civilization, is not dying, only sleepy.

MEANDERINGS

11

THE FRENCH 'FLU[1]

THE people who administer literature in this country — literary editors, critics, essayists: the managerial class on Parnassus — have lately been affected by a new outbreak of that recurrent epidemic, the French 'Flu. Its symptoms are that the patient, ordinarily a balanced, cautious, sceptical man, is lured into un-conditional surrender of his critical faculties when a line of French poetry or prose falls under his eyes. Just as in the case of hay-fever one whiff is sufficient to release the attack, thus a single word like *'bouillabaisse'*, *'crève-cœur'*, *'patrie'* or *'midinette'* is enough to produce the most violent spasms: his eyes water, his heart contracts in bitter-sweet convulsions, his ductless glands swamp the bloodstream with adolescent raptures. If an English poet dares to use words like 'my fatherland', 'my soul', 'my heart', etc., he is done for; if a French one dispenses musical platitudes about *la Patrie*, *la France*, *mon cœur* and *mon âme*, the patient begins to quiver with admiration.

Three works have come during the last year out of France, all three celebrated as literary revelations: Gide's *Imaginary Interviews*, Aragon's volume of poems *Le Crève-Cœur*, and Vercors' *Le Silence de la Mer*. I have read the Gide interviews carefully, nay, greedily: with the greed one would listen to news from the planet Mars. It was distressing reading. Gide's writings have always shown a touch of esoteric arrogance; there is a thin, rarefied atmosphere about him and his books. His influence on the younger French generation was deplorable (not because of his twisted eroticism, for which the Vichy Fascists reproached him: one does not become an invert by reading books), but because of the arrogant spiritualism it imparted, an attitude of being initiated, the illusion of belonging to some exclusive order, of sharing some exquisite values, which, however, if you tried to define them, ran like sand through your

[1] First published in *Tribune*, November 1943.

21

fingers. Gide's message to the young intelligentsia was like the Emperor's new clothes: nobody dared to confess that he could not see them.

These young middle-class Frenchmen lived in a split world of *le bifteck* and *l'esprit*; they counterbalanced their self-indulgence and cynicism with the excuse that all this could not touch their spiritual existence, their sharing of what they called '*le génie français*'; by day they dealt in secondhand cars, at night they donned the emperor's clothes. Judged by his *Imaginary Interviews* Gide has changed little, if not for the worse. There is the same ethereal boredom, a pale fluorescence which throws no shadow and has no substance behind it. I read them some months ago and cannot remember a single phrase or thought; the sand has run away and all that remains is some vague fragrance. Yet if the word 'message' applied to literature has any meaning, it is this, that its gist should remain in your memory, after the words have faded.

About Louis Aragon, we read in the preface to *Le Crève-Cœur*:

> I first met him [Aragon] on a summer evening at the fair of Neuilly, where he and the youthful band of Surrealists, their white cravats luminous in the dark, were paying court to the only woman in the world for them, the charming and intelligent Femme-Tronc, who, without arms or legs, revolved on a pedestal, like a bust, and autographed her photo with a pen in her mouth. He was small, pale, highly strung, with cold eyes, and a shock of dark hair brushed back from a fine brow. Later he went off on the Surrealist expedition to the Marquesas Islands, to which they were commanded by a dream. After a period of disillusion and self-disgust he ... broke with Surrealism on political grounds and joined the more impersonal Communist Party.

For all this, he could still be an excellent poet, and nobody would care about his private and political past; yet the propagators of the French 'Flu feel driven to present Aragon not only as a poet but as a hero and martyr of the Left. They tell us that 'he was arrested for an anti-military poem, went to Russia ...' etc., and that when the war broke out was 'as a Communist placed in a post of particular danger ...' Now the truth is that Aragon's career as a Communist was rather in the surrealist tradition. He toured the Spanish front in a loudspeaker-van dispensing poetry to the militiamen at the time when Malraux organized the International Squadron of the Republican Air Force, and Cornford and Ralph Fox died at the front. I do not mean that all writers should have imitated their example, I only mean that if words have any meaning, *they* were the heroes and martyrs and not the Aragon-type. His arrest 'for an anti-military poem' was a one-day farce; he did not go to Russia as a fugitive as we are given to understand, but as a tourist to speak at a Writers' Congress; he was not placed 'in a post of particular danger', but served as a junior officer in the Medical Corps — where he doubtless did his duty as many others did. I repeat, nobody expects that writers should be heroes, and that Isherwood, for example, should join the Commandos; but the struggle of the Left is no operetta, and the dressing-up of operetta-heroes, which is another symptom of the French 'Flu, makes one feel very nasty indeed, if for no other reason than respect for our dead.

Besides the poems, *Le Crève-Cœur* contains an essay by Aragon, called 'The Rhyme in 1940', which is highly revealing. The author tells us about a number of innovations which he introduced into French poetry; the first is the return from rhymeless to rhymed poetry, which in some surrealist way is linked for him with the French defeat:

> We are writing 1940. I lift my voice and say that it is not true that there are no new rhymes when there is a new world. Who has so far introduced into French poetry the language of the radio or that of the non-Euclidean geometries? (op. cit. p. 45).

And so on. We have heard all this (the use of technical and scientific terms in poems) in the 'thirties from the New Writing group; and Auden's genius made us accept it, whether we agreed in principle or not. Aragon's revelations were always a decade too late: he discovered Communism during the Moscow purges and the lyricism of the non-Euclidean geometries during the French defeat. His second discovery is to do away with punctuation, which makes his sentences all melt into one lump, like chocolates gone soft in your pocket. The third is what are technically called 'imperfect rhymes' (e.g. move — love). Now poets ever since Donne and Goethe have used imperfect rhymes if they couldn't help it — but they never tried to convert a shortcoming into a philosophy; and they certainly never quoted their own miscarried strophes as examples to be imitated, as Aragon does, for instance, with the following specimen:

> Parler d'amour c'est parler d'elle et parler d'elle
> C'est toute la musique et ce sont les jardins
> Interdite où Renaud s'est épris d'Armide et l'
> Aime sans en rien dire absurde paladin . . .

If you don't know French, never mind; the point is that *d'elle* is made to rhyme with *et l'*, which is as if in English you perpetrated the following rhyme:

> . . . . . . rain
> . . . . . . ain'
> t it a pity. . . .

He then quotes a number of further examples of his new rhymes (ivresse — est-ce; Ourcq — vautour — cour), which makes one's hair bristle, and concludes with his usual modesty:

> I shall now stop my examples, convinced of having shown the way to all seekers of new poetic equations, and already anticipating those acquiescent nods, by which, in the spring of 1941, similar considerations will be received. . . .

So far, Aragon's own comments to *Le Crève-Cœur*. As to the poems themselves, they make, given the background of our nostalgia for France, extremely melodious reading. First of all, each line ends in a rhyme, a pleasure which we have been deprived of for a long time. Secondly, they are in French, i.e. they melt in one's mouth like Turkish Delight. 'L'usage du cabinet est interdit pendant l'arrêt du train en gare', means only that you should not use the toilet while the train is standing in a station, but it sounds like the pure harmonics of the spheres, especially if you have been cut off from the Continent for four years. For the frustrated lover of France even the names of Paris underground stations (Vavin, Les Buttes Chaumont, Réaumur-Sevastopol, Porte des Lilas) become the nostalgia-imbued stimuli of conditioned reflexes: first there is that flutter and twitch of the heart, then the mucus of the French 'Flu begins to flow. Stripped of these nostalgia-reflexes and associated over- and under-tones, to the nakedness in which an English poet faces his infallible reviewers, Aragon would probably be judged as a competent craftsman, one among the larger frogs of the smaller puddles, who 'on condition that he succeeded in ridding himself of his mannerisms, facile stunts, his sometimes abstract, sometimes maudlin imagery, and so on, might [pat on the shoulder] one day become a very good poet'. But to call *Crève-Cœur* 'the S O S of all Europe', as has been done, is an insult to Europe and a blasphemy of the dead.

Finally, there is Vercors' *Le Silence de la Mer*. Its author is said to be a well-known French writer hiding behind a pseudonym. The story runs as follows:

A German officer is billeted in a French house in which live an old man and his niece. The officer's name is Werner von Ebrennac. He is a musician, a composer, young, beautiful, cultured, extremely sensitive; he admires and loves France, knows the French classics inside out, and is convinced that the war will end in an eternal reconciliation, a kind of spiritual marriage between Germany and France, under the cultural tutelage of the latter. This is what he talks about, in a low, modest, pleasant voice, his back to the fire of the sitting-room, during all the winter of 1940-41, to the old man and his niece; in spite of the fact that these two never speak a word, never open their mouths, and for over a hundred winter evenings listen to his monologues in the stony silence of deaf-mutes, the old man smoking his pipe, the niece stitching away on some embroidery. Finally Werner goes on leave to Paris, finds out that the Nazis are beasts (in spite of being a supporter of the Weimar Republic, cultured, extremely sensitive, etc. etc., this has never occurred to him before), and decides in despair to get himself killed by volunteering for the Russian front. On announcing his decision, the niece (who is of course in love with him as he is with her) speaks her first and last word to him — 'Adieu'. The story is told by the old man in the first person singular.

Now take this story first from the psychological angle. Can you imagine a sensitive man going on talking for over one hundred nights to people who cut him and never answer? On the second evening, at the latest, his nerves would go to pieces and he would either do something hysterical, e.g. shake the old man by his shoulders, or slam the door, go to his own room and never enter the sitting-room again. Similar considerations apply to the behaviour of the girl and the old man during those 'more than hundred nights'.

Psychologically the whole story is phoney, but politically it is worse. Every word and thought of this enlightened aristocrat is diametrically opposed to Nazism; but the author obviously hates the term anti-Fascist, hates the idea that a man's loyalty to a political conviction may override his patriotic loyalties. Therefore von Ebrennac becomes a kind of schizophrene or sleep-walker, who, in spite of his versatile intelligence has apparently never read a speech of Hitler's, nor seen a newspaper in the ten years between the Reichstag fire and the attack on Poland. Only thus can the contradiction be solved, can all the social implications be dodged, and the issues of the present war reduced to a woolly, patriotic Franco-German allegory in terms of 1870 or rather 1815.

The most exasperating thing in this booklet is its mixture of inferiority complex and arrogance. If ever there was a noble, well-meaning, unselfish friend of France, it is this wish-dream-hero von Ebrennac who carries his devotion to the point of suicide.

Then why punish him with that stupid and arrogant silence? Only because this enlightened anti-Nazi was born of German parents? Here we have the uncannily precise repetition in 1942 of the mentality which in 1939 sent the German anti-Fascists in France to concentration camps. M. Vercors has learnt as little as the squabbling French politicians in exile. Suffering has not necessarily a purifying effect; psychological shocks may produce diametrically opposed results. And it is time that the admirers of the great cultural tradition of France learned to discriminate between the halo of the real martyrs and the prismatic delusions of their own 'flu-smarting eyes.

Others who could legitimately speak in the name of France are silent. They know, as the Chinese proverb says, that there is a time to go out fishing and a time to dry the nets. But there is a black market in literature, on which human sacrifice, struggle and despair are commercialized, and the spirit is turned into hooch. All this literary ballyhoo gives about as true a picture of the common people of France as Hollywood of the underground movement in Europe. It is of no service to the French case, and it dangerously sidetracks people's attention from the real problems which we shall have to face.

THE YOGI AND THE COMMISSAR

III

THE NOVELIST'S TEMPTATIONS [1]

I

ONE of the great Russians — I think it was Turgeniev — could
write only with his feet in a bucket of hot water under his desk,
facing the open window of his room. I believe that this position is
typical for the novelist. The hot water bucket stands for inspiration, the subconscious, the creative source, or whatever you like
to call it. The open window stands for the world outside, the raw
material for the artist's creation.

Let us for once ignore the hot water bucket and assume that our
novelist is a genuine artist, endowed with creative force; and let us
instead concentrate on the open window and its influence on the
man behind his desk.

The first and strongest temptation which the world outside the
window exerts on the writer is to draw the curtains and close the
shutters. Now this apparently so simple reaction has various
interesting aspects. Perhaps the most dangerous one is that the
gesture seems so natural. The writer needs concentration; his
nerves are easily upset. He must make an immense and ever-
renewed effort to bear the open window, to let those piercing
screams into the room, the laughter, the groaning, and those
ephemeral battlecries.

Another aspect of the temptation to close the window is that it
does not at all resemble the traditional form of temptation, but
rather the opposite. The tempter does not appeal to base mortal
desires but to the loftiest regions of the spirit. His lures are: Peace,
Beauty, perhaps even communion with God. The fiend does not
ask you for your soul, he wants to make you a gift of it. He
whispers: 'Shut the window. The world is a hopeless case. Action

[1] Speech at the 17th International Congress of the P.E.N. Club, September
1941.

is evil. Responsibility is evil. Draw the curtains, forget those savage battlecries, fill your ears with stillness and bathe your smarting eyes in the dim light of eternity.'

Behind the closed shutters strange and sometimes beautiful constructions come to life, the growths of the hothouse, plots and characters hatched in the hothouse. The ivory tower was only one passing form of closed-shutter-interior. There are others; for the decoration of the room with the drawn curtains is, strangely enough, subject to the fashion of the time, although fashion and time itself are supposed to be locked out. The ivory tower was an aesthete's creation; others are modelled on ethic principles. Their inhabitants don't fiddle while Rome burns, they pray. The room with the drawn curtains may be changed into the nave of a cathedral where the bearded Russian novelist sings hymns of atonement for his revolutionary past; or a sort of introspective deep-sea-aquarium populated by monsters in phosphorescent light; or the padded cell of Maupassant and Gérard de Nerval. The latest transformation seems to be an exotic hermitage fit for yogi exercises. It almost looks as if the Pink Decade were to be followed by a Yogi Decade. So much about temptation No. 1.

In temptation No. 2 the action of the open window on the novelist is experienced not in the form of pressure but of suction. The man behind his desk is tempted not to close the shutters but to lean right out of the window. He is so fascinated by the events in the street that he begins to gesticulate, shout, and declaim. Before, we had the case of an unimpaired creative force, but no vision of reality; here we have the case of a boiling-hot vision undigested by the creative process. In leaning too far out of the window our author has taken his feet out of the hot water bucket; in technical terms, he has ceased to be a novelist and become a reporter. This seems to be the reason for the failure of many prose writers of the Pink Decade. It was a period in which novels read like dispatches by war correspondents from the fronts of the class struggle. The characters seemed to be flat, two-dimensional beings, fighting their shadow battles against a lurid background. People in the pink novel had a class-dimension (length) plus, say, a sex-dimension (width); the third, irrational dimension (depth) was missing or atrophied.

In the post-pink or yogi decade the irrational dimension takes its revenge by outgrowing all others. The few authors who have survived the pink era are those who, even in the thick of the battle, never forgot the irrational dimension — e.g. Silone and Malraux. But they are exceptions.

Apparently it is very difficult to keep the window open and your feet in the hot water bucket at the same time. Therefore most novelists, past and present, adopt a compromise, and this compromise is the essence of temptation No. 3.

In this case the window is neither open nor closed but left ajar, and the curtains are drawn in such a way as to expose only a limited section of the world outside while hiding the more painful and menacing sights from the author's eye. He may even push a telescope through a hole in the curtain and thus obtain an image with admirably sharp contours of a small and perhaps not very important fraction of the world. Works of incontestable merit can thus be produced in spite of the fact that they are made of fragments only of the phenomena outside — there is love without sex, work without sweat, class distinction without envy, melancholia without constipation. The telescope may also be focused in another direction, or the left window opened instead of the right — then we get sex without love and a sharp telescopic image of constipation, hatred, and sweat. And again works of merit have been produced with this fragmentary optic. Why then call this so successful method a 'succumbing to temptation' and why insist on the fully open window? Because the hole-in-the-curtain method may produce occasional masterpieces of technical virtuosity as in the Victorian novel or in the naturalistic novel, but inevitably leads to a dead end in the development of the novel as an art. Our admiration for Dickens or Zola always has a slight taint of benevolent indulgence.

Indeed, the term 'temptation' presupposes the existence of a road leading to a certain end, a road to perfection from which the tempter tries to lure us to side-tracks. To yield does not necessarily involve artistic failure; but I do believe that there is a main road leading from *Ulenspiegel* and *Don Quixote* to *War and Peace*, *The Magic Mountain*, and *Fontamara*. And I also believe that *Tristram Shandy*, and *Wuthering Heights*, *Swann's Way*, and *The Waves*, are masterpieces at dead ends.

To justify this apparently arbitrary distinction, let us return to our window and watch our fallen author at work. His curtains are closed, but he has made a tiny circular hole in the fabric, with a telescope pushed through, focused on a house and a garden, and a girl with a bunch of roses in her hands, waiting for her betrothed. She is not necessarily the wishdream-girl of suburban circulating libraries — she may be a very sophisticated young lady with, in her free left hand, a volume of Proust. 'Isn't she lovely?' asks our author — who may be a very good author recommended by the Book Society — 'isn't she *alive*? Her name is Sylvia.' And indeed we must admit that house, garden, girl, and roses are perfectly lifelike in spite of the fact that they were produced by the hole-in-the-curtain method. We watch them with admiration until about page twenty-five; and then we horrify the author with the question: 'Excuse us, but haven't you forgotten the factory chimney in the background, the splitting of the atom, Voronoff's apes, and the concentration camps?' 'Are you crazy?' retorts our author, 'do you expect me to drag a German refugee into my picture, with scars on his back?'

The answer, of course, is no. We do not want him to *drag* anything into the picture, not even a chimney as background; that would not help. But there is an alternative in our minds which does require an answer if Sylvia is to be not a puppet but a real being, living in this century, now and here. The alternative is this: either she knows about the concentration camps and still goes on standing there with roses in her hand, then this adds an important feature to her character — not necessarily a derogative feature, but an important one. Or she has never heard or read about them — then this again gives us a cue. And these cues are essential because they show us her relations, or absence of relations, to the essential facts of her time. But these essentials being shielded from the author by the curtain with the one tiny hole — how can he show her to us in true proportion? We do not miss the factory chimney in the picture — we miss it in the author's mind.

The absence of background (not in the picture itself but in the author's mind) makes the house, the garden, and Sylvia with her roses, appear as a half-truth, a lie. It is the author's ignorance of what is going on behind the veiled parts of the window which deprives the picture of its width and depth, of perspective and proportion, and which makes me feel that, the longer we look at the young lady in her garden, the more she resembles a wax figure at Madame Tussaud's.

The perfect novel, then, indeed presupposes a totally open window, and that the author should have an all-embracing knowledge of the essential currents and facts (including statistics), of the ideas and theories (including the natural sciences) of his time. This knowledge is not for actual use — that would produce an encyclopedia, not a novel. It is for use by implication. It has to act as a catalytic agent, as the saliva in the process of creative assimilation. Without it, the characters will be distorted and the story arbitrary like a Victorian plot. The act of creation presupposes omniscience.

III

But is not all this rather abstract? In hundreds of novels, with some quite good novels among them, the young lady still stands triumphantly in her garden and still clasps those roses in her outstretched hand. Our objection to her was that the author did not, or did not want to, see her in the perspective of her environment, the world of the split atom and the flame-throwers. But what if the narrow surroundings which conditioned her character bear in fact no relation whatever to those unpleasant events which we obstinately call the essentials? Do not millions of Sylvias exist unscorched by flame-throwers and the problems of their time? And is it not possible to write quite good books about them?

Let us imagine a human being living on an island isolated from the rest of the world, and with no knowledge of the rest of the world. His *real* character is of course conditioned by his immediate environment. Yet as a *novel* character the most interesting thing about him will be his ignorance of the essentials of his time, his (negative) relation to the background. We see him in the specific novel-perspective: that is, *we know more about him than he knows about himself.* We have included in our vision the background of the towns, mountains, and rivers unknown to him; and only by seeing him in proportion to these towns, rivers, and mountains did we give him novel-life. In other words: his novel-character is conditioned not by his narrow island-surroundings which condition his real life, but by distant surroundings with which he has no point of contact whatever. If I cut these distant surroundings out of my mind he will in reality be still alive, but for the novel he is dead. And are the concentration camps, the factory chimneys, and the flame-throwers less real or significant than the rivers and mountains?

The law of the novel-perspective prescribes that it is not enough for the author to create 'real life', he must also locate its geometrical place in a co-ordinate system, the axes of which are represented by the dominating facts, ideas, and tendencies of his time; he must fix its position in an n-dimensional space-time continuum. The real Sylvia spins around the centre of a narrow family-vortex of conditioning factors, whereas the author, in promoting her to novel life, places her in the centre of a vortex formed by the great trade winds, typhoons, depressions, and hurricanes of her time. Of course he need not describe or even mention them. But implicitly they must be there.

Only this way, it seems, can the novelist keep on the main road,

33

avoid the side-tracks and dead ends. His greatness is in direct proportion to the width and depth of his vision. His window has to be filled with an all-embracing view even if his subject is only a garden with a girl in it. His ears have to be filled with the harmonies and discords of the great symphony, even if his attention is concentrated on the voice of a single flute. 'Where there is hope in the air he will hear it; where there is agony about he will feel it.' (C. Day Lewis.)

IV

Being a contemporary of ours, what he feels will be mainly agony. In other periods it may seem that to care for politics is a temptation for the artist. In periods like the present the temptation is not to care for politics.

Yet whatever his convictions may be, any idea — political, philosophical, scientific — has novel-life and *raison d'être* only if assimilated by the characters of the novel. In the true novel, as opposed to reportage and chronicle, the main action takes place inside the character's skull and ribs. Thus both facts and ideas are conveyed only after a double process of digestion.

It is a strange and sometimes painful process. When I think of the species Novelist, I am always reminded of certain strange practices of the Australian white ant. The normal ants of this species are not able to benefit by the food within their reach owing to an insufficiency of their digestive apparatus. They would all die of starvation but for the existence of certain specialized workers who gather the harvest, devour and digest the food, and feed all the others, the queen, the workers, and the winged adults, with the contents of their stomach. In some species these workers never leave the nest; they hang head downwards in the dark vaults and tunnels of the termitary, and in the absence of other receptacles, become living reservoirs, cisterns, honey-pots — with enormous elastic, distended bellies into which the harvest is poured, to be pumped out when folk are hungry.

34

Hanging head downwards in the dark vaults of our termitary, feeding warriors and winged adults with the assimilated products of a bitter and poisonous harvest, the artist of to-day is inclined towards rather sinister thoughts. At times he feels as if he were the only adult surrounded by beings still at the stage of befouling themselves. Hence his urge and duty in a world where nobody is well: *the duty not to accept.*

In fact all the temptations I mentioned have one common denominator: the temptation to accept. To close the window 'pour embrasser l'absolu', means to accept the madness outside as incurable, to shirk responsibility. To leave the window ajar and hide the more unpleasant sights means acceptance by complacency. Complacency is passive complicity, and in this sense all art is propaganda, by omission or commission. But only in this sense. Conscious propaganda means the artist's abdication and is only another form of escape — escape into the happy fields of dilettantism where all problems and difficulties are easily solved.

The artist is no leader; his mission is not to solve but to expose, not to preach but to demonstrate. 'We make out of our quarrels with others rhetoric, but with our quarrels with ourselves, poetry,' said Yeats. The healing, the teaching and preaching he must leave to others; but by exposing the truth by special means unavailable to them, he creates the emotional urge for healing.

Thus the writer has a definite social task and function to fulfil. When embarking on a novel the author is not unlike the captain of a vessel setting out on a voyage with sealed orders in his pocket. But when he opens the envelope after having put out to sea, he finds that the order is written in invisible ink. Unable to read it, he is yet constantly aware of a duty to perform. For he is a captain of a warship, not of a pleasure-cruiser. The indecipherable yet imperative orders in his pocket fill him with the consciousness of his responsibility. This is the greatness of the writer's mission; this is his predicament.

THE READER'S DILEMMA[1]

DEAR Corporal Jeff,

I received your alarming letter and shall try my best to answer it. You write:

> I am twenty-two. Before I was called up I was a radio mechanic in L. I am writing to you to ask you which reviewer's column I should read to have a reliable guide for buying books. I can only afford to buy one book a month, and I am putting aside 2s. a week for it. I read the *News Chronicle* and sometimes I get hold of *Tribune* or the *New Statesman*. But, mostly, the reviews are a bit too clever for me ... There is hardly anybody in my unit interested in books ... Our camp is on a rather lonely site. ...

People will probably think that to call your letter 'alarming' is exaggerated. I don't think it is. For.I am only partly concerned with the technical question in your letter, and mainly with the pathetic appeal which I read between its lines. As an army lecturer during the last three years I have come across hundreds of men in your condition and of your type: the 'Thoughtful Corporal belt' of the conscript army. Reliable and serious-minded, you soon get your two stripes, but, except in the R.A.F., rarely the third. While I was reading your letter you began to take bodily shape for me, though I have never met you. I imagined seeing you, on Saturday afternoons, scanning the dismal Y.M.C.A. library, or asking the lymphatic girl at the W. H. Smith bookstall for a Penguin which is out of print. You feel vaguely attracted by Common Wealth and Federal Union, while the name of the Labour Party tastes to you like stale beer; you keep a diary at irregular intervals, plan to write a short story on army life for *Tribune* or *New Writing*, and at lectures ask carefully-

[1] First published in *Tribune*, April 1944.

prepared questions about the Curzon Line and how to re-educate the Germans. Some years ago you were a subscriber to the Left Book Club, but gave it up because of that same taste of staleness on your tongue and/or because of the Stalin-Hitler pact. At dances you pick out a serious girl who is, alas, mostly skinny and anaemic and, in contradiction to the law of supply and demand, more virtuous than her prettier sisters. You see your future in a rather grim perspective of W.E.A. evening classes, night reading, and an elaborate saving plan for a week's visit to France. You do not envy the rich but you bitterly resent poverty. 'Class struggle' is for you an abstract term, and 'barricades' a romantic word associated with Paris and the last century. The common denominator of your thoughts and emotions is one enormous, grey, brooding mass of frustration.

But we shall return to your personal problem later; first let us deal with your technical question. There is a short answer to it and a long one. The short one is: for fiction read Betjeman in the *Herald*; for non-fiction the *Observer*'s book page; and if you want to check by a more detailed review, take the *Listener*. Their judgment is not infallible but generally sound and independent; they are to the point, neither facetious nor dull; they rarely miss an important book; and that is all that matters to you. And now to the longer answer.

First of all, I believe that criticism in this country is on the whole not too badly off compared with other countries. In Russia, for instance, the line of literature is decreed by government spokesmen, and literary debates are spiced with accusations of 'counter-revolutionary deviations'; to give Gide a bad review during the ballyhoo of his Moscow visit would have meant 'Sabotaging the International Cultural Relations of the U.S.S.R.'; to give him a good review after he became a heretic would have been equally suicidal for reviewer and editor. A leading literary organizer in Moscow (J. R. Becher) once told me: 'We build up the reputations of writers whom we think useful; we destroy writers whom we consider harmful; aesthetic considerations are petit-bourgeois prejudice.'

In Germany, needless to say, things are even worse. Criticism is subject to racial and Party considerations; Heine the Jew, Thomas Mann the Liberal, Silone the Socialist are banned on these grounds, regardless of literary merit.

In France the Press never took book-reviewing very seriously; the British papers devoted to books considerably more space and care. Intrigue and corruption permeated literary politics; the yearly prizes (*Goncourt, Femina*, etc.) were the trophies of clique-struggles; the success of a book depended to a much larger extent on the publisher's pushing (which sometimes included bribing reviewers) than here. I remember, when my first book came out in France, how my publisher, the late Albin Michel, made me spend a whole day in his office signing about three hundred copies to be sent to reviewers, editors and influential people in general. He had a long typewritten list from which he dictated the varying formulae of dedication — 'hommage de l'auteur' — 'hommage distingué' — 'hommage *très* distingué' — 'hommage distingué et respectueux' and whatnot, according to the addressee's social status. This sort of thing at least is, thank God, unknown in this country. There are, of course, luncheons between publishers and reviewers; there is advertising which sometimes expands a discreet, soothing film of oil over the stormy book-columns; there are cliques and personal friendships between author and critic; but all this within reasonable limits, and criticism in England is on the whole more decent and honest than anywhere else in (pre-war) Europe.

But this is only a relative merit. Ploughing through the book-columns, especially the fiction columns, I felt that your complaint was justified, that the effect was more confusing than helpful if it came to making up one's mind which book is worth buying. The main trouble is, I believe, that most professional novel-reviewers lose their standards of values after a time. Of course, one can't have a fixed yard-stick to measure literary merit, nor a thermometer for emotional heat; but one does expect a critic to have a sense of proportion as to the importance of the work reviewed. Take as an example Mr. Ralph Strauss's column in the *Sunday*

Times; in the last issue before me (April 9th, 1944) he reviewed three novels; the closing lines of each review respectively read as follows:

> . . . exceedingly good company and there is not a dull page in her book.
> . . . reads unusually well and may be warmly recommended.
> . . . heartening and fine. A good piece of work.

Picking at random another week (March 19th), there are five reviews, which end in turn:

> . . . it is a pleasure to make her [the author's] acquaintance.
> . . . pursues a highly picturesque course.
> . . . an interesting and sympathetically told story.
> . . . delightfully easy to read.
> . . . her dialogue is easy and natural.

I thought of your two shillings a week and my heart filled with dismay; how can you know how to invest them, reading these clichés turned out by the sausage-machine, each to the same prescription: one introductory sentence, the story retold in three or four; a word of mild criticism and a gentle wind-up as above? The sausage is filled, sealed with three asterisks, the next follows. Let us assume that among the newly published novels of the week there is one called *Roses from a Kentish Garden* by some Miss Margery Edwardes, and another called *Crime and Punishment*. Each would get about twenty lines, divided by asterisks; approximately thus:

> . . . of the delightful Kentish landscape. Her characters are neatly drawn and the story, if sometimes halting, is gracefully and adroitly told.

*　　*　　*

Mr. Dostoevsky, a Russian, lacks Miss Edwardes' delicate humour. An excitable young student kills a usuress with an axe . . . somewhat morbid effect. But the characters are neatly drawn, the dialogue is fluent, and, on the whole, the story is told with adroitness and skill.

39

On these scales a ton weighs the same as an ounce; and though I admit that Mr. Strauss is an extreme example, this lack of perspective and proportion is, in varying degrees, the main weakness of the book-columns in the daily and Sunday papers. To go through them one by one would be tedious; so let us get on to your main grievance, the highbrow weeklies. You say that they are 'a bit too clever for you', and this is where your personal problems come in — that feeling of resentment and frustration which cried out between the lines of your letter.

I believe I can guess what you feel. You start eagerly to read an article, let's say in the *New Statesman*; let's say by Raymond Mortimer or Stonier; after a few lines you stumble over an allusion which you don't understand — a reference to Proust, or Kafka, or Péguy — authors whom you have never read. But the writer of the article seems to assume that everybody has read, or at least ought to have read, them; and so you begin to feel like a schoolboy who hasn't learnt his lesson, or, rather, like the uninvited guest at a party; left in the cold, humiliated, envious, resentful. And here we are at the crucial point: we are facing the wall, the tragic barrier which separates the progressive intelligentsia from the educated working class.

Let us not be hypocritical about it. The wall is there, and the more we try to explain it away, the harder we bump our heads against it. In the 'thirties Left intellectuals tried to masquerade as proletarians; it was a farce. They tried to write down 'to the masses'; it was a failure. They derided the highbrows; it was self-derision. It's no good trying to jump over the wall; our task is to abolish it. But that is a political, not a literary, task. It is, I believe, the main and ultimate task of Socialism.

All this talk about highbrows and lowbrows is a smoke-screen. The brutal facts are that your critic's parents were able to pay during an average of sixteen years so that he should read, browse, learn at his leisure and soak in that spiritual nourishment for which you crave. You could only go to school for about nine years — and it was a different school and there was less leisure. This is what stands between you and him, between you and me. When we get tight, or sentimental, or rub shoulders at a meeting, the barrier seems to melt; but when we return each to our own routine it's there again. It's neither my fault nor yours; it does not help if I feel guilty towards you, nor you towards me. I share your feeling of frustration; I loathe the order which is its cause; but don't expect me for that reason to join in the popular game of highbrow-bating. Wipe out the highbrow, and you will soon march the goose-step. It is a Fascist diversion; our way is to attack the wall. As long as it stands, democracy is a sham.

And now to return to your question. Who told you that in order to enjoy reading you have to torture yourself with that type of sophisticated review? It seems to me an utterly false approach. Reversing the proverb, you force yourself to eat the grapes *because* they taste sour. My advice is, regard reading as a pleasure, and not as a task to be pursued with clenched teeth.

May I tell you a story? I lived for a long time in France and I am very fond of wine. Some friends of mine, French writers, grown up among the vineyards, had the admirable faculty of telling you after a sniff and a sip in what district that wine had grown, and the year of the vintage. When we dined together they had long arguments about this château and that year, and about rare vintages I have never heard of. I felt out of it, humiliated, envious, resentful. Those tipple-highbrows were, as you said, just a bit too clever for me. I tried to imitate them in a frantic, snobbish effort — to drink wine with clenched teeth as it were. But I have not grown up among the vineyards; my first twenty years were spent in countries where little wine is drunk. One night I got thoroughly and happily tight after drinking everything in the wrong order and with the wrong food. Since then I only drink for my enjoyment. I can tell a claret from a burgundy, a young wine from an old one, a good wine from a bad one; and that is all I need to get joy out of the blessed liquid.

Don't misunderstand me. I recognize that the connoisseur's enjoyment is on a higher plane than mine; and that goes for art, music, books alike. Our aim is that everybody should have a chance to attain that higher plane in the particular field he chooses; that we should all grow up among the vineyards. But meanwhile we can make the best of our limited possibilities instead of making the worst of them.

Read for pleasure, man, and don't bother about Péguy and *Finnegans Wake*! Go to the public library or the bookstall, open a book at random, browse, read a page, and you will see whether you want to read that book or not. Never force yourself to read a book — it is a wasted effort. That book is right for you which needs just the amount of concentration on your part to make you turn the radio off. Read fiction only if it excites you; all great works of fiction, even *Pilgrim's Progress*, are exciting reading for a certain type of reader at a certain period of his life. If the right book falls into your hands at the right time, you won't be able to put it down. At any other time it is wasted on you. And the same goes for essays, history, philosophy. If you don't feel that it has a direct bearing on your own personal interests, worries, problems — put it away. But never, never read with clenched teeth for reading's sake. For what, after all, is the aim of literature and art — if not to imbue the world with feeling and meaning, to broaden and deepen our understanding of ourselves and the things around us? All this is within your reach.

And, mind you, I don't preach resignation. It is your right and duty to feel frustrated and resentful — but on a political plane. Watch carefully what you do with your resentment — it is the only historical asset of the poor; without it they would still live in serfdom. The others would like to deflect it into the wrong direction, against 'cleverness', culture, art; to make you spit on those values of which they deprive you. It is a subtle manœuvre of diversion; the Nazis were not the first and not the last to succeed with it. Don't fall into the trap. Your opponent is not the highbrow, but the rich.

THE GREAT CRANK[1]

THE one entirely self-revealing sentence he wrote has never been exactly translated. The original says: *In der Groesse der Luege liegt immer ein Faktor des Geglaubtwerdens.* An exact rendering is difficult because the sentence has no logical structure; it is a mystic's proposition in his own grammar. The nearest approximation would be: 'The greatness of a lie always contains an element of being believed.' Note that the verb 'contains' is related not to 'lie' but to 'greatness'. 'Greatness' here has a mystical double meaning: it stands both for quantity (a big lie) and for grandeur, majesty. Now this majestic lie, the apotheosis of the Absolute Untruth, is said to *contain* the quality of being believed. In other words, the lie is not laboriously constructed so as to be believed; it is born by intuition and its very greatness automatically compels adoration. This is one of the keys to the Crank's mysticism; actually the one which opened for him the door to power. Obviously, if the key was strange, the lock must have been even stranger.

But the lock is a problem for the historian; we are only concerned with the key. The Crank in his unhappy youth knocked at many doors, and was always refused. He tried his hand as an artist, but his sunsets in aquarelle did not sell. He worked on a building site, but was refused the fraternity of his fellow workers because he drank milk instead of beer, and made crankish speeches. He joined the Army, but never got further than his first stripe. He lived in Salvation Army shelters, under bridges, and in casual wards; he mixed with the *Lumpen-proletariat*, the nomadic outcasts in the no-man's-land of society. This period lasted for several years; it was a unique experience for a future statesman. Here the master-key began to take its first rough shape, the shape of a sovereign contempt for the people. True, he mistook the refuse

---

[1] First published in the *Observer* (Profiles series), October 1942.

for the substance, but this mistake proved to be an asset, not a liability. He divined that the mentality of the crowd is not the sum total of the mentality of the individuals which form it, but their lowest common denominator; that their intellectual powers are not integrated by contact but bewildered by the interference of their minds — light plus light resulting in darkness; that their emotional vibrations, however, increase by induction and self-induction like the current in a wire coil. By descending into the bottom strata of society the Crank made the discovery of his life: the discovery of the lowest common denominator. The master-key was found.

Its magic worked first on its owner. The frustrated Crank became the inspired Crank. His face in those early years, an unshaped pudding with a black horizontal dot, came to life as the lights of obsession were switched on behind the eyeballs. The features of it retained their crankish ridiculousness, with the black dot under the upturned nose and the second black dot pasted on the forefront, but it now assumed the grotesque horror of a totem-mask worn at ritual dances where human sacrifices are performed. His shrill voice became even shriller, an entranced incantation, while the catchwords it conveyed were simple in their ever-repeated monotony, like the rhythmical beating of the tom-tom in the bush. He knew it and in those early days called himself the Drummer.

He first spoke at small meetings and tried the formula: disintegration of the intellect by interference, increase of the crowd-emotion by induction. It worked. Now those were the days after his country's defeat, when certain powers were on the search for useful cranks to divert the energies of the embittered populace, and they discovered that this was a very useful crank. Though its effect became visible only later, this was an historic event: the key had met the lock.

History is always written in terms of keys and locks; the keys are shaped by subjective individual factors, the locks by objective constellations in the structure of society. If the course of history is determined in its broad outlines, there is always a margin left for the undetermined. It is the margin of chance in all probability calculations; the chance of a given lock constellation meeting a key which fits, and vice versa. How many potential Wellingtons died as retired colonels in Cheltenham we cannot know. And vice versa: if the Gracchi had been a little less dilettanti, Rome might have survived; and if this Crank had been killed in time, Weimar might have survived and the present war might have been postponed or even avoided. As it is, men must die with open eyes to fill in the blind margin of chance; and the danger that this may happen again, that another future Crank may discover the master-key to the masses, will persist — until the lowest common denominator of men has gradually been lifted to a level beyond his reach. This, perhaps, is the basic issue between Democracy and the Crank.

VI

IN MEMORY OF RICHARD HILLARY[1]

WRITING about a dead friend is writing against time, a chase after a receding image; catch him, hold him, before he becomes petrified into a myth. For the dead are arrogant; it is as hard to be at ease with them as it is with someone who has served with you in the ranks after he received his commission. Their perverse silence has a numbing effect: you have lost the race before it started, you will never get hold of him as he was. Already the fatal, legend-forming mechanism is at work: those pleasant trifles are freezing into Biographical Anecdotes, and weightless episodes hang like stalactites in the caves of your memory.

In times of war the dead recede quicker and myths form faster; already there is one growing around Hillary and it is easy to foresee that it will wax and expand, until his name has become one of the symbolic names of this war. The growth of a myth cannot be influenced and one should not attempt it. For myths grow like crystals: there is some diffuse emotion latent in the social medium which strives for expression as the molecules in a saturated solution strive to form a coherent pattern; and as soon as a suitable core is found, they group themselves around it and the crystal is formed, the myth is born.

The question, of course, is who makes a suitable core. Obviously he must have some affinity with that vague, diffuse sentiment, that craving for the right type of hero to turn into a myth; obviously he must express something which is the unconscious content of that craving. Now Hillary's life and death was in a way symbolic and he knew it — but a symbol for precisely what?

[1] First published in *Horizon*, April 1943, under the title 'The Birth of a Myth'. Richard Hillary, author of *The Last Enemy*, had joined the Royal Air Force as a fighter pilot in 1939, aged nineteen. He was shot down in the Battle of Britain and severely burned. Despite physical unfitness he insisted on returning to active service and was killed by an unexplained accident during a night training flight on January 8th, 1943, at the age of twenty-three.

That is what he could not, and would have so much liked to, know:

> ... I am writing this just before going to bed and I feel a little sick, for I have learned to-day that Colin Pinckney has been killed in Singapore. You do not know him, but you will, and I hope, like him, when you read the book. His death makes an apt postscript and it raises in my mind yet again the question which I have put in the book and attempted to answer, of what is the responsibility of the man who is left. I say man and not men, for I am now the last. It is odd that I who always gave least should be the one who remained. Why, I wonder. . . .[1]

What kind of responsibility was this that fell to him? What was the symbol he stood for? A myth may grow and appeal to us, may make us respond like tuning-forks to the vibration of the right chord — and yet we may not know why; we may sense the symbol without having deciphered it. After all it took over two thousand years until somebody explained to us why the myth of Oedipus Rex makes us hold our breath.

In the last two years of his twenty-three, Hillary was much concerned to find that answer, to analyse the core of the legend which he felt closing in around him. He knew he was going to die, and he wanted to find out why. In fact he had deliberately chosen a course of which he knew that it could not end otherwise but by his death:

> ... You ask me to have faith, darling.[2] Yes, but faith in what? 'That things will be all right', you say. Depends what you mean by all right. If you mean faith that some miracle will happen and that I shall be ordered to do some job which I could not only do well, but enjoy, then I say No: it is bad to have that faith and very undermining. If you mean faith that I have done the right thing in coming back,[3] then Yes. But if you mean faith that I shall survive, why then again No. If

---

[1] To 'X'. 1.3.42.   [2] To 'X'. 1.12.42.
[3] i.e. back to flying two years after his first crash.

this thing plays to its logical conclusion there is no reason why I should survive. After a few hours' flying my instinct will tell me that I shall survive, while my reason will tell me that I shall not — and this time reason will be all right.

And again:

... As before, the more I fly the more my instinct will tell me that I shall get through, while my reason telling me that I shall not, will grow fainter.
But this time my reason will be right. I know too much not to doubt it. . . .[1]

Now this is rather odd, isn't it? For normally it is our instinct which warns and scares us, and reasoning which reassures us. With him it is the other way round. But there is something even odder to come. We have seen how treacherous this instinct was. He knew it and repeatedly emphasized it; e.g. '. . . already the potion is beginning to work. My walk as I enter the Mess is jaunty', etc. And yet he takes the fatal decision to return to flying, deliberately following his instinct and against his reason. A few days after his arrival at the station he writes:

One can rationalize for ever and one's reason finally tells one that it is madness, but it is one's instinct to which one listens. . . .[2]

And in another letter:

This is indeed a queer place for journey's end.[3]

Thus he distrusts his 'instinct' when it tells him that he shall survive; but trusts it when it pushes him to his journey's end. Who cheats here whom? Apparently the 'instinct' cheats its victim: it lures him into the death-trap with the mirage of his jaunty invulnerability. But at closer view we find that the victim lets himself be led into the trap with open eyes, and even with his tongue in his cheek:

I feel like the Hollywood gangster hero, who voluntarily

[1] To A.K. 2.12.42.   [2] To A.K. 3.12.42.   [3] To 'X'. 25.11.42.

walking back into gaol, hears the prison gates clang behind him for the last time. . . .[1]

That strange and suspect 'instinct' whose sentence he accepts and whose consolations he discards — resentfully, wistfully, arguing, grimacing and even 'weeping as a child', but finally submitting in humbleness and acceptance — that 'instinct' now appears to us as a very strange force indeed. We have no scientific term as yet to name it; but it seems oddly akin to that other force which makes the core the captive of the crystal, closing in around it to fulfil its predestined pattern.

II

We see here indeed with almost clinical precision how the myth invades and destroys its chosen object. We see in his letters as under a microscope how the hero-craving, symbol-eager expectations of his Time creep like microbes under his skin, penetrate the blood-stream and burn him out, in order to preserve the symbolic shell.

But all this does not answer our question: a symbol for what? After all, Pat Finucane shot down thirty-two 'planes and he only five (with three probables). He wasn't even given a medal. And *The Last Enemy*, the most promising book that came out of his generation, was promise and not fulfilment. What was it then — what attitude, idea, state of mind, latent hope did he express? Young Hillary himself would have given anything to know, but he was not allowed to. It would have been against the rules of the game; for in these dim realms the right thing has always to be done for the wrong reasons. All he knew was that 'his instinct was right about this thing',[2] and with the writers' passion to formulate he made one attempt after another to explain why it was right. He could not succeed, for had he succeeded the 'instinct' would have

---

[1] To 'X'. 25.11.42.
[2] '. . . I know that my instinct is right about this thing and you have never questioned my decision. Bless you for that.' (To 'X'. 19.11.42.)

died and he survived. As it was, he had to die in search of his own epitaph.

The first he proposed for himself were four lines from Verlaine:

> Quoique sans patrie et sans roi
> Et très brave ne l'étant guère,
> J'ai voulu mourir à la guerre.
> La mort n'a pas voulu de moi.

But that was still in his early period, a hang-over from adolescence, the nihilistic post-puberty pose. It is written in retrospect and closes the first chapter of *The Last Enemy*. Then comes the turning point: 'I see they got you too'; the 'lifting of the veil on possibilities of thought so far beyond the grasp of the human mind'. And in the last chapter the epitaph has changed:

> 'Le sentiment d'être tout et l'évidence de n'être rien' — that was me.

In that last chapter the dazzling facility of the previous parts of the book turns into almost helpless stammering. But once the crisis is over — that inevitable process of breaking up and reforming of the personality — he sets out again to discover what he stands for:

> It was with some hesitation that I sat down to write the book, for I felt that when someone finally pointed out that the impact of this war was something more than a series of movie climaxes on the youth of the country, that it had some mental impact, the thing should be done well and worthy of the subject. Whether I succeeded I don't know. Finally I got so sick of the sop about our 'Island Fortress' and 'The Knights of the Air' that I determined to write it anyway in the hope that the next generation might realize that while stupid, we were not that stupid, that we could remember only too well that all this has been seen in the last war, but that in spite of that and not because of it, we still thought this one worth fighting.[1]

[1] To L.D., Autumn 1941.

It isn't much of an explanation, except for one turn of phrase. 'In spite of that and not because of it . . .' — that somehow sets the tuning-forks in us into faint vibration; for we all more or less feel that we fight this war rather *in spite of* than *because of* something. The big words and slogans rather embarrass us, we don't like to be thought quite so naïve as that. This tongue-in-the-cheek patriotism, the attitude of the sceptic knight, the heretic crusader, is as typical for the mental climate of this war as the stoning of the dachshunds for the last; and we get a hint of the quality of the forces which select this specific type of hero for their purpose. But it is merely a hint, not more. It is somewhat elaborated in another letter, written after the torture of one of those monotonously repeated operations by which they re-made his face patch by patch until, as on a used coat, there were more patches than original tissue on it, and is dated:

> In Hospital,
>> In bed,
>>> In anger.
>
> . . . Humanity is irony from the neck up. I guess that's the first thing you've got to realize if you want to fight for it. You'll get nothing out of it, and if you don't find virtue being its own reward sufficient, you have to be human enough to be amused by it, otherwise God help you.[1]

Six weeks later, after another operation — this time a new arm splint for his hands — he tries to formulate that same elusive craving from another angle:

> What is the particular quality of the Air Force? I find it hard to analyse. I suppose it . . . has something which sets its members very distinctly apart from the other services. To say that it is an ethereal quality is both whimsical and untrue, yet I can think of no better word. It is something, some knowledge, not understood if you like, which can only be born of the combined humility and supreme self-confidence which every combat pilot feels. Perhaps in the end it is this.

[1] To 'X'. 19.4.42.

Any human being lies closer to the unseen than any organization, but as an organization the Air Force leaves more scope for the human being as such than any other. And yet if they do feel this thing, it must be unconsciously, for they are strangely disappointing — like one of Mr. Morgan's novels — the theme is sublime, but in the attainment of it something is lacking. Will the time come in the days of peace, as Mr. Harrison asks, 'when they will conquer something more than fear'? . . . .[1]

How jealously he guards the integrity of his scepticism! He sets it like a watch-dog before his door-step. It barked all the time — furiously, excitedly, amusingly. But it didn't bite, and behind it the door was open, the house without defence.

Five months later the 'instinct' had its way and he was back at flying — although his hands, which looked like bird-claws and held knife and fork like chop-sticks, had not the strength to work the brake of the heavy twin-engined craft on which he was trained; they had to fit an extension to the brake lever.[2] He couldn't release the under-carriage either — he had to take up somebody to do it for him.[3] Sometimes he could not fix the straps and flew unstrapped ('. . . by now I really don't care. If we do a crash landing, we do a crash landing. If I go through the windscreen, I go through the windscreen'[4]); sometimes his damaged eyes, fitted with artificial eyelids, misread the altimeter.[5] He suffered from splitting headaches, the altitude made him sick,[6] the struggle of taxying the heavy engine in a gale took the skin off his burned hands.[7] Somehow he succeeded in fooling the medical board, but not to fool himself. His last night-training-flights were a chain of close escapes; and sooner or later the chain had to break.

But why then, in God's name, did he go back?

Was it vanity? 'I wonder if that is true of me, or whether, as

[1] To 'X'. 5.6.42.
[2] Cf. letter to 'X'. 1.12.42.
[3] Cf. letter to 'X'. 30.12.42.
[4] To 'X'. 30.12.42.
[5] Cf. letter to 'X'. 3.1.43.
[6] Cf. letter to 'X'. 3.1.43.
[7] Cf. letter to 'X'. 7.3.43.

some silly girl said, I am going back purely out of vanity. I think not; because implicit in my decision was the acceptance of the fact that I shall not come through.' You can be clever and twist this around and say that the quotation does not disprove the charge, *qui s'excuse s'accuse*, and so on. Granted; but then you have to find a more illuminating name for an urge which accepts destruction to get satisfied. Narcissus did not burn himself alive to preserve his image in the stream.

Urge of self-destruction, masochism, morbidity? . . . 'My darling, I am like a man, who, travelling through a dark tunnel and seeing a pinpoint of light ahead, has shouted for joy, then hesitated, stricken for fear it may be a mirage. Reassured, he presses forward, silent, his heart hammering, and it is only when he stumbles out into the light that he relaxes and, weeping for joy, pours out his heart. Richard.'[1] A boy who writes this kind of love-letter does not seem a morbid masochist. But again one may argue that the one does not exclude the other, *les extrêmes se touchent*, etc.; and again granted.

Fanatical devotion to a cause? . . . 'I could not immediately disabuse my sympathizers of their misplaced pity without appearing mock-modest or slightly insane. And so I remained an impostor. They would say, "I hope someone got the swine who got you: how you must hate those devils!" and I would say weakly, "Oh, I don't know", and leave it at that. I could not explain that I had not been injured in their war, that no thoughts of "our Island Fortress" or of "making the world safe for democracy" had bolstered me up when going into combat. I could not explain that what I had suffered I in no way regretted; that I welcomed it; and that now that it was over I was in a sense grateful for it and certain that in time it would help me along the road of my own private development.'[2] But perhaps this too is just modesty after all, or inverted pride; the young Englishman's love to over-state his understatements.

Thus we can go on being clever and analytical, and stick labels on our victim until he looks like a globetrotter's cabin trunk.

[1] To 'X'. 12.2.42.   [2] *The Last Enemy*, p. 206.

There will always be a certain amount of truth in such statements; they fit in a loose way everybody, like shilling horoscopes; and if one of our clinical adjectives does not fit directly, we can always turn it round by putting a minus sign before it and call it over-compensation or 'the revenge of the repressed'. We are, of course, fond of our little adjectives; they save us from pathos and embarrassment, from the threat of having to face the tragic implication. We prefer to let our lights shine like candles under the stars. But once they have burned down we are back where we started, under a sky too large for us. Our adjectives fade, the labels peel off, only the subject remains, alone under the stars, faced with that nameless force which is set to destroy him. We watch the struggle, his reason against his fate, the man against the myth; and the myth devours the man.

> I shall go back, I think. I can rationalize no further. I must let instinct decide. Maybe it is for this that I have withdrawn into myself. I don't know. I can make nothing of this letter. (You perhaps will.) And yet in some way it seems an explanation ... It is those circles of peace again. They must return — they must. . . .[1]

How he struggles in the net! To escape, to live; after all, one is only twenty-two:

> Do not, darling, I beseech you, pucker your lovely brows at this levity for it is not what it seems; but cloaking lightly the agitated palpitations of a bewildered heart. . . .
> Were I Mr. Beverley Nichols, had I any suède shoes, and were there any daffodils, I would now trip lightly outside and prance among them for the sheer joy of living. Thwarted by all three factors, I will content myself with a stoop of port in the mess, a slightly smug expression being the only visible sign that inwardly I am hugging myself with joyful anticipation. . . .[2]

After all, one is only twenty-two and one still has the undrawn cheque for about twice as many years in one's pocket. But there is no escape, and he feels it; so he goes on trying at least to name the nameless force which destroys him. We have followed his various attempts from that first 'Quoique sans patrie et sans roi' to that final 'I can rationalize no further. I must let instinct decide'. Yet once the decision is taken he once more tries, *post factum*, to rationalize it. This last attempt to decipher the oracle dominates his letters in the last few weeks before he is killed:

> Funny about your instinct about Kennington. Had I not stayed with him I should not have read *The Mint* and had I not read it I should not have come back (perhaps).[1]

The meaning of this becomes clear from the following passage, written one week later:

> When I was still waffling I read *The Mint*, T. E. Lawrence's unpublished agony in the Air Force, describing his first period at Uxbridge as an Air Force A.C.2. This, I confess, influenced me strongly, as it was what I was looking for. He found amongst those airmen and the ordinary things he shared with them, the petty tyrannies, etc., some kind of fellowship and happiness which before had been denied him.
> As much as anything I came back for that, and yet. . . .[2]

So that is what he came back for: fellowship and happiness. It is a long way from 'Humanity is irony from the neck up', written seven months ago; those who die young, walk fast. But this is not the last station either. There is a strange irony behind this last attempt to explain the motives of his return, for the letter goes on as follows:

> . . . and yet it is difficult to reorientate oneself to three years ago. The young pilots are the same and yet not the same — less fine somehow. I am outside still . . . I look up sometimes in an armament lecture and expect to see Noel Agazarian sitting beside me, instead there is some pimply youth picking his nose . . .

[1] To 'X'. 25.11.42.　　　　[2] To A.K. 3.12.42.

And earlier in the same letter:

> Wretched I am that this station should be so utterly cold and
> bare, not only of trees and houses, but of all human contact
> ... My first two nights I crept back to my hut and wept like
> a child, much to my own surprise, as I thought I had steeled
> myself for this ...

Even Lawrence, who had such a decisive influence on him, lets
him down. The first book he discovers, the day after his arrival,
in the station library is Lawrence's Letters, edited by David
Garnett; this appears to him fraught with a curious significance:
'I took the book out and, believe it or not, opened it at this page
...'[1] He then quotes Garnett's comment on Lawrence's desire to
go back to the R.A.F.:

> One wonders whether his will had not become greater than
> his intelligence. The courage of the boy too proud to make a
> fuss is something we admire; in an educated man it is ridicul-
> ous and a sign of abnormality.

This judgment on Lawrence he applies, *mutatis mutandis*, to
himself; it is a devaluation, a terrible debunking of his motives,
of the search for 'fellowship and happiness'. He does not cease
complaining about his disappointment and loneliness:

> Perhaps it is merely the fear of being so much alone — a bitter
> pill when I always thought I liked it so much. But the total
> lack of human contact is awful — they are machines, not
> men. At Fighter Command they were people. One could
> talk to them and like them ... I love you so very much that
> at moments I think my heart will break. You are everything
> that is not here — warmth, humanity, humour and intellig-
> ence.[2]

There are, of course, moments of exhilaration, as when the
younger pilots congratulate him on his first solo-flight in a twin-
engined plane:

[1] To 'X'. 25.11.42.   [2] Ibid.

... So they are human after all. I feel a new-old warmth begin to course through me; the potion is already at work.

I pick up a newspaper — Beveridge Report? Oh the fellow is thinking about after the war — what do we care about after the war; we'll be dead anyway. Let's find out what Jane's doing in the *Daily Mirror*. We turn to the page — we comment on her legs, and I look closely at the faces around me, and what I see pleases me. I am happy.

We wander in to dinner and afterwards we crowd round the fire, order beers, more beers, and talk shop. Time passes. Am I bored? A little, but only a very little, for to-morrow I shall be up again.[1]

But these moments of fellowship and happiness are short, and of a somewhat hectic, artificial character; then the solitude closes in once more on him. His days are now counted; he has but ten more left to live:

I ponder K.'s theory that l'espoir de la fraternité is always a wild goose chase unless one is tight or physically exhausted in a crowd — as after long marches.

To-night I am almost convinced he is right. But he must not be — for it was for that reason that I returned.[2]

Ten days more and the wild goose chase is over. But is it true that he returned for that — *l'espoir de la fraternité*? And fraternity with whom? Behind the pimpled youth there is the image of Noel Agazarian, of Peter Pease and Colin Pinckney and the others, of whom he alone survived, the 'last of the long-haired boys', the flying undergraduates of the Battle of Britain. The young pilots at the station are 'somehow not the same' — at twenty-three he feels like an anachronism, a survivor from another generation. One after the other they had been killed; there is a sentence which runs like a monotonous row of tombstones through his book: From this flight Broody Benson did not return. From this flight Bubble Waterston did not return. From this flight Larry Cunningham

[1] To 'X'. 3.12.42.　　[2] To 'X'. 30.12.42.

did not return. 'Each time they climbed into their machines and took off to combat, they were paying instinctive tribute to their comrades who were dead.'[1] He was the only one left, and he had to go on paying the tribute; for the survivor is always a debtor. He thought he came back for fellowship with the living, while already he belonged to the fraternity of the dead.

We find, then, that this last attempt to explain and rationalize his motives is as true as his earlier ones, but not the final truth. The final truth is probably a pattern composed of all the threads we have picked up, and followed for a short while and dropped again. For the pattern is more than the sum total of the threads; it has its own symbolic design of which the threads know nothing. They are ordinary strings, woven of cause and effect; but in the completed design the effect seems to operate the cause. The threads are subject to causality; the pattern to finality.

III

Perhaps I shall be accused of romanticizing. There are those who like their heroes as idols of clay, and those who like them cut into slices for examination under the microscope. The latter will be delighted and the former shocked by the publication of Hillary's letters; for those of his last period are terrifying to read. They are the letters of a very young man who knows that he is doomed, looking into a mirror:

All day my eyes have pricked with tears, and now at last in the privacy of my room I have been weeping like a child for an hour. Why? Is it fear? I have not yet seen an aeroplane and I know not yet whether the night will terrify me or not. Is it just the atmosphere? Very largely I know. But perhaps this is what they mean in the Air Force by 'lack of moral fibre'. I have often wondered. Maybe this is what happens when a man's nerve goes. And yet I am not consciously frightened of anything, merely unutterably wretched. . . .[2]

[1] *The Last Enemy*, p. 220.   [2] To 'X'.   25.11.42.

This wretchedness is mainly due to physical reasons:

> ... Being a rather selfish fellow, however, what is of far more
> interest to me is how to keep the extremely bitter cold not
> only from petrifying the burnt skin on my hands and face,
> but from prying its way into my very soul ... I suppose the
> atmosphere brought to the surface the subconscious dread
> of dying up here, at night and in the cold.[1]

Of course he does not give himself away; nobody on the station
can guess his agonies; he is a popular figure and they think him a
'rather droll fellow' as he stalks the aerodrome with his burnt face
and hands, the constant, boyish pout on his grafted lips. There is
the routine, the bull-shit, the dances, the average number of
crashes; one might as well walk one's calvary between Oxford
Circus and Marble Arch.

Those moods of complete despair alternate with moments of
elation; with the elusive touch of those Circles of Peace travelling
past in the air:

> Much better to-day, for I have actually flown ... Were it not
> that one's chattering teeth force one to walk on, it would be
> time well spent just to sit on the aerodrome and look out
> across the great stillness — for it is still; the roar of machines
> taking off and landing only seeming to emphasize it.
>
> It's curious psychologically that I have only to step into an
> aeroplane — that monstrous thing of iron and steel just
> watching for its chance to down me, and all fear goes. I am
> at peace again.[2]

And there are other moments of a great weariness — almost
amounting to a desire that it may be over, and over soon. Talking
of a dance on the aerodrome, a week before his death:

> I want to go to bed, but I stay on watching people getting
> drunk — talking of the 'blacks' they put up the night before,
> etc. At 2.30 I am still there. Why? I don't know. I've long
> ago got over that distressing emotion which should be con-

[1] To A.K. 2.12.42.   [2] To 'X'. 1.12.42.

fined to middle-aged women and very young boys — the fear of missing something — and yet I stayed.[1]

The worst is that he has what the French Catholics call *la maladie du scrupule*; he despises himself for his 'egotistical meanderings'. 'Forgive me this long and (yes, I believe it's true) self-pitying epistle. Don't be ashamed of me if you can help it.'[2] The fraternity of the dead has its peculiar etiquette; one has not only to live up to one's form, one has to die up to it. But then again, there is the writer's curiosity which forces him to feel his own pulse, to jot down on long rambling pages of pencil-scrawl the minutes of his agony; there are the nerve-tearing oscillations between cant and introspection, acceptance and revolt, arrogance and humility, twenty-three years and eternity:

> Koestler has a theory for this. He believes there are two planes of existence, which he calls the *vie tragique* and the *vie triviale*. Usually we move on the plane of the *vie triviale*, but occasionally in moments of elation, danger, etc., we find ourselves transferred to the plane of the *vie tragique*, with its un-common-sense cosmic perspective. One of the miseries of the human condition is that we can neither live permanently on the one nor on the other plane, but oscillate between the two. When we are on the trivial plane, the realities of the other are non-sense—overstrung nerves, etc. When we live on the tragic plane, the joys and sorrows of the other are shallow, frivolous, trifling. Some people try all their lives to make up their minds on which plane to live — unable to recognize that we are condemned to live alternatingly on both in a biological rhythm. But it happens that in exceptional circumstances — for instance if one has to live through a long stretch of time in physical danger, one is placed as it were on the intersection line of the two planes; a curious situation which is a kind of tight-rope walking on one's nerves. As few people can bear it for long, they elaborate conventions and formulae — e.g. R.A.F. slang and understatement. In other words, they

[1] To 'X'. 30.12.42.   [2] To 'X'. 25.11.42.

try to assimilate the tragic with the trivial plane. *Au fond*, he thinks, that is one of the main mechanisms of the evolution of civilization: to petrify the violent and tragic into dignified conventional formulae. I think he is right.[1]

Actually I still believe that this is true, as metaphors go. It is this jump from one plane to the other which transforms undergraduates into heroes, psychology into mythology, a thousand individually conditioned reflexes into the Battle of Britain. The mere passing of time has cumulatively a similar result — for the present is mainly on the trivial, history always on the tragic plane. Wars and catastrophes accelerate this process by producing what one might call the Pompeii-effect: schoolboys playing with marbles are caught by the lava and petrified into monuments.

But perhaps some will say that the lava romanticized the boys.

I V

There is another type of person condemned to walk the tightrope on the intersection-line of the two planes: the artist, particularly the writer. The pilot can only stand the strain by projecting the tragic on to the trivial plane. The artist proceeds the opposite way: he tries to see the trivial from the perspective of the tragic or absolute plane.

Does Hillary, as a writer, succeed in that? The promise is there, and the fulfilment, I believe, would have come. Among all the writing airmen, Hillary, with St. Exupéry, form a category apart. The others he compares to 'people who happened to be watching an accident with a camera in their hands and they got a good picture'; whereas he is the professional cameraman who always will get a good picture, even if there is no accident.

The professional touch in *The Last Enemy* is unmistakable. There is a dazzling facility of expression very rare in a first book. It has all the qualities of first-rate reportage — precision, vividity, brilliancy, economy, excitement. But for two chapters, I would

[1] To 'X'. 10.12.42.

call it the best reportage that has come out of the war. And it is precisely these two chapters — 'The world of Peter Pease' and 'I see they got you too' — which, through their failure, prove that he was more than a reporter. In these two chapters he tries to tackle the problem of ethical values *sub specie aeternitatis*, and here all facility and glibness suddenly leave him, the language becomes flat, the thought disarmingly naive. One feels that there is an overwhelming emotion which cuts his breath to helpless stammering:

> ... I would write of these men, of Peter and of the others, I would write for them and would write with them. They would be at my side. And to whom would I address this book, to whom would I be speaking when I spoke of these men? And that too I knew. To Humanity, for Humanity must be the public of any book. Yes, that despised Humanity which I had scorned and ridiculed to Peter.[1]

If one compares this with the accomplished virtuosity of the reportage chapters, one realizes where the promise lacks fulfilment. The violence of emotional perception, and the facility to report the factual, are basic qualities which make the writer; in *The Last Enemy* these two still lead a somewhat separated existence. But there are passages in the book, a good many of them, where they actually meet. There is, for instance, his recollection of the first fatal crash in the squadron:

> Of crashes. It was after an armament lecture in one of the huts when we heard, very high, the thin wailing scream of a plane coming down fast. The corporal sat down and rolled himself a cigarette. He took out the paper and made of it a neat trough with his forefinger, opened the tin of tobacco and sprinkled a little on to the paper, ran his tongue along the paper edge and then rolled it. As he put it in his mouth we heard the crash, maybe a mile away. The corporal lit a match and spoke: 'I remember the last time we had one of those. I was on the salvage party. It wasn't a pretty sight.' We learned later that the man had been on a war-load height

---

[1] *The Last Enemy*, p. 221.

test and had presumably fainted. They did not find much of him, but we filled up the coffin with sand and gave him a grand funeral.[1]

There it is — the interlacing of the tragic and the trivial. We find it again in the puzzling effect of 'The beauty shop' — of that horror-cabinet of plastic surgery in the hospital, where noses grow from foreheads, grafted white lips are painted red with mercuro-chrome, grafted eyelids which have not taken are torn off again and thrown into the bucket. But all this is told with such a superbly grotesque twist that instead of being sick we chuckle and grin in blasphemous hilarity. How does he achieve this? It is the effect of walking on the intersection line; for what strikes us as grotesque is the reflection of the tragic in the distorting mirror of the trivial.

Passages like this are strewn all over the book; one meets them on every second or third page — memories of Oxford, a regatta in Germany, the first contact with a Spitfire, panic during a night-flight, the children of Tarfside, portraits of pilots, samples of R.A.F.-atmosphere bottled on the aerodrome, crashes, death, drunkenness, operations and more operations, blindness, quarrels with nurses and philosophical talks. The two planes are not yet assimilated, but while moving on one, he keeps a feeler on the other plane. And that gives one confidence that, granted to live a few more years and write a few more books, the promise would have been fulfilled.

As it is, his place in literature can only be marked by a blank; and yet we can at least define with some probability the position of that blank on the map. With the 'bourgeois' novel getting more and more exhausted and insipid as the era which produced it draws to its close, a new type of writer seems to take over from the cultured middle-class humanist: airmen, revolutionaries, adventurers, men who live the dangerous life; with a new oper-ative technique of observation, a curious alfresco introspection and an even more curious trend of contemplation, even mysticism, born in the dead centre of the hurricane. St. Exupéry, Silone,

[1] *The Last Enemy*, p. 44.

Traven, Hemingway, Malraux, Scholochow, Istrati may be the forerunners; and Hillary might have become one of them. But one slim volume, a packet of letters, two short stories are all that is left; and that is not enough to fill in the blank.

Thomas Mann says somewhere that to leave a trace behind him a writer must produce not only quality but bulk; the sheer bulk of the *œuvre* helps its impact on us. It is a melancholy truth; and yet this slim volume of Hillary's seems to have a specific weight which makes it sink into the depth of one's memory, while tons of printed bulk drift as flotsam on its surface.

v

We started from the question: What makes this young author-pilot's life and death into a symbol? and have not answered it. For the question what ideas or values he represents must finally merge into that of the ideas and values latent in his generation and class. This is what he has to say about them:

> The seed of self-destruction among the more intellectual members of the University was even more evident. Despising the middle-class society to which they owed their education and position, they attacked it, not with vigour but with adolescent petulance. They were encouraged in this by their literary idols, by their unquestioning allegiance to Auden, Isherwood, Spender, and Day Lewis. With them they affected a dilettante political leaning to the left. Thus, while refusing to be confined by the limited outlook of their own class, they were regarded with suspicion by the practical exponents of labour as bourgeois, idealistic, pink in their politics and pale-grey in their effectiveness. They balanced precariously and with irritability between a despised world they had come out of and a despising world they couldn't get into . . .[1]

This is how he saw his background; but we get a curiously

[1] *The Last Enemy*, p. 14.

different impression of the atmosphere and of himself in a letter of condolence from the Vice-President of Trinity to Hillary's father:

> ... Then Dick arrived with his great charm and great personality, and at the end of his first year he had achieved a feat which will go down to posterity ... for he was the stroke of an VIII which was the best College VIII that has ever been seen, and which, in making five bumps to go to the head of the river ... achieved a feat which is never likely to be eclipsed. In 1939 again, his indomitable spirit and skill kept us in the position which his leadership had won for us the year before. Then came this cruel war ...

This, I suppose, is what one might call a counterpoint; but without it there would be no fugue. Auden and the five bumps complete each other in a singular way; without the bumps no Battle of Britain, without Auden no *The Last Enemy*. The very violence with which these youngsters reacted against their tradition proves how strong its hold on them still was. But tradition might act on a man in two ways: either as a sterilizing, or as a catalysing agent. With the majority the first is the case; Hillary belonged to that lucky minority to whom Shrewsbury plus Oxford becomes not a liability but a basic asset. This is how, in a few remarkably measured lines, he sums up what Oxford did to him:

> As it was, I read fairly widely, and, more important, learned a certain *savoir faire*, learned how much I could drink, how not to be gauche with women, how to talk to people without being aggressive or embarrassed, and gained a measure of confidence which would have been impossible for me under any other form of education.[1]

And then, without transition, in between two bumps on the river — Pompeii. He was just learning 'a certain *savoir faire*', when:

> ... Here in a clearing of the woods in Devon, I heard of the

[1] *The Last Enemy*, p. 18.

last flight of Richard Hillary. I sat in a stillness of the spirit and watched great hawks wheeling in the wind, poised to strike then suddenly swooping down upon their prey. So had he manœuvred his Spitfire, fearlessly braving elemental dangers and man-made devilries to keep us, and England, safe.[1]

Another counterpoint. Our highbrow-hawk pulls a face — for in his own eyes it looked like this:

> ... This then was the Oxford Generation which on September 3rd, 1939, went to war ... We were disillusioned and spoiled. The press referred to us as the Lost Generation and we were not displeased. Superficially we were selfish and egocentric without any Holy Grail in which we could lose ourselves. The war provided it, and in a delightfully palatable form. It demanded no heroics, but gave us the opportunity to demonstrate in action our dislike of organized emotion and patriotism, the opportunity to prove to ourselves and to the world that our effete veneer was not as deep as our dislike of interference, the opportunity to prove that, undisciplined though we might be, we were a match for Hitler's dogma-fed youth.[2]

What meticulous efforts to keep a clean head and dodge *la gloire*! There are those who die with their boots clean, and those who die with their minds clean. For the former it is easier — their life and death are ruled by exclamation marks. For the Hillarys it is harder; their curriculum is punctuated by question-marks which they have to unbend, straighten, point all by themselves.

But the aim at which they point we can only guess. We can guess it, not from his formulations and ratiocinations, but from those parts in his writings where he is un-selfconscious and inarticulate. 'In an age when to love one's country is vulgar, to love God archaic, and to love mankind sentimental, you do all

---

[1] From an appreciation (unpublished), by Lady Fortescue.
[2] *The Last Enemy*, pp. 28-29.

three', he says to Peter Pease — to the same Peter whom he admires most of all his friends, whose death he sees in a vision under the anaesthetic and whose memory becomes a cult and an obsession for him. And through that one sentence with its three disparaging adjectives, we get a glimpse into the concealed nostalgia, the *mal du siècle* of those who die with their minds clean.

For, in spite of all intellectual camouflage and nimbleness of formulation, one does not let one's body go up in flames thrice out of sheer 'dislike of organized emotion and patriotism'. It sounds all very well, and it is not true. But one does it — perhaps, if one is exceptionally sensitive and exceptionally brave, and if one caught the bug of the great nostalgia of one's time — in search of a redeeming emotion; of a credo, neither sentimental, vulgar nor archaic, whose words one could say without embarrassment or shame. When all isms become meaningless and the world an alley of crooked query-marks, then indeed a man's longing for the Holy Grail may become so strong that he flies like a moth into the flame; and having burned his wings, crawls back into it again. But this, of course, is the one instinct in man's condition which he cannot rationalize.

Richard Hillary was burnt thrice. After the first time they brought him back and patched him up and made him a new face. It was wasted, for the second time his body was charred to coal. But to make quite sure that the pattern be fulfilled, it was his wish to be cremated; so they burned him a third time, on the twelfth of January, 1943, in Golders Green; and the coal became ashes and the ashes were scattered into the sea.

There the man ends and the myth begins. It is the myth of the Lost Generation — sceptic crusaders, knights of effete veneer, sick with the nostalgia of something to fight for, which as yet is not. It is the myth of the crusade without a cross, and of desperate crusaders in search of a cross. What creed they will adopt, Christ's or Barrabas', remains to be seen.

VII

THE INTELLIGENTSIA[1]

I

'INTELLIGENTSIA' is one of those terms difficult to define but easy to associate. It is logically blurred but emotionally vivid, surrounded with a halo, or rather several halos which overlap and vary according to period and place. One may list as examples the romantic salon; the professional middle classes; terroristic organizations of students and aristocracy in the second half of nineteenth-century Russia; patriotic University Corps in post-Napoleonic Germany; the Bohemians of Montmartre, and so on. There are also evocative geographical names like Bloomsbury, Montparnasse and Cagnes; and certain typical attitudes to life including clothing, hair-fashion, drink and food. The aura of the intelligentsia changes all the time; its temporary representatives are subdivided into classes and groups, and even its limits are blurred by a host of camp followers and hangers-on: members of the aristocracy, Maecenases, tarts, fools, admirers and Earnest Young Men. Hence we won't get far with impressionistic judgments, and had better look up the *Oxford Dictionary* for a solid definition.

There we find:

> INTELLIGENTZIA, -sia, The part of a nation (esp. the Russian) that aspires to independent thinking.

Thus the *Concise Oxford Dictionary*, 3rd edition, 1934.

By 1936, in the climate of the pink decade and the popular front, the definition has undergone a significant change:

> The class consisting of the educated portion of the population regarded as capable of forming public opinion.

(*The Shorter Oxford Dictionary*, 2nd edition, 1936.)

[1] First published in *Horizon*, March 1944.

This second version has since obviously been proved too optimistic, and we had better fall back on the first which is excellent. Historically, it is indeed the 'aspiration to independent thinking' which provides the only valid group-characteristic of the intelligentsia.

But how does it happen that an 'aspiration towards independent thinking' arises in a part of a nation? In our class-ridden world this is obviously not a matter of a spontaneous association of the gifted — enlightened dukes, plus miners' sons plus General Practitioners. The intelligentsia of a given period and place is of a fairly homogeneous social texture: loose threads only appear on the fringes. Intelligence alone is neither a necessary nor a sufficient qualification for a member of the Intelligentsia. Instead, we have to regard the formation of this particular group as a social process which, as far as modern society is concerned, begins with the French Revolution.

II

The Intelligentsia and the Third Estate

Among the upper strata of the Third Estate the aspiration to independent thinking was not a luxury but a dire necessity of survival. The young bourgeoisie, hemmed in by the stultifying feudal structure, had to conquer its historic lebensraum, and this conquest was only possible by blowing up the feudal totems and taboos with the dynamite of 'independent thought'. The first modern intellectuals were the Encyclopaedists, and they enter the historical stage as the great debunkers and iconoclasts. Goethe resurrected is unimaginable in our time, but Voltaire would be within a fortnight acclimatized in Bloomsbury, winning all week-end competitions of the *New Statesman*. For Goethe was the last Renaissance genius, a direct descendant of Leonardo, and his attitude to Society that of a courtier of some enlightened Florentine prince; whereas with Voltaire, the great debunking of feudal values begins.

The intelligentsia in the modern sense thus first appears as that part of a nation which by its social situation not so much 'aspires' but is *driven* to independent thought, that is, to a type of group-behaviour which debunks the existing hierarchy of values (from which it is excluded) and at the same time tries to replace it with new values of its own. This constructive tendency of the intelligentsia is its second basic feature. The true iconoclasts always had a prophetic streak, and all debunkers have a bashfully hidden pedagogic vein.

But where had these new values of their own come from? This is the point where Marxist analysis ends in over-simplified schemata:

> The bourgeoisie, historically, has played a most revolutionary part... Constant revolutionizing of production, uninterrupted disturbance of all social conditions, everlasting uncertainty and agitation distinguish the bourgeois epoch from all earlier ones. All fixed, fast-frozen, relations, with their train of ancient and venerable prejudices and opinions, are swept away, all new-formed ones become antiquated before they can ossify. All that is solid melts into air, all that is holy is profaned, and man is at last compelled to face with sober senses his real conditions of life and his relations with his kind...
>
> And as in material, so also in intellectual production. The intellectual creations of individual nations become common property. National one-sidedness and narrow-mindedness become more and more impossible, and from the numerous national and local literatures there arises a world literature.
>
> (Manifesto of the Communist Party, 1848.)

The first paragraph quoted shows Marx and Engels at their best; in the second they take the fatal short cut from Economy to 'Superstructure': that is culture, art, mass psychology. Marxian society has a basement-production, and an attic-intellectual production; the staircase and the lifts are missing. For it is not as simple as that: the triumphant class creating its own philosophic superstructure to fit its mode of production like a tailored suit. The Encyclopaedia was not commissioned by the National

Assembly. Whenever a class or group emerged victorious from its struggles, it found the befitting ideology already waiting for it like a ready-made suit in a department store. Thus Marx found Hegel, Feuerbach, and Ricardo; Mussolini had only to pick Sorel and Pareto; Hitler discovered Gobineau, Houston Stuart Chamberlain and Jung; Stalin revived Machiavelli and Peter the Great. This, of course, is a mixed bag of examples of progressive and regressive movements which, strictly speaking, should be kept apart. For regressive movements need simply to fall back on superannuated values — not on the last, but on the last-but-one or last-but-two, to perform a romantic revival, and derive a lot of pseudo-revolutionary gusto out of this 'revolution à rebours'. And there is always a part of the intelligentsia which, abandoning its aspiration to independent thought and detaching itself from the main body, lends itself to such romantic revivals. They are the tired and the cynics, the hedonists, the romantic capitulators, who transform their dynamite into Bengal lights, the Juengers, Montherlants, Ezra Pounds.

Discarding these, there still remains the problem of how and why the true, emergent, progressive movements in history, those which led to the Rights of Man and to the founding of the First Workers International, those who have no last-but-one precepts to fall back on, invariably find the right ideology waiting for them at the right moment. I repeat that I do not believe any more that the economic process by itself creates its own superstructure. Orthodox Marxism has never produced historical evidence for this postulate. Nor, of course, is it a matter of coincidence. It seems rather that political economy and cultural development are merely two aspects of the same basic process, which we are as yet far from being able to define.

Two examples from other spheres may help to bring this vague-sounding assertion into relief. The first is the old mind-body problem where the antithesis between materialistic and idealistic schools was much the same as between historical materialism and historical idealism, until the double-aspect theory brought the quarrel about which is the cause and which the effect, which is the hen and which the egg, to at least a temporary close. Thus your gastric acid is neither the cause nor the effect of your nervous state, but both are aspects, consequences of your total mode of living. The second example is the relation between physics and mathematics. When Einstein was faced with the contradictory evidence of two perfectly sound physical experiments (Michelson-Morley and Fizeau) he was able to develop the theory of Relativity only because the apparently abstract and useless non-Euclidian mathematical fantasies of Bolyai, Riemann and others were waiting for him just at the right moment, ready-made around the corner. The mathematical and the physical elements of Relativity were developed quite independently, and their coincidence would appear miraculous, without the recognition of a fundamental trend of evolution in scientific thought, of which the various faculties are merely isolated aspects.

The rise of the Third Estate and of the progressive middle classes was thus neither the cause nor the effect of humanistic liberal philosophy. The two phenomena sprang from the same root, they were entwined and correlated like colour and shape in the same object. *The basic function of the Encyclopaedists and of all later intelligentsias was this correlating of social and intellectual evolution; they were the self-interpreting, introspective organs of the social body;* and this function automatically included both the iconoclastic and the pedagogic, the destructive and the constructive element.

III

The Decay of the Third Estate

This function gives a clue to the always peculiar structure of the intelligentsia.

Social behaviour has a much greater inertia than thought. There is always an enormous discrepancy between our collective ways of living and the accumulated data of science, art, technique. We wage wars, go to church, worship kings, eat murderous diets, conform to sexual taboos, make neurotics of our children, miseries

of our marriages, oppress and let ourselves be oppressed —
whereas in our text-books and art galleries there is embodied the
objective knowledge of a way of living which we shall put into
practice only after decades or centuries. In everyday life we all
behave like creatures in a period piece, anachronistic caricatures
of ourselves. The distance between the library and the bedroom
is astronomical. However, the body of theoretical knowledge and
independent thought is there, only waiting to be picked up, as the
Jacobins picked up the Encyclopaedists.

This picking up, however, is the function of a special type of
people; the liaison agents between the way we live and the way
we *could* live according to the contemporary level of objective
knowledge. Those who are snugly tucked into the social hierarchy
have obviously no strong impulse towards independent thought.
Where should it come from? They have no reason to destroy their
accepted values nor any desire to build new ones. The thirst for
knowledge is mainly confined to situations where the unknown is
disquieting; the happy are rarely curious. On the other hand, the
great majority of the oppressed, the underdogs, lack the opportunity or the objectivity or both, for the pursuit of independent
thought. They accept or reject the existing values; both attitudes
are inarticulate and unobjective. Thus the function of co-
ordination between the two concepts *Homo* and *Sapiens* falls to
those sandwiched in between two layers, and exposed to the
pressure of both. The intelligentsia is a kind of sensitive, porous
membrane stretched between media of different properties.

One should not however confound them with the middle classes
as such. Sensitivity, searching and groping are attitudes which
presuppose a certain amount of frustration — not too much and
not too little; a kind of moderate unhappiness, a harmonious
disequilibrium. The upper strata which accept the traditional
values, lack this frustration; the bottom strata have too much of
it — to the degree of being either paralysed or discharging it in
convulsive fits. Further, it must be a *specific* frustration — the discontent of the professional man, writer, artist, who rebel not
because society has deprived them of every chance, crushed and

buried them in pit or workshop, but because they have been given a margin large enough to develop their gifts but too narrow to make them feel smug and accept the given order of things. For the smug, thinking is a luxury, for the frustrated a necessity. And as long as the chasm between thought and tradition, theoretical insight and practical routine prevails, thinking must necessarily be directed by the two poles of debunking and Utopianism.

All this does not apply any more to the bulk of the middle class. It did as long as their climate was 'Commonwealth' and Jacobinism. Meanwhile the once revolutionary urban bourgeoisie has become a conservative force. No more a sensitive membrane, but an inert sticky glue which holds the social body together. Their frustrations are repressed, their aspirations are not towards new hierarchies of values, but towards climbing to the top of the existing hierarchy. Thus the intelligentsia, once the vanguard of the ascending bourgeoisie, becomes the Lumpen-Bourgeoisie in the age of its decay.

IV

The Intelligentsia and the Fourth Estate

As the Third Estate gradually loses its progressive character to become first stagnant then regressive, the intelligentsia becomes more and more detached from it and driven to the quest for more vigorous allies, capable of fulfilling its task of demolition and construction.

The most fascinating example for this quest is nineteenth-century Russia. '... Whether they (the revolutionary intelligentsia) spoke of the necessity of political liberty, of the plight of the peasant or of the socialist future of society, it was always their own plight which really moved them. And their plight was not primarily due to material need: it was spiritual' (Borkenau, *The Communist International*).

This spiritual plight of the Russian intelligentsia was yet another form of the duality I mentioned: the contradiction between the inert, stagnant, habit-conditioned form of everyday life on the one hand, and the accumulated data of objective knowledge lying fallow as 'theory' and 'ideology' on the other. For the nineteenth-century Russians this latter principle was embodied in Western European civilization: in British Parliamentarism, French literature, German philosophy. For them, the West was the incarnation of *Homo Sapiens* as opposed to the Barbarians of the steppes; just as, by an ironical turn of history, the Western intelligentsia of the two post-war decades became spellbound by Russian Communism which seemed to incorporate the truly human Utopia, as opposed to the decay of Capitalism.

There is, however, a fundamental difference between the early Russian revolutionary intelligentsia — the Shelabows, Sonja Petrovskajas, Bakunins, Nechaews, Kropotkins, and the Bloomsbury of the Pink Decade. It is easy to sneer at the comparison and to contrast the futility of the latter with the heroism of the assassins of Alexander II, the martyrdom of the Siberian exiles and the prisoners of Schluesselburg. Racial comparisons between the undeniably greater endurance and fatalism of the semi-asiatic Russians and the highly strung Westerners provide one differential factor, but not the basic one. The basic point is that people grow under the burden of their responsibilities and shrink if the burden is taken from them. Nechaew lived for a number of years chained to the wall of a humid cell and when his comrades succeeded in establishing contact and offered to liberate him, refused because he preferred them to concentrate on more important tasks. But later, in the émigré atmosphere of Geneva, he became involved in the most squalid quarrels and died an obscure nobody. The venerable and justly venerated Russian student heroines and martyrs were not less hysterical than any character of Huxley's or Evelyn Waugh's; Lassalle was a snob who got himself killed in a quixotic duel, Marx a pathologically quarrelsome old sponger, Bakunin had an incestuous fixation on a sister, was impotent and died a virgin; Trotsky at a certain period spent all his afternoons and evenings playing chess in the Café Central in Vienna — a typical figure from an Osbert Lancaster Café Royal

Landscape; Lenin suffered a traumatic shock when his brother Alexander was hanged — hence his fanatical hatred of the bourgeoisie of which, in analytical terms, the Russian revolution was merely a 'projection'. Neurosis is inherent in the structure of intelligentsias (I shall come back to this point in a moment): history, however, is not interested in a person's motives, only in his achievements. But why is it that the burden and bliss of responsibility is given to the intelligentsia in certain periods and in others not, condemning the latter to barrenness and futility? This is the question to which the comparison between the early Russians and Bloomsbury boils down; more precisely to the question of the historical constellation which accounts for the sharing-out of responsibilities.

The answer becomes at once obvious by a comparison of the two countries' sociological structure. Nineteenth-century Russia had no Trade Unions, no Labour movement or Co-operatives. Serfdom was only abolished in 1862. In that drowsy, inert giant-country there was no gradual transition from patriarchal feudalism to modern Capitalism; I have spoken to peasants who took aeroplanes for granted, watching them each day fly over their heads but had never seen a railway or motor-car; others who had travelled in a car but wouldn't believe that such a thing as a bicycle existed.

What a paradise for intellectuals with pedagogical yearnings! When the first of them, the martyrs of Narodnaya Volya, started what they called 'going among the people' dressed as peasants, preaching the new gospel, they trod on virgin soil; they found no competition in the shape of Trade Unions and Labour politicians telling them to cast off their masquerade and go back to the Bloomsbury of Petrograd or Moscow. The mushik proved apathetic and did not respond to their appeal; but the crusading intelligentsia was not discouraged because they had no rivals; they changed their tactics from mass-appeal to terrorism, from terrorism to work among the industrial proletariat, the landless peasants, among the soldiers. They quarrelled, they split, they ramified; but all the time they could work in the untouched raw material of History, could project their spiritual plight, their desire to destroy and rebuild on to a gigantic historical plane. Their faïth moved rocks because there still were unhewn rocks to move.

In contrast to them, the Western intelligentsia found no virgin fields to plough, no natural allies to realize their aspirations. According to Marxist theory the intelligentsia was to join the ranks of the working class and to become their strategists and tacticians. There is no evidence that the intelligentsia lacked the courage or the ability to do so. In 1848 students and workers fought together on the barricades; in the French Commune and in the revolutionary movements after the last war in Germany, Austria, Hungary, Bulgaria, and even in the International Brigades of Spain, they gave an excellent account of themselves. But from the middle of the nineteenth century onward, the workers of Central and Western Europe had rapidly developed their own organizations, parties, trade unions, produced their own leaders and, above all, their own bureaucracy — men with iron wills and wooden heads. In an age of accelerated developments, the organized Fourth Estate had become stagnant much quicker than the Third in its time, and without even ascending to power. The crumbs of material improvements and the shadow of political influence which various Sections of the Second International had wrung from the rulers, were enough to paralyse their impetus. Members of the Western intelligentsia could become Labour members of Parliament, editors of Left papers, lecturers in dreary evening classes; but there were no rocks to move with the lever of 'independent thought'. Towards the end of the century the Western intelligentsia had only the choice to be either bourgeois decadents or proletarian schoolmasters. Their groups and cliques developed according to these alternative poles, with a spectrum ranging from the French Symbolists through the 'George-Kreis' to the Fabians. Compare Shaw with Voltaire, Leon Blum with St. Just, and you get the difference — not so much in stature as in historical opportunity.

The shake-up of the First World War seemed to create a new

opportunity for a general debunking and rebuilding. The whole body of ideas had undergone a radical transformation: Relativity and Quantum mechanics, Hormonology and Psycho-analysis, Leninism and Behaviourism, Aviation and Wireless, Expressionism and Surrealism — a completely new universe had taken shape in the library; and the dazzling light it radiated drove the intelligentsia half crazy by its contrast to the anachronistic, dusty-musty traditions still governing everyday conduct and beliefs. What an historical opportunity for debunking and rebuilding; but where were the allies to carry it out? The sensitive membrane vibrated wildly; but there was no resonance-body attached to it. Utopian striving during those two decades was monopolized by the Third International, whose blue-print for the European revolution was shaped on the conditions of a country with 80 per cent illiterates and a ratio of rural to urban population of ten to one. During the two decades of its existence the revolutionary movement was focused on and governed by that semi-asiatic dictatorship. Its European extension needed not intellectuals, but a ruthless and uncritically obedient bureaucracy. The few members of the Western intelligentsia who were accepted into its ranks lost first the right, and soon even the desire for 'independent thought'; they became fanatic sectarians and Party-hacks, while the best among them met a tragic end. Particularly tragic was the fate of the revolutionary intelligentsia in the country where revolution seemed almost within reach, Germany. Liebknecht and Luxemburg were murdered in '18, Paul Levy committed suicide after his expulsion from the C.P., Ruth Fischer, also expelled, vanished into obscurity, Toller hanged himself in New York, Muehsam was murdered in a Nazi concentration camp, Max Hoelz was drowned under dubious circumstances in Russia, Heinz Neumann, the last surviving C.P. leader who came from the intelligentsia, was liquidated.

But the bulk of the Western intelligentsia were never admitted to this bloody Olympus. They were not wanted, had to remain fellow-travellers, the fifth wheel to the cart. The intelligentsia of the Pink Decade was irresponsible, because it was deprived of the privilege of responsibility. Left in the cold, suspended in a vacuum, they became decadents of the bourgeoisie. It was nobody's fault; for they were the mirror, not the light.

I am trying neither to whitewash nor to accuse. The intelligentsia is part of the social body, its most sensitive part; when the body is ill, the skin develops a rash. The deterioration of the intelligentsia is as much a symptom of disease as the corruption of the ruling class or the sleeping sickness of the proletariat. They are symptoms of the same fundamental process. To sneer at the intelligentsia and, while depriving it of the responsibility of action, shove on to it the responsibility of failure, is either thoughtless stupidity or a manœuvre with obvious motives. Nazism knew exactly what it was doing when it exterminated the intelligentsia of the European Continent.

v

The Intelligentsia and Neurosis

This sensitive membrane not only stretches between heterogeneous social classes, but between the social body as a whole and its environment. It is tempting, and perhaps not entirely futile, to follow up this metaphor for a while. It is the surface, the ectoderm, philogenetically the rind of the plasmatic bubble, which provides the tissues for the nerves, the spinal cord and the brain in the embryo. The central nervous system is derived not, as one would expect, from the inside, the sheltered parts, the core; but from the exposed surface, permanently submitted to the bombardment of external stimuli, to irritation and excitement, some lust and much pain. Under the influence of this permanent buzzing shower-bath of stimuli the surface-tissue gradually loses its obtuseness and undergoes that strange transformation, that 'burning through' process which finally gives rise to the elusive, first faint glow of consciousness. The grey matter of the brain-rind was originally skin-tissue, exposed and brow-beaten, transformed by a unique organic metamorphosis. Even Freud, that giant of profanity, became almost lyrical where (in *Beyond the Pleasure Principle*) he dealt with this aspect of the biology of the mind.

However, man developed a skull, in which his precious grey matter is safely packed like caviar in a box. No such casing is provided by society for its nervous tissues. They are rather treated like corns on the toes, a nuisance permanently trampled on and permanently hitting back with mean little stabs.

To return from metaphor to fact: the relation between intelligentsia and neurosis is not accidental, but functional. To think and behave independently puts one automatically into opposition to the majority whose thinking and behaviour is dependent on traditional patterns: and to belong to a minority is in itself a neurosis-forming situation. From the nonconformist to the crank there is only one step; and the hostile pressure of society provides the push.

When a man in a concert hall coughs, everybody will cough, and one feels the physical itching in one's throat. Group-mimicry is a real force; to resist it means getting out of tune with one's social environment, creates neurotic tensions and feelings of guilt. One might in theory be a thousand times in the right, and yet feel guilty for butting against the accepted wrong, sanctioned by a tradition whose roots have sprouted in one's own unconscious self. To quarrel with society means to quarrel with its projections in one's self, and produces the classical neurotic split patterns. Oedipus situation and inferiority complex, timidity and arrogance, over-compensation and introversion are merely descriptive metaphors for various deformations with a common denominator: maladjustment. An intelligentsia deprived of the prop of an alliance with an ascending class must turn against itself and develop that hot-house atmosphere, that climate of intellectual masturbation and incest, which characterized it during the last decade.

And it must further develop that morbid attraction for the pseudo-intellectual hangers-on whose primary motive is not the 'aspiration to independent thought' but neurosis pure and simple, and who crowd around the hot-house because the world outside is too cold for them. They infiltrate, and gradually outnumber the legitimate inhabitants, adding to their disrepute, until, in periods of decadence, the camp-followers gradually swallow up the army. It is a sad transformation when social protest dissolves into a-social morbidity.

But even for the 'real' intelligentsia, neurosis is an almost inevitable correlate. Take sex for example. On the one hand we know all about the anachronistic nature of our sex-regulating institutions, their thwarting influence, and the constant barrage of unhappiness they shower on society. On the other hand, individual experiments of 'free companionship', marriages with mutual freedom, etc. etc., all end in pitiful failure; the very term 'free love' has already an embarrassingly Edwardian taint. Reasonable arrangements in an unreasonable society cannot succeed. The pressure of the environment (both from outside and from inside our conditioned selves) is enormous; under its distorting influence the natural becomes cramped, even in writing. You feel it even in such accomplished craftsmen as D. H. Lawrence and Hemingway. You hear, when the critical situation approaches, the author saying to himself: 'Damn it, it is an act of nature and I am going to put it as easily and naturally as if the two of them were having a meal.' And then you watch him, the author, rolling his sleeves up and setting himself to the task; sweat pours down his brow, his eyes pop out of his head, the nib of his pen breaks under the pressure of his desperate efforts to be 'easy and natural about it'. Hence the cramped dialect of Lady Chatterley's lover and that preposterous rabbit in the bag for which no bell would ever toll, in an otherwise masterly novel.

The pressure of the environment cramps art as it cramps behaviour. One may challenge this environment, but one has to pay for it, and the price is neurotic guilt. There never was an intelligentsia without a guilt-complex; it is the income-tax one has to pay for wanting to make others richer. An armament manufacturer may have a perfectly clean conscience, but I have never met a pacifist without a guilty look in his eyes.

Those who attack the intelligentsia for its neurotic dispositions might as well attack the miners for their susceptibility to T.B. It is a professional disease and should be recognized as such, without scorn or shame.

V I

The Intelligentsia and The Future

The old, liberal and socialist intelligentsia of the Continent is no more; though we still fail to realize how thoroughly Nazism implemented its poet laureate's programme 'When I hear the word culture I fire my pistol'. A new intelligentsia may be growing underground, a new seed beneath the snow; but in spite of newspaper articles, intelligence-digests, radio, etc., we know at present as little about the mental climate of the people beyond the Channel, about how the past, present and future looks, smells, tastes to them, as we know about the planet Mars. Samples of literature which reach us from France do not seem to me very encouraging; but then, I am perhaps prejudiced against what I believe to be the growing French intellectual predilection for melodious bombast. Yet in Italy and the Balkans, in Austria and Norway, a process might already have started which one day will come into the open as a brand-new movement, a fresh attitude to life which will make all of us appear like old Victorian dodderers; and any of us who earn a patronizing pat will have got all the credit which historically we deserve.

This is all speculation; it is easier to prophesy in terms of decades than in terms of years. One may have some ideas as to the historical curve along which we move; but the oscillations and ripples of the curve are completely unpredictable. If, in the long run, Burnham's diagnosis comes to be true (as I believe it well may), and if, after some intermediary oscillations, we are in for an era of managerial super-states, the intelligentsia is bound to become a special sector in the Civil Service. This is less far-fetched and fantastic than it sounds; in Russia during the past twenty years this state of affairs has been realized to a very large extent, and Germany during the last ten years was on the way to imitate it. Russian publishing houses, theatres, building trusts, research laboratories, universities and medical services are all owned by the State; the author, actor, architect, scientist, is in fact a civil servant, though the atmosphere is not exactly that of Whitehall. But even the literary movements in Russia — 'Revolutionary Romanticism', 'Socialist Realism', 'Operative Literature', 'New Patriotism' have not spontaneously, organically grown, but were decreed at Party-Congresses and by utterances of government spokesmen; and the same applies, in varying degree, to poetry, drama, architecture, films, not to mention historical research and philosophy. The successive philosophical and artistic movements in the Soviet State look as if they were performed to the pattern 'Left turn — Right turn — As you were'. In the German Reichskulturkammern the transformation of Parnassus into a barrack-square was equally thorough.

In the Anglo-Saxon countries a similar development is difficult, but not altogether impossible to visualize. Above all, a number of different roads may lead to the same goal. Total mobilization during the present war was a kind of dress-rehearsal for the Western version of the bureaucratized state, and during the last two years the intelligentsia has to a large extent been absorbed as temporary civil servants in the Ministry of Information, as Public Relations Officers, in the B.B.C., etc. For the time being 'job' and 'private production' are still kept in separate compartments (with the result that the latter is becoming more and more atrophied); but it is imaginable that a situation may arise in which the two merge; when, instead of regarding the former as a kind of patriotic hacking and the latter as the real thing, the energies become suddenly canalized into one stream. A few may start the new mode, and the rest follow suit; the individuals concerned may believe that they are following a personal impulse, whereas in reality it would be a process of adaptation to the changed social situation of the managerial state. The danger of this happening is all the greater as conformity is often a form of betrayal which can be carried out with a perfectly clean conscience; and the temptation to exchange the miseries which intellectual honesty entails for the heart-warming satisfactions of managerial efficiency is great. The collapse of the revolutionary movement has put the intelligentsia into a defensive position; the alternative for the next few years is no more 'capitalism or revolution' but to save *some* of the values of democracy and humanism or to lose them all; and to prevent this happening one has to cling more than ever to the ragged banner of 'independent thinking'.

It is not, at present, a very popular banner; and unique in this respect, that on its cloth the spittle of derision has clotted together with the blood of our dead.

PART II

EXHORTATIONS

———————

I

SCUM OF THE EARTH — 1942 [1]

FROM time to time just as, after many a year, one hears bits of news and gossip from one's old school, bits of news and gossip reach me from my old concentration camp. It is one of the most distinguished camps of the good old Continent and those of us who survived it wear the old school tie in the shape of some scar on the body, or an ulcer in the stomach or at least a solid anxiety neurosis. As to the news, it is not exactly of the type 'B., the little rotter, is now a dentist in Glasgow', but rather: 'B., the one with the bullet from Guadalajara in his knee, hanged himself in the latrine facing Hut No. 34.'

The latest bits of news reached me through an Englishman who arrived in this country a few weeks ago. He was brought to my old concentration camp at the time of the fall of France, that is, five months after I left it, and spent a year there. He brought me news of those friends of mine who are still alive, from the International Brigaders, the inhabitants of the Leper Barrack, the Gendarmes, the bugs, the rats, from Mimi the Cantinière who stole my wristwatch and Lieutenant Comps who beat Klein with his riding-crop. He brought back to me the smell of the latrines during an epidemic, the smell of the damp straw in the huts and the smell of the men who had been rotting on it for years; the hunger, the cold, the beatings, the fear; the look in the eyes of men the day before they go mad, and the look in the eyes of a gendarme when he puts on your handcuffs.

I said it was a very distinguished camp; its name is Le Vernet

[1] First published in the *Evening Standard*, June 1942.

and it was the only disciplinary camp in France to which prisoners from other camps were transferred for punishment, a sort of Devil's Island north of the Pyrenees. It was originally created during the Spanish prelude to this war to bestow French hospitality upon the defeated Republican militiamen. In those early days accommodation in Le Vernet consisted of trenches dug into the frozen earth, in which the wounded were allowed to die and the healthy to get sick. The first installations in the camp were the barbed wire around it and the cemetery next to it, where the first rows of wooden crosses all bear threefold Spanish names. There are no inscriptions, but one of them, some José or Diego or Jesus had scratched into the wood with his pocket knife: '*Adios, Pedro. Los fascistas* wanted to burn you alive but the French allowed you to freeze to death in peace. *Pues viva la democracia.*'

Later a number of wooden huts were built, each to provide two hundred men with a living space of twenty-one inches in width; and when they were completed, the whole camp was evacuated because some inspecting commission found it uninhabitable for human beings. For a few months it stood empty except for the rats and bugs; then war broke out, and it was filled again with a strange crowd of men from all over Europe whom the French newspapers had graciously labelled the Scum of the Earth.

They were partly the last Mohicans of the International Brigades and partly politically active exiles from all countries under Fascist rule. The French Sureté Nationale, which had never ceased to be an instrument of the Bonnet-Laval policy and which had had Vichy all bottled and ready for sale since September 1939, decided that the first thing to do in a war against Hitler was to lock up all the notorious anti-Hitlerites. To make this private anti-Left pogrom of the Sureté more palatable to the public, the 'Scum' was given a fair sprinkling of about twenty per cent of genuine criminals, pimps, dope peddlars, nancy-boys and other types of the Montmartre underworld.

But the remaining eighty per cent of us, whom they had thrown on the dung heap, were those who had started the present war on our own as far back as 1930 and even earlier; who had drunk of

Mussolini's castor oil and had lain on the torture racks of the Siguranza in Bucarest and sat on the Ghetto benches of Lvov and known the steel whips of the S.S. in Dachau; who had printed secret anti-Nazi leaflets in Vienna and Prague and, above all, had fought through the prelude to the Apocalypse in Spain. Yes, I am rather proud of my old school tie of Le Vernet.

I was released in January 1940 and though I have heard vague rumours of what has happened there since, the first authentic report comes through this young Englishman who was brought into the camp five months after I left. As he still has relatives in France I shall call him by the assumed name of 'Murdoch'. He was arrested in Paris a few days after the German occupation, sent to a prisoners-of-war camp near Rheims, escaped, managed to get into non-occupied France, was arrested by Vichy gendarmes for crossing the demarcation line without permission and sent as a 'suspect' to Vernet, where he arrived, complete with handcuffs, in the first days of July 1940.

His narrative contains all the familiar features of a year's curriculum in Vernet. After three months his weight had gone down from one hundred and fifty to one hundred and twenty pounds. After six months he caught typhoid fever, but unlike those whose strength had been sapped by up to ten years of previous detentions, survived it. After twelve months he had reached a point where he thought that a short agony is better than a long one and embarked on a hunger-strike which, after twenty days proved successful, thanks to the exceptional circumstances of his having a passport and a consul in Marseilles to raise a fuss about him. The characteristic of the ordinary member of the Scum is that he has no passport, no consul and nobody to care twopence for his existence.

Murdock arrived in the camp just at the time when the first rumours about the terms of the Armistice treaty, and of the fatal nineteenth Paragraph of the treaty, began to circulate. Paragraph nineteen provided for the extradition of any German-born subject the German authorities asked for — in other words, the handing over of anti-Nazi refugees to the Gestapo.

And yet when the terms of the Armistice were published there was no panic in the camp. The men got together and appealed to the Commander, asking him to let a few of the most exposed escape before the Germans got them. The Commander refused. As an officer he probably disliked the job he had to do; but after all he had a salary of about ten pounds a month to lose. Next, a delegation of the prisoners asked that their files in the camp office be destroyed before the Gestapo arrived. This the Commander promised; but when the first German commission arrived, the lists of prisoners were complete.

The first Nazi commission arrived at the camp some time in July. And now the tragedy became a sinister farce. For two days before the visit there was, by the Commander's orders, a feverish activity of spit and polish going on. The straw was changed, the huts disinfected, the latrines cleaned. When the commission arrived the whole camp, except a dozen or so who had hanged themselves or cut their veins in time, were lined up for inspection on the parade ground. There they stood for hours, grouped by nationalities, all washed and brushed, with clean ears and finger-nails, in perfect military order, lambs waiting for the butcher. The commission consisted of sixteen smart German officers in various uniforms, including Gestapo and S.S. Correct and impersonal, like cattle-dealers taking stock, they reviewed the parade of their victims. The French gendarmes and officers accompanied them, beaming with smiles.

Surprisingly enough the Germans were in no hurry to get their pound of flesh. Altogether not more than about thirty of the politically most eminent refugees were taken away in small batches of three or five during the following months. Among them were Hans Dahlem and other members of the Central Committee of the German Communist Party, and Hans Schultz who had taken a leading part editing the famous 'Brown Books on the Nazi Atrocities'. He had been one of my dearest friends, and secretary to Willi Muenzenberg, propaganda chief of the West Bureau of the Communist International and perhaps the only match for Goebbels the Comintern ever produced. (Muenzenberg was found hanged in a forest near Grenoble during the days of the collapse; whether he was killed or committed suicide has never been established.)

Apart from the most prominent cases, the Nazis seemed to have lost interest in getting their refugees back. Probably they thought that these wretches could do no more harm, now that Europe was theirs. What they were after instead was human labour. The famous Todt Commission (named after the recently killed builder of the Siegfried line), set up an office in Le Vernet to recruit volunteers for their labour camps, to work on fortifications, in factories, mines, etc. So desperate seemed to be their need for labour that they took anybody, regardless of political faith, 'provided that the candidate was of Aryan descent, medically fit and willing to work hard', promising a fantastically high pay of one hundred and twenty francs, about thirteen shillings a day.

Well over a thousand desperate men enlisted with the Todt Commission. Most of them belonged to the criminal and non-political element. The International Brigaders refused *en bloc.* My informant heard one of them answer to the Commission's question whether he wanted to return to Germany: 'With pleasure — after Thaelman has been made President.' (Thaelman is the leader of the German Communist Party imprisoned since 1932.) Strangely enough, nothing happened to him.

Another thousand or so were shipped by force by the French authorities to North Africa, to work in the modern slave gangs of the Trans-Sahara railway. These deportations were as much dreaded by the camp inmates as extradition to Germany. The victims were selected apparently at random, nobody knew whether his turn would come next. Letters which reached Le Vernet succeeded in conveying, despite the censorship, an idea of the horrors of the Moroccan slave gangs, of men dying like flies from undernourishment, exhaustion and epidemics in the murderous climate. When Murdoch was released he was escorted to Marseilles by a gendarme who had accompanied one of the deportation transports to the embarkation port of Sette. 'We had them all handcuffed', he told Murdoch. 'But they would not keep quiet.

One of them tried to jump out of a window in the train. I just grabbed him by his pants in time. Before we got them on board six escaped, but once we had them aboard we locked them up in the hold with a machine gun on top, and then we had no more trouble with them.'

Extradition to the Gestapo or deportation into the Sahara hung as constant menaces day and night, week after week, month after month, over the heads of the men in Le Vernet. They had no hope for the future; and the past, after years of hunted, outcast life, had become more and more unreal to them. And yet, not more than a dozen went insane and not more than a score committed suicide. The rest not only kept their morale but incredibly opposed their gaolers in a bloodless revolt, scoring a victory over them.

The revolt was organized by the backbone of the community, seven hundred International Brigaders, who had been transferred to Le Vernet from another camp after I had left. 'Without them', says my informant, 'we would all have been dead.'

The unrest started in the fall of 1940. By then the food shortage in the camp had developed into acute starvation. The bread ration was cut down to nine ounces, and the rest of the diet consisted of a half pint of black coffee in the morning and about a pint of soup per day. The little food which reached the camp was for the larger part stolen by the quartermaster and partly sold on the black market, partly sold by the camp canteen for fantastic prices to the wealthier inmates. This canteen was run by a woman named Mimi Dejeune, who slept with Lieutenant Comps, the most notorious sadist in the camp, and split the profits with him. To replace the stolen potatoes and carrots the prisoners' soup was cooked with frozen turnips. On a certain day in December, 1940, the prisoners in common accord buried the frozen turnips in a ditch and started to shout in chorus: 'Nous avons faim' and 'Respectez nos droits'. This went on for hours. Finally the Commander marched into the barbed-wire enclosure at the head of a platoon with cocked rifles. He said: 'I will count up to three and you will disperse.' He counted to three and nobody moved.

He hesitated; if he gave the order to fire he could kill as many prisoners as he liked, but half of his platoon would have been killed too, which probably meant losing his job. While he hesitated a polite voice asked: 'Why don't you start counting once more?' The Commander and his platoon left the enclosure.

The first victory was won. The frozen turnips were thrown away and the prisoners were granted the right to appoint delegates to check the weight of the rations at the quartermaster's stores.

A couple of months later the delegates of two barracks found a deficiency in the rations allotted to them, and refused to accept it. A complicated and lengthy struggle followed, during which first the two barracks in question, and then half of the camp went on hunger strike. All this time the prisoners, with remarkable discipline, avoided any act of violence, refused to fall for any provocation, did not resist when the guards attacked them, and fought by the sole means of depriving themselves of food and of repeating for hours on end, with the monotony of a jungle tom-tom, their two slogans: 'We are hungry' and 'Respect our rights'. The end of it was that the Commander collected about half a regiment of gendarmes from the neighbouring villages, who raided the camp without warning, assaulted the non-resisting crowd with their rifle butts and dragged away one hundred and six men, selected at random. These hundred and six were taken to the local gaol, beaten up all night and sent to prison. His prestige thus re-established, the Commander started negotiations with the prisoners' delegates which ended in the granting of practically all their claims. This victory of sheer will power was the more fantastic as the Commander of Le Vernet at that time was the same Squadron-Leader Pratz of the Garde Mobile who, during the demonstrations on February 6th, 1934, had ordered his men to fire into the crowd at the Place de la Concorde.

When Murdoch was freed, there were about two thousand men left in Vernet. Some Belgians, Swiss and Dutch had been repatriated, over one thousand had gone to slave for Germany under the Todt Commission, about eight hundred were deported to Africa; but new prisoners were brought in all the time. The majority of the newcomers were foreign volunteers who had fought through the battle of France; some had been wounded, some decorated for conspicuous bravery. Now they paraded their Croix de Guerre on the famous latrine fatigues of Vernet. There were even two Chinamen there and an Abyssinian tribesman who had escaped from an Italian prison-camp in 1935 and had since lived in Marseilles until the police rounded him up as 'suspect of anti-fascist activities'. He died of tuberculosis in the hospital of Vernet.

As to genuine Fifth Columnists, only three or four are known to have dishonoured my old concentration camp by a short stay. Leon Degrelle, the Belgian Rexist leader, was locked up for a few days in barrack 17, amongst the Internatoinal Brigaders. He feared that the red savages would kill him. They did not even touch him. They looked through him as if he were transparent. He was released before the armistice was even signed; the camp Commander in person came to announce the good news to him which he did in the classic sentence: '*Monsieur Degrelle votre voiture est arrivée.*'

For my old friends, however, no car arrived; if they left, they left on the stretcher. Mario is the only one of them who, almost by a miracle, managed to get free after having been deported to Morocco. He is now in Mexico, continuing to write his book on Benedetto Croce which he began in Vernet. Publishers who are interested can get in touch with him through me. But old Poddach is still there with his asthma and his despair, and Klein, the Rumanian model shoe-designer; and Yankel was also still there when Murdoch arrived — Yankel, the little boy of nineteen, with his ever-dripping nose and the red scarf around his neck, who had lived through two pogroms and had served two prison sentences for distributing leaflets in Cracow. Murdock thinks he was one of the three who were shot when a party of twelve tried to escape in November, but he is not sure. 'Such a decent little Jew with lots of pluck' is his description. But there were many decent little Jews with lots of pluck in Le Vernet.

EXHORTATIONS

The very last news I had from the camp after Murdoch left was printed in the confidential report of an international philanthropic organization:

> An epidemic has occurred in Le Vernot. During the months of September and October 1941 there was an average of two or three deaths a day due to the absence of the most elementary sanitary care. The internees are allowed to die of hunger in the literal sense of the word. Only in the last extremity are they admitted to the camp infirmary where they die in large numbers.

Pues, viva la democracia. It is June, 1942, and I wonder how many of them still survive. From the barbed-wire fence of Section C they can watch the number of the wooden crosses in the cemetery grow day by day and row by row. It is probably the most cosmopolitan collection of skulls since the mass graves of the crusaders. And crusaders they were, the pride and the heroes of a declining Continent, pioneers in the fight to safeguard the dignity of man. But perhaps future historians will unearth their story, the saga of the International Brigades and of my old concentration camp; and perhaps they will alter the label attached to them, and call them what they really were: 'The Salt of the Earth'.

II

ON DISBELIEVING ATROCITIES[1]

THERE is a dream which keeps coming back to me at almost regular intervals; it is dark, and I am being murdered in some kind of thicket or brushwood; there is a busy road at no more than ten yards distance; I scream for help but nobody hears me, the crowd walks past laughing and chatting.

I know that a great many people share, with individual variations, the same type of dream. I have quarrelled about it with analysts and I believe it to be an archetype in the Jungian sense: an expression of the individual's ultimate loneliness when faced with death and cosmic violence; and his inability to communicate the unique horror of his experience. I further believe that it is the root of the ineffectiveness of our atrocity propaganda.

For, after all, you are the crowd who walk past laughing on the road; and there are a few of us, escaped victims or eye-witnesses of the things which happen in the thicket and who, haunted by our memories, go on screaming on the wireless, yelling at you in newspapers and in public meetings, theatres and cinemas. Now and then we succeed in reaching your ear for a minute. I know it each time it happens by a certain dumb wonder on your faces, a faint glassy stare entering your eye; and I tell myself: now you have got them, now hold them, hold them, so that they will remain awake. But it only lasts a minute. You shake yourself like puppies who have got their fur wet; then the transparent screen descends again and you walk on, protected by the dream barrier which stifles all sound.

We, the screamers, have been at it now for about ten years. We started on the night when the epileptic Van der Lubbe set fire to the German Parliament; we said that if you don't quench those flames at once, they will spread all over the world; you thought we were maniacs. At present we have the mania of trying to tell

[1] First published in the *New York Times Magazine*, January 1944.

you about the killing, by hot steam, mass electrocution and live burial of the total Jewish population of Europe. So far three million have died. It is the greatest mass-killing in recorded history; and it goes on daily, hourly, as regularly as the ticking of your watch. I have photographs before me on the desk while I am writing this, and that accounts for my emotion and bitterness. People died to smuggle them out of Poland; they thought it was worth while. The facts have been published in pamphlets, White Books, newspapers, magazines and whatnot. But the other day I met one of the best-known American journalists over here. He told me that in the course of some recent public opinion survey nine out of ten average American citizens, when asked whether they believed that the Nazis commit atrocities, answered that it was all propaganda lies, and that they didn't believe a word of it. As to this country, I have been lecturing now for three years to the troops, and their attitude is the same. They don't believe in concentration camps, they don't believe in the starved children of Greece, in the shot hostages of France, in the mass graves of Poland; they have never heard of Lidice, Treblinka or Belzec; you can convince them for an hour, then they shake themselves, their mental self-defence begins to work and in a week the shrug of incredulity has returned like a reflex temporarily weakened by a shock.

Clearly all this is becoming a mania with me and my like. Clearly we must suffer from some morbid obsession, whereas the others are healthy and normal. But the characteristic symptom of maniacs is that they lose contact with reality and live in a phantasy world. So, perhaps, it is the other way round: perhaps it is we, the screamers, who react in a sound and healthy way to the reality which surrounds us, whereas you are the neurotics who totter about in a screened phantasy world because you lack the faculty to face the facts. Were it not so, this war would have been avoided, and those murdered within sight of your day-dreaming eyes would still be alive.

I said *perhaps*, because obviously the above can only be half the truth. There have been screamers at all times — Prophets, Preachers, Teachers and Cranks, cursing the obtuseness of their contemporaries, and the situation-pattern remained very much the same. There are always the screamers screaming from the thicket and the people who pass by on the road. They have ears but hear not, they have eyes but see not. So the roots of this must lie deeper than mere obtuseness.

Is it perhaps the fault of the screamers? Sometimes, no doubt, but I do not believe this to be the core of the matter. Amos, Hosea, Jeremiah were pretty good propagandists and yet they failed to shake their people and to warn them. Cassandra's voice was said to have pierced walls, and yet the Trojan war took place. And at our end of the chain — in due proportion — I believe that on the whole the M.O.I. and B.B.C. are quite competent at their job. For almost three years they had to keep this country going, on nothing but defeats, and they succeeded. But at the same time they lamentably failed to imbue the people with anything approaching a full awareness of what it was all about, of the grandeur and horror of the time into which they were born. They carried on business-as-usual style, with the only difference that the routine of this business included killing and being killed. Matter-of-fact unimaginativeness has become a kind of Anglo-Saxon racial myth; it is usually opposed to Latin hysterics and praised for its high value in an emergency. But the myth does not say what happens *between* emergencies and that the same quality is responsible for the failure to prevent their recurrence.

Now this limitation of awareness is not an Anglo-Saxon privilege, though they are probably the only race which claims as an asset what others regard as a deficiency. Nor is it a matter of temperament; stoics have wider horizons than fanatics. It is a psychological fact, inherent in our mental frame, which I believe has not been given sufficient attention in social psychology or political theory.

We say: 'I believe this' or 'I don't believe that'; 'I know it' or 'I don't know it', and regard these as black-and-white alternatives. Now in reality both 'knowing' and 'believing' have varying degrees of intensity. I know that there was a man called Spartacus who led the Roman slaves into revolt; but my belief in his one-time existence is much paler than is that of, say, Lenin. I believe in spiral nebulae, can see them in a telescope and express their distance in figures; but they have a lower degree of reality for me than the inkpot on my table. Distance in space and time degrades intensity of awareness. So does magnitude. Seventeen is a figure which I know intimately like a friend; fifty billions is just a sound. A dog run over by a car upsets our emotional balance and digestion; three million Jews killed in Poland cause but a moderate uneasiness. Statistics don't bleed; it is the detail which counts. We are unable to embrace the total process with our awareness; we can only focus on little lumps of reality.

So far all this is a matter of degrees; of gradations in the intensity of knowing and believing. But when we pass the realm of the finite and are faced with words like eternity in time, infinity of space, that is, when we approach the sphere of the Absolute, our reaction ceases to be a matter of degrees and becomes different in quality. Faced with the Absolute, understanding breaks down, and our 'knowing' and 'believing' become pure lip-service. Death, for instance, belongs to the category of the Absolute and our belief in it is merely a lip-service belief. 'I know' that, the average statistical age being about 65, I may reasonably expect to live no more than another 27 years, but if I knew for certain that I should die on November 30th, 1970, at 5 a.m., I would be poisoned by this knowledge, count and re-count the remaining days and hours, grudge myself every wasted minute, in other words, develop a neurosis. This has nothing to do with hopes to live longer than the average; if the date were fixed ten years later, the neurosis-forming process would remain the same.

Thus we all live in a state of split consciousness. There is a tragic plane and a trivial plane, which contain two mutually incompatible kinds of experienced knowledge. Their climate and language are as different as Church Latin from business slang.

These limitations of awareness account for the limitations of enlightenment by propaganda. People go to cinemas, they see films of Nazi tortures, of mass-shootings, of underground conspiracy and self-sacrifice. They sigh, they shake their heads, some have a good cry. But they do not connect it with the realities of their normal plane of existence. It is Romance, it is Art, it is Those Higher Things, it is Church Latin. It does not click with real y. We live in a society of the Jekyll and Hyde pattern, magnified into gigantic proportions.

This was, however, not always the case to the same extent. There were periods and movements in history — in Athens, in the early Renaissance, during the first years of the Russian Revolution — when at least certain representative layers of society had attained a relatively high level of mental integration; times, when people seemed to rub their eyes and come awake, when their cosmic awareness seemed to expand, when they were 'contemporaries' in a much broader and fuller sense; when the trivial and the cosmic planes seemed on the point of fusing.

And there were periods of disintegration and dissociation. But never before, not even during the spectacular decay of Rome and Byzantium was split thinking so palpably evident, such a uniform mass-disease; never did human psychology reach such a height of phoneyness. Our awareness seems to shrink in direct ratio as communications expand; the world is open to us as never before, and we walk about as prisoners, each in his private portable cage. And meanwhile the watch goes on ticking. What can the screamers do but go on screaming, until they get blue in the face.

I know one who used to tour this country addressing meetings, at an average of ten a week. He is a well-known London publisher. Before each meeting he used to lock himself up in a room, close his eyes, and imagine in detail, for twenty minutes, that he was one of the people in Poland who were killed. One day he tried to feel what it was like to be suffocated by chloride gas in a death-train; the other he had to dig his grave with two hundred others and then face a machine gun, which, of course, is rather unprecise and capricious in its aiming. Then he walked out to the platform and talked. He kept going for a full year before he collapsed with a nervous breakdown. He had a great command of his audiences, and perhaps he has done some good, perhaps he brought the two planes, divided by miles of distance, an inch closer to each other.

I think one should imitate this example. Two minutes of this kind of exercise per day, with closed eyes, after reading the morning paper, are at present more necessary to us than physical jerks and breathing the yogi way. It might even be a substitute for going to church. For as long as there are people on the road and victims in the thicket, divided by dream barriers, this will remain a phoney civilization.

III

KNIGHTS IN RUSTY ARMOUR [1]

I

I HAVE been asked by the editor of this paper to write an article, 'based on personal experience, on what gives men faith to fight to the end for the democratic way'. I quote the question because I feel that, in a negative form, it contains in itself part of the answer. Most of the men whom I have seen dying or going to their death on battlefields, in hospitals, prisons and concentration camps since Badajoz certainly did not part from life out of enthusiasm for an abstract 'democratic way'; and I wonder how many of the men who do the real fighting in this war can tell you even the difference between a British Trade Union and the German Workers Front; not to speak of more complicated constitutional questions.

Take one of the great epics of this war, the tiny Greek Army, of which nobody ever heard before, beating up Mussolini's crack regiments. It was almost a miracle — and yet the Greeks fought under the fascist dictatorship of the late Metaxas, a tryanny so stupid and narrow that it put Plato's *Republic* on the list of forbidden books. Again, take the latest miracle, the defence of Stalingrad. We look with humility, gratitude and admiration at the men and women of the Soviet State. Those who try to divide us from them are playing Hitler's game; but those who pretend that Uncle Joe's ways are democratic ways are either trying to be very clever or are just innocent fools.

II

I am not saying all this for the sake of the cheap pleasure of debunking. I only mean that this war turns out to be a more complicated affair than it looked at the beginning; and that we

[1] First published in the *New York Times Magazine*, January 1943.

should try to focus our eyes on real people, not on the glamour-soldiers and soldierettes of propaganda posters. Talking of real people, we may distinguish two main categories: those who have personally experienced the Nazi-Fascist ways, and those who have not.

The first category — that is, the people on the European Continent — know exactly what they are up against; they know it as intimately as the sufferer knows his pains. But do they also know the remedy? Does the experience of pain provide you with the doctor's insight? The more you talk to people who have recently escaped from the dark Continent, the more you doubt it.

For the Czechs, Poles, Frenchmen, Belgians, Dutch, etc., this war is literally a fight for physical survival. They hate, not the abstract term 'fascism', but the concrete German who destroyed their homes and killed their friends. They fight, not for the abstract term 'democracy', but for the concrete aim of national liberation. If you talk to them of the United States of Europe they look askance at you. One of the main curses Hitler has brought on us is that, by trying to unify Europe in the wrong way, he has caused such a recrudescence of nationalistic, chauvinistic feeling, that the clock of European evolution has been put back for at least fifty years. Whether you like it or not, the wish-dream of the martyrized Continent is a super-Versailles, and 'national sovereignty' is the great slogan of the hour.

As to those who have had no personal experience of fascism — the common people in Anglo-Saxon countries — the term democracy has very little real meaning to them. They are as unaware of the basic constitutional liberties they enjoy as they are unaware of the composition of the air they breathe.

And this, if you reflect upon it, is perhaps the proudest achievement of the liberal era. Indeed, the ideal for a well-functioning democratic state is the same as for a gentleman's well-cut suit — it should not be noticed. For the common people of Britain, Gestapo and concentration camps have approximately the same degree of reality as the monster of Loch Ness. Atrocity propaganda is helpless against this healthy lack of imagination. I have tried my hand at it. Whenever I have lectured to the troops on fascist concentration camps I have had the distinct feeling that as long as I had a grip on the audience they believed me, but that as soon as I had gone they did not believe me any more than one believes in yesterday's nightmare, and started happily to sing 'Who's Afraid of the Big Bad Wolf?'

Thus the great majority of the people in this country has still not the faintest idea of what this bogy of fascism means. On the other hand, they have a very clear idea of what German aggression and the German Air Force mean; here their thoughts move along the well-established association-tracks of 1914; and since the blitz on Coventry those who try to discriminate between 'Germans' and 'Nazis' are fighting a losing battle. Soon they are going to be buried with military honours in the columns of the *New Statesman and Nation*; and the nearer victory comes in sight, the clearer the character of the war reveals itself as what the Tories always said that it was — a war for national survival, a war in defence of certain conservative nineteenth-century ideals, and not what I and my friends of the Left said that it was — a revolutionary civil war in Europe on the Spanish pattern.

And this is so not because the Tories are cleverer than the Left, or because Mr. Churchill has more 'massivity' than Mr. Attlee, but because the great majority of ordinary people of all classes still think more in terms of the nineteenth century than of the twentieth, and of wars more in terms of the Charge of the Light Brigade than of the International Brigade. The last Gallup poll revealed that 91 per cent of the British people approved of Mr. Churchill's policy after his famous 'we are going to hold what we have' speech. Let us be frank; and while we rejoice over the victory of our arms, let us recognize the defeat of our aims.

III

So far I have spoken about the non-political majority. Now what about us, the conscious minority who dreamed and worked for a unified, fraternal, socialist Europe? It must be admitted that we are beginning to look rather silly, and personally I am getting sick of my own and my friends' wailings and moanings. Let us instead face the facts and see where we stand.

The great international movements have failed. The Second International failed in its mission when it failed to prevent the war in 1914; the Third International when it failed to prevent Hitler's ascension to power in 1933 and became a mere extension of the Russian Foreign Office. Thus the defensive coalition of conservative and progressive forces which the Nazi menace brought into being stood from the very beginning under conservative leadership. It was the Appeasers, not the Crusaders, who led us into the war — because the Crusaders, even if they were a thousand times right, had been too often defeated to be trusted by the people, whereas the Appeasers, with all their past blunders, had the solid forces of inertia behind them.

In consequence the war was waged from the very beginning not only strategically but ideologically on defensive lines. We were and are fighting 'in defence' of conservative values that are expressed in nineteenth-century terms against a ruthlessly offensive 'new order'. And while recently the Allied coalition switched to the offensive in the military field, its ideology is still conservative and defensive, even more pronouncedly so than before. The American elections, the burlesque Darlaniad, the melancholy Crippsiad and other events make it increasingly clear that the scales are moving more and more to the conservative side, almost in direct proportion to the approach of victory; and that the people do not seem to mind very deeply — they are much more interested in the Eighth Army's advance than in Cripps' retreat.

Thus, if nothing unexpected happens, the coming victory will be a conservative victory and lead to a conservative peace. It will produce no lasting solution of the minority problems in the European jigsaw puzzle. It will provide no cure for the inherent disease of the capitalistic system. It will not mark a decisive step in the ascent of the human race. But it will bring an enormous temporary relief to the people of the Continent, it will bring salvation to millions whose life seemed doomed, and a certain minimum of liberty, decency, security. Briefly, it will be a new, perhaps slightly improved, edition of the pre-Hitlerian old order, a nineteenth-century postscript to the first half of the twentieth, which history has written in such abominable style. And I hope, and believe, that this anachronistic patchwork, if it is achieved with good craftsmanship, may give Europe a breathing space of perhaps a couple of decades, with at least a chance of averting the next fatal plunge.

That means that we are beginning to realize that this war is not the final cataclysm, not the ultimate showdown between the forces of darkness and light, but perhaps only the beginning of a new series of convulsions, spread over a much larger period of history than we originally thought, until the new world is born. The task will be to use the coming breathing space as best we can. And, incidentally, to give praise every morning we awake without a Gestapo sentry under our window, for this nineteenth-century postscript, our own physical survival. Who among those who lived through the French collapse two years ago believed in it? I for one did not.

IV

I am aware that this is a very modest credo for a member of what you call the 'Left intelligentsia', and that my friends are going to throw stones and call me names. The more so as they too must feel, more or less consciously, that we have manœuvred ourselves into a political vacuum — a vanguard cut off from its sources of supply.

We have thought of the Battle for Progress in the classical terms of Socialist trench warfare with neat, tidy front lines between the classes — and are caught in a perplexing fluid war of social movements with mobile units breaking loose from their social bodies; large sections of the working class joining the fascist ranks, radical wings of the younger Tory generation operating on the Left of the Trade Unions, bureaucracies and managers establishing themselves in vital hedgehog positions. And there we stand in no-man's land, dazzled knights in rusty armour, with a well-thumbed handbook of Marx-Engels quotations as our sole guide — the truest and profoundest social guide of the last century, but, alas! of modest use on this topsy-turvy battleground of to-day.

There is, however, a more encouraging aspect of this picture. For the last fifteen years those knights in rusty armour with Liberty, Equality, Fraternity written on their shields have always fought on the losing side. Shanghai, Addis Ababa, Madrid, Vienna, Prague — one long chain of wretched debacles, until it became a habit with us to live in a climate of constant defeat, a kind of permanent apocalypse. Defeat taken in large doses is a dangerous drug; it becomes an addiction.

Now for the first time it seems that we shall be on the winning side. And though this victory will be very different from what we dreamed, it might produce an enormous change — get us out of the habit of defeat. And once we get into the habit of winning, with our armour brought up to date, who knows where we shall stop?

IV

THE FRATERNITY OF PESSIMISTS [1]

IN this war we are fighting against a total lie in the name of a half-truth. This is a more modest formulation than those currently used, but if we tentatively accept it, the present will probably appear less confused and the future less depressing.

We call Nazism's New Order a total lie because it denies the specific ethos of our species, because by proclaiming that might is right it reduces Civil Law to Jungle Law, and by proclaiming that race is all reduces Sociology to Zoology. With such a philosophy there can be no compromise; it must unconditionally surrender.

We, on the other hand, live in a climate of half-truths. We fight against Racialism and yet racial discrimination is far from abolished in the Anglo-Saxon countries; we fight for Democracy and yet our mightiest ally is a dictatorship where at least two of the four freedoms are not operating. But such is the sticky, all-pervading influence of our climate that even to mention these facts, undeniable though they are, has the effect of a provocation.

'So why rub it in?' some will probably say. 'This is a battle-field, not a public confessional.' The answer is that on both sides of the Atlantic people are getting more restive the nearer victory approaches. There is a strange mood of uneasiness everywhere — the hangover seems to precede the celebration.

After Dunkirk, at a time when America was still neutral and Russia still waiting for Hitler to open a second front in the East, many of us in this country felt that only a miracle could save us. Like a patient before a desperate operation, we thought: Lord, if I survive this I'll start a new life — and what a life it will be! Well, the miracle came, the operation succeeded and the patient was discharged from hospital — only to discover that his house is still in the slums, the letter-box still full of creditors' bills, his wife's voice still as strident and her eyes as squinting as before,

[1] First published in the *New York Times Magazine*, November 1943.

and the awful child's nose still drips all day. Is he ungrateful to fate if the next morning he starts grumbling and swearing again?

Ever since the critical operation succeeded in North Africa, the bills kept coming in and the voices became more strident, the looks more squinting in the allied family apartment. But sentimental appeals for more goodwill and co-operation between the competing partners who to-morrow will rule the world are naive and pointless. Governments have only a narrow margin for manœuvring within the fatal automatism of the economic and social forces behind them. For at least fifty years it has become increasingly clear that only a vigorous international, i.e. 'horizontal', organization could end the global muddle by global solutions. In the first decades of this century, and particularly between the two wars, there was an immense hope that such a horizontal force would emerge and sweep away the vertical structures of competing national egotisms. Progressive people all over the world set their hopes on the League of Nations, the Second and Third International; and even the more conservative clung, consciously or unconsciously, to 'horizontal' hopes such as the Vatican, some other Church or a masonic brotherhood.

The outstanding feature of our days is the collapse of all horizontal structures. That our truths are half-truths is a direct consequence of it. And unless we overcome our reluctance to chew, swallow and digest the bitter pill, we shall not be able to see clearly either where we stand or whither we drift.

Seen from the melancholy angle of a Continental (or rather of that bunch of homeless Leftists to whom I belong, and whom the Stalinites call Trotskyites, the Trotskyites call Imperialists, and the Imperialists call bloody Reds), the bankruptcy of Left horizontalism is becoming increasingly apparent. The corpse of the Comintern, in an advanced stage of decomposition, has at last been officially interred; Mr. Lewis' complicated game of stick-up-chess with President Roosevelt was a memento of the state of affairs in the American Labour movement; in Russia the wheel is coming back full circle to the traditional values of the Fatherland, the Cadet Schools and the Orthodox Church; the British Labour

Party dropped its last pretence of Socialist horizontalism when it adopted a Vansittartite resolution which made the German people, including the thirteen million workers who at the last free elections voted against the Nazis, collectively responsible for the Nazis' deeds.

If ever there was a chance for Socialism in Britain, it was in the period from Dunkirk to the fall of Tobruk. Popular discontent against the conduct of the war seemed at its peak. In a dozen or so by-elections the Government was defeated. The Government had been invested with the power of nationalizing all individual property in the country; the transition to State-Socialism could have been achieved merely by political pressure, without revolution or civil war. For, in contrast to French Big Business, which when faced by the dilemma 'Hitler or the Popular Front' opted for Hitler, the British ruling class, with dwindling exceptions, seemed prepared to live rather in a red Britain than under Nazi domination. (This difference in attitude between the British and French ruling classes is of historical importance; it was the crucial test of Britain's fitness for survival.) However, the working class lacked the political maturity to grasp its opportunity. Intelligent Tories have to this day not recovered from the surprise that capitalism survived the Dunkirk to Singapore crisis.

This was only a link in the chain of Socialism's missed opportunities. Before, there was the Weimar Republic, the American slump, the Popular Front victories in France and Spain. What an enormous longing for a new human order there was in the air between the two wars, and what a miserable failure to live up to it! Fascism was the profiteer of this failure. Again and again the Socialist movement played the rôle of what the French call a *séducteur jusqu'au bord du lit* — a seducer who loses heart at the bedroom-door (to put it politely). History is a capricious belle, and if the suitor goes on missing the rare chances accorded to him, the damage becomes irreparable. After a while the courtship turns into mere pretence, and nothing would embarrass the aged wooer more than if she suddenly threw herself into his arms — imagine Mr. Attlee as Britain's Marxist premier....

Political movements, it seems, have their own organic laws. They grow, and if at the time of their maturity they don't attain fulfilment by seizing power, they decline and wither away. That is what happened to the horizontal movements in this century. The League of Nations died of consumption, the official Churches are politically paralysed, the Second International developed arteriosclerosis, the Third decayed. The only survivors of the age of the ascending power of the workers are the Trade Unions. I am far from underrating their enormous importance and the positive function they fulfil. But they are an economic safeguard, not a creative political force.

The failure of 'horizontalism' in our time is more than a momentary set-back; it reveals the inadequacy of a method of approach which dominated the Liberal and Socialist movements for the last century. To talk of 'ups and downs' is self-deception; we are not on a mountain-railway but in a blind alley. To-day we are farther than twenty years ago from the realization of a truly new human climate, from thinking, feeling, acting in inter-continental terms adequate to the speed of communications. All our post-war planning has the character of designing makeshift bridges from one vertical power-centre to the other; they are half-honest, half-earnest attempts to get somehow over the next decade or two which, everybody vaguely feels, will not be an era of long-term solutions but an intermediate, transitory period, an interregnum of half-truths and twilight, fraught with the danger that the bridges may crack and the fatal mechanism may push the vertical giants once more on their blind march of destruction.

So far this is a pessimistic picture, but based, I believe, on objective facts. What follows is a purely subjective assessment of future trends, which some will say is crankish. But I know that many others have the same vague feelings in their bones; I am talking to those others.

Interregnums — i.e. periods of transitory chaos which follow the collapse of the traditional values of a civilization — are of limited duration. I believe that the day is not far when the present interregnum will end, and a new 'horizontal' ferment will arise — not a new party or sect, but an irresistible global mood, a spiritual spring-tide like early Christianity or the Renaissance. It will probably mark the end of our historical era, the period which began with Galileo, Newton and Columbus, the period of human adolescence, the age of scientific formulations and quantitative measurements, of utility values, of the ascendancy of reason over spirit. Its achievements were gigantic; the spasms of its death struggle are terrifying. But they can't last much longer; as the frequency of the convulsions increases, the amplitude of their violence grows; the point of exhaustion has come within almost measurable range. There might be one or two more world-wars but not a dozen; it is a question of decades, not of centuries.

What will the new age after the interregnum be like? One thing is certain: it will not be the Brave New World with which Huxley frightened us. It is Hitler's historic merit that he immunized us against Totalitarian utopias, as a dose of cholera-vaccine immunizes against cholera. I do not mean that similar attempts will not be made in other parts of the world during the remaining decades of the interregnum. But they will be mere episodes, symptoms of the agony of the dying age.

The clue to the values of the coming new global mood is provided by historical analogy. We can discern in the past a succession of levels of social awareness, like an ascending staircase. The age of religious wars ended when secular politics began to dominate human consciousness; feudal politics ended when economic factors assumed overriding importance; the struggles of Economic Man will end by the emergence of the new ethical values of the new age. The great disputes are never settled on their own level, but on the next higher one. The Second and Third Internationals got into the blind alley because they fought capitalism in its own terms of reference, and were unable to ascend to that spiritual climate the longing for which we feel in our bones.

Seen from the perspective of the next-higher historical level, the old controversies lose interest, appear drained of their meaning; and conversely, the exact properties of the succeeding period cannot be formulated from the lower level. Such attempts lead to mystic dilettantism, like Heard's yogi journalese. All we can say is that the new movement will re-establish the disturbed balance between rational and spiritual values, or, in Auden's words, *rally the lost and trembling forces of the will — Gather them up and let them loose upon the earth.* But as yet we live in the interregnum.

Those who are basically optimists can afford to face facts and to be pessimistic in their short-term predictions; only basic pessimists need the dope of the half-truth. The interregnum of the next decades will be a time of distress and of gnashing of teeth. We shall live in the hollow of the historical wave. Does this mean that we should lie low and wait fatalistically until the time is ripe?

I believe the contrary. What we need is an active fraternity of pessimists (I mean short-term pessimists). They will not aim at immediate radical solutions, because they know that these cannot be achieved in the hollow of the wave; they will not brandish the surgeon's knife at the social body, because they know that their own instruments are polluted. They will watch with open eyes and without sectarian blinkers, for the first signs of the new horizontal movement; when it comes, they will assist its birth; but if it does not come in their lifetime, they will not despair. They will not necessarily expect the new movement to arise from this or that section of the working or professional classes; but certainly from the ranks of the poor, from those who have suffered most. And meanwhile their chief aim will be to create oases in the interregnum desert.

Oases may be small or big. They may consist of only a few friends as in Silone's great book *The Seed Beneath the Snow*; or they may embrace whole countries — countries situated on the periphery of the great fields of force, for instance Italy, Norway, Spain. It is quite possible that in the coming world of bellicose managerial giant States of the Burnham pattern such marginal oases survive; that, although submitting to the general social-economic trend, they will be able to afford a greater amount of tolerance and old-fashioned humaneness than the main competitors; Switzerland during the last three hundred years is an obvious example. And it may further be possible to create enclaves, and to a certain extent to influence the climate, within the competing giant-States themselves. During an earlier interregnum, in the so-called dark ages between the decline of Rome and the dawn of the Renaissance, such oases assured the continuity of civilization: the monasteries first, and later the Universities with their more or less extra-territorial Alma Mater on which no gendarme could set boot.

Among the great Powers, Britain, thanks to the obstinacy of her traditions and the great inertia of her body social, is probably the most capable of developing an oasis-climate. Interregnums are downward slopes of history; and at this point of our journey the brakes of the train are more important than the engine. During the last century our ethical brakes were more and more neglected, until totalitarian dynamism made the engine run amok. In plain language, that means that if I have to choose between living under a Political Commissar or a Blimp, I unhesitatingly choose Blimp. He will treat me as an annoying kind of oddity and push me about from sheer lack of imagination; the imaginative Commissar will politely shoot me because I disagree with him. In other historical situations, on the upward grade, Blimp might again become the main enemy of progress. For the next decades, his muddled decency and clinging to traditional values (even if it is partly pretence) will be a great asset, to mollify the impact.

In 1917 Utopia seemed at hand. To-day it is postponed for the duration of the interregnum. Let us build oases. . . .

V

LE ROI EST MORT

I

'LE ROI EST MORT, VIVE LE ROI', the French courtiers used to cry
when the pox finally had the better of the king. 'Hitler est mort,
vive le Fascisme' is a possible variation for the next few years to
come, and we had better get this straight in our minds lest we
find ourselves as painfully surprised as the keeper who went to
sleep with his head in the lion's mouth. Fascism can't be defeated
on the battlefield alone; it has to be defeated inside people's brains,
hearts and glands; for it is merely a new word for a very old state
of mind. Wherever there is talk of niggers, sheenies and kikes;
wherever there is snooping, official or private, into citizens'
amorous habits and political creed; wherever a demand for better
wages is called the Red Menace and a legal strike is smashed with
lead pipes and shot-guns — wherever these things happen, fascism
is there, straight under your nose; you don't need to go to the
pictures and look at the technicolour-Gestapo to find it.

Freedom is a matter of degrees. The prisoner in solitary confinement is less free than the one allowed exercise; an internment
camp is paradise compared with prison; fascist Italy was a free
country compared with Nazi Germany and an unfree one compared with France; but French democracy denied women the
right to vote — or to keep a bank-account without the husband's
gracious permission. This of course seems a very barbarous thing
to Americans and confirms them in their smug conviction of living
in the freest country in the world. I knew of a man who committed
suicide because, having been driven through the streets of Vienna
with a sandwich-board round his neck which said: 'I am a filthy
Semite, please spit at me', and having reached the blessed shores
of America, he was turned out of a restricted hotel. He obviously
didn't know that such a thing existed; he liked American films,

and the tough Sergeant had never mentioned it when he quoted the Gettysburg speech in the Jungle of Bataan.

Now when I say that the difference between fascism and democracy is merely a matter of degrees, you will probably object by referring to constitutional guarantees — freedom of the Press, parliamentary representation, and so on. This is of course true, and whoever has lived under a dictatorship knows the vital importance of democratic institutions — knows it even better than those who always use this argument to prove that everything is all right. But he also knows the difference between the letter of the law and the spirit in which it is applied. One would blush to quote such a platitude but for that Sergeant in Bataan who seems always apt to confound Abraham Lincoln with President Harding. Let us dot the 'i's then (the trouble with the Atlantic Charter and the Dumbarton Oaks plan is that they they consist mainly of undotted 'i's and uncrossed 't's) and get it straight that Hitler too has a parliament which is theoretically free to sack him any time; that under Horthy's rule the Hungarian Labour Party was allowed to remain legal and even to publish a daily paper until a few months ago; and that the most democratic constitution in the world, the Soviet constitution of 1936, is apparently compatible with a one-party system and the banning of all oppositional activities.

In other words, one can't rely on constitutional guarantees and use them as an excuse for complacency. We always think of fascism as of something solid, palpably different from our forms of life. It would be more correct to compare it with a gas which can be put into any container regardless of its shape. And once you get into the habit of living amidst a moderate amount of stink you won't notice it when you become completely poisoned. The danger is not that we may wake up one morning to find a fascist world; that would be easy to prevent. The danger is that we went to bed the previous night in a world which was already turning fascist without our noticing it.

I wish you wouldn't think that these are the exaggerations of a professional Cassandra. The European Cassandras between the two wars did not shout because they were pessimists, or masochists, or scaremongers, or for the pleasure of saying afterwards 'I told you so'. They can't say it anyway because few of them survive. They warned you, not because they were visionaries, but because they had seen reality — and suffered it on their own body. The socialists warned you against Hitler because they knew Dachau and Oranienburg. The French clamoured for security because they knew what invasion meant. The small nations warned you against power-politics, the conception of the Big Three (or Four or Five) because they knew they were going to pay the bill. The Jews warned you against racialism because they knew that what starts as Calling Names ends in lynching and massacre, whether in Calcutta, Warsaw or Detroit. And to-day those of us who saw Fascism grow and know its first symptoms warn you against the pious error of calling the pox a pimple.

Suffering alone, of course, does not produce wisdom; so do not think us arrogant or patronizing when we point to the difference between our experience and yours. Not every martyr is a saint; and often he behaves like a fool. The Poles, second only to the Jews, had suffered the worst tragedy; they were butchered by the enemy and let down by their allies; and look how they succeeded in spoiling their own case. It seems as if they were incapable of learning their lesson — but it would be more correct to say that History is a bad teacher: it inflicts the punishment first and leaves it to the pupil to find out why. And the Poles are not the only bad pupils; on the greater part of the devastated Continent nationalism and blind vindictiveness are on the increase, and even the guerrillas and resistance movements fight among themselves, openly or covertly, both in the liberated countries and in those still occupied.

But nevertheless there is a difference between those who have suffered and those who remained relatively untouched. Among the millions of Europe who have experienced famine, terror and degradation, there is a conscious minority who did learn at least a thing or two. They are the only asset left on a bankrupt continent and its strongest hope. They should not be identified with this or that party or group, though they are more numerous in the groups of the Left than of the Right; they are as yet no more than individuals with a common denominator, and it is possible that for some time the old parties and new foreign allegiances to East and West will superimpose their pattern. That they are still a minority does not matter. Whatever progress there was achieved in History has always been initiated by such conscious minorities — if and when they succeeded in grafting their awareness on the inert mass, in pointing out to them where their own interest lay. Without them the Bastille would never have been stormed and the United States would never have been united. They are the good pupils of History who draw and interpret the lesson.

Now such minorities exist of course everywhere — among the American intelligentsia as in the maquis of Norway and France. But that is precisely the point where the difference between the Haves and Have-nots of suffering and experience comes in. Among the Have-nots the intelligentsia is a small and rather isolated body. Their Cassandra-cries are prompted by vision, not by experience. They may shout themselves hoarse and yet find no resonance, because the masses have not been tuned to the same wave-length by suffering and experience, because they lack the visionaries' imaginative gifts and have simply no idea what the fellow gets so excited about. This lack of response influences in turn the character of the intellectual Cassandra; he becomes lonely and bitter and gets even more out of tune with the ordinary man. Had the French peasants in the eighteenth century not been prepared by suffering and starvation, Danton and St. Just would have had to spend their lives editing some equivalent of the *New Republic* or *Partisan Review*.

Obviously, on the continent of Europe climate and conditions are different. At least the people there have lost their callowness —

that charming, disarming monstrous ignorance of what it's all about which characterizes the average American soldier and officer abroad. Have you seen photographs of American tanks surrounded by natives in a French or Belgian village? Those people who stretch out their hands for a bar of chocolate or throw flowers at the turret are each one of them a century older than the boys inside. You see it in their eyes, even if they smile. You see it even in the young girl who kisses the driver. They are the Haves of experience. And that conscious minority among them on whom our hopes are based are not isolated individuals sprung from the intelligentsia, but men of action and sensitivity who sprang mainly from the resistance movements. Their number is much greater in proportion, their ties with the masses are more human and intimate, and their chance to be heard is better, even if that takes some time. For the broad inert masses themselves have not only been fanaticized but also sensitivized; that is what makes the people on the photographs look older and more mature than the boys in the turret.

'Souffrir passe; avoir souffert ne passe jamais.' This residue of their sufferings will remain, even if it finds no immediate political expression, even if it remains for some time an under-current waiting for the chance to break through the chaotic surface. They may commit follies and mistakes, but these will not be quite the same mistakes as before. And perhaps they will not even be their own mistakes, but imposed upon them from outside: false polarizations and national splits which merely reflect latent conflicts between the great Powers competing for zones of influence. After all, if the Poles had acquired all the wisdom of this earth, their fate would still have been much the same. Thus if you hear about the quarrels among Greek partisans or French maquisards, don't say smugly: These people are the same fools they were before, their sufferings haven't changed them. The change is there and will bear its fruit in time — if power-politics gives them a chance. And if this chance is denied them as it has been in the past, they have at least an excuse for going temporarily mad.

But you have no such excuse. You are not sandwiched in

between big neighbours who decide your fate either by bullying or by washing their hands of you. A Venezuelan invasion of the States is rather unlikely for the next few hundred years. Nor will the Canadian government finance a movement in your midst to pose as a national revolutionary party. You are the richest country in the world. Twice within a generation you have saved Western Europe from subjugation. After the first time you have robbed yourself and your dead in the French cemeteries of the moral credit of their sacrifice. The people of Europe are asking themselves whether this time you are going to do the same.

III

Freedom being a matter of degrees, the great danger for those who have not been immunized by experience is the smoothness of transition to successive degrees of unfreedom. This goes for the whole of our Western civilization. The great catastrophes of history, like the decay of Rome, did not come in one spectacular crash, but by a smooth tobogganing down the slope, which may last centuries or decades.

It seems a curious law of human nature that the real tragedies are camouflaged by a smooth triviality. The first symptoms of tuberculosis are much less dramatic than whooping cough. Mental disease starts with quite harmless signs compared with the violence of a nervous breakdown. Every soldier knows that the sky and the fields never look so dreamy, peaceful and safe as in the lull of a battle. Every psycho-analyst knows that the real conflicts of the patient lie behind those ideas and dreams which he dismisses as trivial and unimportant. And if one re-reads the entries of one's diary after a year, one is surprised to find that those events which mattered most to one are all strangely under-emphasized; the same applies to many autobiographies.

Curious as this phenomenon appears, its reasons are obvious. The mind can only maintain its balance by surrounding itself with a kind of protective filter which reduces the great, tragic tides of reality to a trivial spray. Without it, we would all go off our heads in our 'teens. It is a necessary device, but it has its drawbacks. In a crisis it preserves our sanity; when all seems to be going well it makes us callously self-satisfied. The English habit of 'under-statement' has its unconscious roots in the same tendency to filter down the tragic to a cant-spray of banality; it dates from the late Victorian period when England became a bastion of power and complacency.

Suffering enlarges the holes of the filter; that is the great advantage of the Haves over the Have-nots. The essence of all moral teaching and exhortation is to make us perform the same operation by a voluntary effort. But that is an arduous task; that's why it is so much easier to wage war than to wage peace. . . .

PART THREE

EXPLORATIONS

I

ANATOMY OF A MYTH

'The unbelievable epochs are the cradles of new superstitions.' — AMIEL

I

NEWTON wrote not only the *Principia* but also a treatise on the topography of Hell. Up to this day we all hold beliefs which are not only incompatible with observable facts, but with facts actually observed by us. The hot steam of belief and the iceblock of reasoning are packed together inside our skulls, but as a rule they do not interact; the steam does not condense and the ice does not melt. The human mind is basically schizophrenic, split into at least two mutually exclusive planes. The main difference between 'pathological' and 'normal' schizophrenia lies in the isolated character of the irrational component in the former, as opposed to the collectively accepted irrationality of the latter.

Typical examples of socially approved split-mind patterns are the Astronomer who believes both in his instruments and in Christian dogma; the Army padre; the Communist who accepts 'proletarian millionaires'; the psycho-analyst who gets married; the determinist who abuses his opponents. The Primitive knows that his idol is a piece of carved wood, and yet he believes in its power to make rain; and though our beliefs underwent a gradual refinement, the dualistic pattern of our minds remained basically unchanged.

There are indications that this dualism is correlated to specific neural processes. Recent progress in neurology established the thalamus (the philogenetically older central organ of the midbrain) as the seat of feeling and emotion, and the pallial cortex (the rind of the relatively new brain-hemispheres) as the seat of discriminative ('logical') thought. Animal experiments and the study of certain types of brain-injuries during the last war (e.g. Head's thalamic syndrome) disclosed two mutually inhibitive tendencies of reaction to a given situation: the 'thalamic' and the 'cortical' type of behaviour. Thalamic behaviour is dominated by emotion, cortical behaviour by formal reasoning. Irrational beliefs are rooted in emotion; they are *felt* to be true. Believing may be defined as 'knowing with one's viscerae'. Behaviour under thalamic domination is accompanied by affective, that is, wishful or fearful thinking; the type of thinking we find in monkeys, savages and infants; and in twenty-three out of twenty-four hours in ourselves. Cortical, i.e. detached rational thought, is a new and fragile acquisition which breaks down at the slightest irritation of the viscerae, reported by the autonomous system to the thalamus, which, once aroused, dominates the scene.

Both anthropology and psychology have during the last fifty years led to convergent results. Levy-Bruehl proved that the mentality of the primitives is pre-logical; the Kantian categories of (homogenous) space, time and causality do not exist in the primitive mind; it is controlled not by formal reasoning but by ready-made beliefs (pré-liaisons collectives). Freud demonstrated the affective roots of thought and followed them down to Totem and Tabu; Jung showed that certain archaic or archetypal images and beliefs are the collective property of our race. Even modern philology came more or less independently to the same results; Ogden and Richards proved the emotional fetish-character of words and tautological statements. Science has at last reached a stage sufficiently rational to be able to see the irrationality of the mind's normal functioning.

The science which has so far been least affected by these developments is politics. The ultimate reason for the failure of the Second, Third and Fourth Internationals, and of international socialism in general, is their disregard of the irrational factor in the human mind. Socialist doctrine and Leftist propaganda remain based on the assumption that man is an entirely rational being who only needs convincing by logical arguments, evening classes, pamphlets, Penguins, etc., to recognize his own interests and to act accordingly. The subconscious, the older half of the brain, the archetypes, the world of the dream the ductless glands, the autonomous nervous system, the id, — that is, ninety per cent of what constitutes the real *Homo Sapiens*, was left out of the picture. Hence the total failure of the Left to analyse, explain and counteract the phenomenon of Fascism. Hence its self-deceiving, shallow optimism even on the present verge of the abyss.[1]

I I

This basic shortcoming of the Left cannot be explained by individual shortcomings of their leaders. Its roots lie much deeper.

Up to the end of the eighteenth century, revolutionary movements had either a religious basis, or at least strong religious ties. They satisfied both the rational desire for a better life and the irrational craving for an Absolute. In other words, they were emotionally saturated movements. The French Revolution brought a radical change.

The Reformation had attacked the corrupt papist clergy in the name of God; its secular struggle had left deity intact. The French Revolution was a frontal attack not only against the clergy, but against God. Robespierre's attempt to provide a synthetic substitute in the 'Goddess of Reason' proved a failure.

[1] Fascism, on the other hand, despite its emphasis on the irrational and the myth, is no nearer to scientific truth. It errs on the other side; the rational element is underplayed, its sociology is based on an untenable race-theory, its political economy is rudimentary and eclectic, its society static.

The only scientific attempt at a synthesis between the Marxian approach to history on the one hand and the 'neo-machiavellian school' – Michel, Pareto, Sorel, Mosca – to which Fascism is the heir, on the other hand, was made by Burnham; and he was promptly stoned by the Left. Burnham's conclusions are often sweeping and it is easy to criticize him in detail; but the originality of his approach and its immensely stimulating character come at once into relief if one contrasts the *Managerial Revolution* or *The Machiavellians* with, say, Professor Laski's *Reflections on the Revolution of our Time*. They compare as an aphrodisiac with an aspirin tablet.

Fortunately, however, other Absolutes substituted themselves: Liberté Egalité Fraternité was not a mere slogan but a fetish; so were the Tricolor and the Phrygian çap. Roman tradition — Consuls, Patriots, the new calendar, etc. — provided the mythology of the new cult. The Church as a secular vehicle of deity was superseded by *la patrie* as an instrument for the spreading of the new gospel of the Rights of Man. The American Constitution contains the words: 'We hold the truth to be self-evident that all men are created equal.' The emphasis is on 'self-evident'; it is the operative word for axiomatic belief, for a Revelation beyond the reach of logical reasoning.

But the direct emotional appeal of the new deities was of short duration; it wore off in less than a century as compared with almost two millennia of the Christian myth. The reasons are obvious. The myths and rites of Christianity had a continuous ancestry back through Judea, Sumeria, Babylon, to neolithic man, to magic and animism. Its roots were in the deepest archetypal layers of the unconscious. But the tenets of 1789 were a product of conscious reasoning. For a short time they were capable of filling the sudden vacuum, of serving as idols *faute de mieux*. But they were not capable of personification, they could not serve as a projecting screen for man's craving for the Absolute. They could not provide mystic compensation for his feelings of cosmic inadequacy and frustration, for his archaic fears. They had no thalamic roots, they were secular and synthetic ersatz-deities. Gods reside in clouds and twilight; the 'mystique' of the Left, as the French call it, was born in the sharp clarity of the Age of Enlightenment.

About the middle of the nineteenth century, after 1848, the new Creed had lost its religious fetish-character. The epigones of the French Revolution — Proudhon, Fourier, Saint Simon — were not prophets but cranks. There was no movement with an irresistible emotional appeal to take over the heritage of declining Christianity.

The founders of modern socialism thought that an appeal of this kind had become unnecessary. Religion was opium for the people and was to be replaced by a rational diet. The rapid advance of all sciences, with Darwinism making the pace, created a general optimistic belief in the infallibility of reasoning, in a clear, bright, crystalline world with a transparent atomic structure, with no room for shadows, twilights and myths. In this atmosphere was Marxian scientific socialism born; in a period when the relations between rational and affective behaviour were looked upon much as the relation between rider and horse; the rider representing rational thought, the horse what was then called the 'dark instincts' and 'the beast within us'. To-day we have become more modest, and inclined to think that the mythological Centaur would be a more fitting comparison. But meanwhile it had become a tradition in the Left to argue with the rider while others whipped the horse.

The results were what one would expect. In the century and a half since the storming of the Bastille, Movement followed Movement and withered away. Jacobinism, Fourierism, Utilitarianism, the First and Second Internationals, Owenism, Trade Unionism, Anarchism, Fabianism, Wilsonism, the League of Nations, the Weimar Republic, the Third International — they were all branches of the same tree rooted in the Age of Enlightenment, and they had all become dead branches within a decade or two.

The practical achievements of these abortive movements were nevertheless enormous and unparalleled in History. Those who sneer and talk in sweeping negations about the concrete progress achieved should read the chapter in Marx's *Kapital* about child-labour in English factories at the beginning of the last century, or the story of the mutiny on the Spithead and Nore, or even Maugham's *Liza of Lambeth*. Those hundred and fifty years of profane movements brought more tangible improvements in the lot of the common people than a thousand and five hundred years of Christianity. But this applies only to material reality. The reflection of this reality in the People's minds was different. Measured by its original aims, each of these progressive movements was a failure. None of them had set out to achieve the limited results which it did achieve; each started by promising the Golden Age, with utopian fervour. Their concrete achievements were more or less by-products of their ideological failure; the residue which the executors save after the death of a bankrupt millionaire. *Thus while in the material sphere the cumulative effect of Left attempts was a slow and steady improvement of social conditions, its cumulative effect in the psychological sphere was a growing frustration and disillusionment.* There was nothing to replace the lost absolute faith, the belief in a higher reality, in a fixed system of ethical values. Progress is a shallow myth because its roots are not in the past but in the future. The Left became emotionally more and more rootless. The sap was drying up. At the time when British Labour and German Social-Democrats came to power, all vitality had already run out of them. The communications with the unconscious layers were cut; their ethos was based on purely rational concepts; the only reminder of French revolutionary tradition was the caustic Voltairian tone of their polemics.

At a Communist writers' Congress, after hours of speeches about the brave new world in construction, André Malraux asked impatiently: 'And what about the man who is run over by a tram-car?' He met blank stares and did not insist. But there is a voice inside all of us which does insist. We have been cut off from the belief in personal survival, in the immortality of a self which we love and hate more intimately than anything else, and the scar of that amputation has never healed. To be killed on a barricade or to die as a martyr of science provides some compensation; but what about that man who is run over by the tram-car, or the child who is drowned? Gothic man had an answer to this question. The apparently accidental was part of a higher design. Fate was not blind; storms, volcanoes, floods and plagues all conformed to a subtle pattern; you were looked after in higher quarters. Cannibals, Eskimos, Hindus and Christians — all have an answer to this question of all questions which, however repressed, pooh-poohed, shamefully hidden, still remains the last decisive regulator of our actions. But the only answer which Malraux, after a painful silence, received was:

'In a perfect socialist transport-system, there would be no accidents.'

EXPLORATIONS

III

After world war number one the accumulated frustration exploded. The neglected craving for Faith, for something absolute and unquestionable to believe in, swept over Europe. It was the Return of the Repressed; the cortex had had its say and failed, the thalamus took its revenge. The electrical storm discharged itself in different forms according to different local conditions. In some countries it was delayed by the soothing effects of victory; in some it blew over in a hedonistic wave, an orgy-porgy of Jazz and copulation. The historically relevant phenomena in which the return to Faith crystallized were two: Fascism and the Soviet myth.

I should emphasize at once that by 'Soviet myth' I do not mean the developments in the Soviet Union, but their psychological reflection in the European Left. I shall try to prove that, like all genuine myths, it responded to certain deep and unconscious cravings, almost independently of the historical reality which it was supposed to reflect; just as the Christian myth remains unaffected by any historical discoveries about the real personality of Jesus of Nazareth and his intimates.

IV

Both the Fascist and the Soviet myths were not synthetic constructions, but revivals of archetypes, and therefore both capable of absorbing not only the cerebral component but the total man; both provided emotional saturation.

The fascist myth is undisguised and explicit. The opium is doled out by the leaders to the masses quite openly. The archetypes of Blood and Soil, of the dragon-slaying Superman, the deities of Valhalla and the satanic powers of the Jews are systematically called up for national service. One half of Hitler's genius consisted in hitting the right unconscious chords. The other half was his alert eclecticism, his flair for hyper-modern avant-garde methods in Economy, Architecture, Technique, Propaganda and Warfare. The secret of Fascism is the revival.of archaic beliefs in an ultra-modern setting. The Nazi edifice was a skyscraper fitted with hot water pipes which drew on underground springs of volcanic origin.

On the other hand, the water supply of the socialist movement consisted of a cistern on the roof which it was hoped would one day fill with rain. The Russian revolution brought not only rain but a tropical cloud-burst. Suddenly the hitherto dry taps began to gush and spout.

During the first few years Soviet myth and Russian reality were fairly congruent. It was the heroic age in which legends are generated. Behind the smoke there was a real fire.

And what a fire! The People had seized the power and had maintained itself in power on one sixth of the earth. Private ownership, the profit motive, sexual taboos, social conventions were abolished practically in one stroke. There were no more rich and poor, masters and servants, officers and men. The husband had no longer authority over his wife, the parent over his child, the teacher over his pupil. The history of *Homo Sapiens* seemed to start from scratch. There was a thunder behind the words of those unheard-of decrees like the voice from Sinai which gave the Ten Commandments. Those who listened felt as if some rigid crust inside them, the parched crust of scepticism, frustration, resigned common sense had suddenly burst open; they felt an emotional surge of which they had not thought themselves capable. Something had been released in them, something so deeply repressed that they were unaware of its existence; a hope so deeply buried that they had forgotten it. The Left had talked of the coming revolution for years, for decades, for more than a century; but when it came they were as stunned by the event as a country parson who, after delivering his weekly sermon before an empty church, learns from his curate that the Kingdom of Heaven has been announced on the wireless.

In terms of the Left, it was indeed a messianic prophecy come true. All the stock phrases from the text-books: the Government of the Workers and Peasants, the Expropriation of the Expropriators, the Dictatorship of the Proletariat, had changed from dry ink into blood. The myth of the Left was, as we saw, not derived from the past, but adduced from a hypothetical future. This future had now materialized. A bloodless Utopia had changed into a real country with real people; sufficiently remote in space to give freedom to imagination; with picturesque costumes and nostalgic songs to feed it. Progress, Justice and Socialism were abstractions which provided no fuel for dreams, no opportunity for worship, love and identification. Now the homeless, dispersed movement had gained a motherland, a flag, and the bearded silhouette of a father with humorous twinkling eyes and Mongolian features. The epic struggle of a great people, fighting their battles of freedom and playing the balalaika in between, satisfied all the starved emotions of that centenarian spinster, the European Left, which had never known the embrace of Power.

Thus was the Soviet myth born — or rather re-born. For Russia was merely the new occasion for the revival of an archetype as old as humanity. Like its past symbols, the Golden Age, the Land of Promise and the Kingdom of Heaven, it offered glorious compensations for a life of frustration and the pointlessness of death. Those of us who had lived in the Communist movement know how completely the Soviet myth fulfilled this function — not for the Russian but for the worshippers outside.

An essential feature of this archetype is, that the fulfilment of the promise should be preceded by violent upheavals: the Last Judgment, the advent of the comet, etc. Hence the instinctive rejection by full-blooded communists of all reformist ideas about a smooth transition to Socialism. The revolutionary apocalypse is necessary to fulfil the pattern of the Advent.

The Western Powers' half-hearted attempts to quell Bolshevism by military intervention only increased the fervour of the disciples and invested Russia with an aura of martyrdom which was to persist even after she had become the greatest military power of Europe and swallowed half Poland and the Baltic States. 'Hands off Russia' started as a political slogan and soon became a religious tabu. In a similar way, the vituperations of the reactionary Press led to an extension of the tabu to criticism and debate. The official explanation of this was that criticism of Russia, however friendly and objective, played into the hands of Reaction. But this was obviously a mere rationalization of the attitude involved; for even in private, with no *Daily Mail* reporter present, any critical utterance was regarded by the worshippers as blasphemy and crime. The urge to defend Russia became detached from reality and turned into the mental defence of a creed against the foreign intervention of doubt.

Progress had recovered its lost religion: Soviet Russia became the new 'Opium for the People'.

v

The revolutionary wave which swept over the Continent in the wake of the Russian Revolution ended in a series of defeats in Germany, Italy, Hungary, the Balkans. From the early 'twenties onward it became clear that the hope for an early European revolution had to be abandoned. Up to then the Soviet State had been regarded as the spearhead of the revolutionary movement. Now the movement became the rearguard of the Soviet State. In a series of tragic episodes from China to Spain the rearguard had to act as suicide squads. The interests of the world-proletariat were subordinated to the interests of the Soviet Union, and the Communist International became an auxiliary lever of the Russian Foreign Office. The abrupt changes of Party line in the various countries of Europe were but the amplified results of the subtle manœuvrings of Soviet diplomacy — like the jerks and jumps of a trailer attached to a motor car.

This development was rationalized as the doctrine of 'Socialism in One Country'. The Motherland of the Proletariat was the bastion which had to be preserved even at the price of sacrificing those outside it — that is, the *élite* of the revolutionary movement in Europe. At a future date, after the bastion had been sufficiently strengthened, the garrison would sally out and liberate those *extra muros.* Their sacrifice was in reality a long-term investment which was to find its glorious reward at the hour of reckoning. Thus the element of messianic promise became even more pronounced. The withdrawal of Soviet Russia from the European working class, even the inaccessibility of their territory except for carefully staged Mecca-pilgrimages — all helped to make Russia more remote in the field of reality and to feed the imaginative sources of the myth.

VI

The disastrous results of this policy for the European Left are on the records of history. All over Europe the Communist parties played the role of involuntary midwives to Fascism. Those among the leaders and rank and file who had the sense and courage to protest were expelled, killed or denounced to the police. The Byzantine structure of the Comintern reflected the structure of the Soviet dictatorship; the Communist approach to the workers and the intelligentsia of Europe was modelled on the Russian way of handling a semi-asiatic and practically illiterate population, and applied with total disregard of Western conditions and mentality. All this has been expounded in detail by critics of the Comintern from Trotsky to Borkenau. But their analysis is confined to the political plane; the psychological reasons why the majority of Communists and fellow-travellers outside Russia accepted this state of affairs remain to be explained.

Constant purges, the monotonously recurrent excommunication of the popular leaders of yesterday, the absence of any rank-and-file influence on the party-line, the sacrifice of thousands in hopeless adventures alternating with capitulations to and alliances with the enemy; the twisting around of slogans to mean the exact opposite of what the words conveyed, indignant denials of the truth of yesterday, an atmosphere of slander, denunciations and Byzantine worship — how can it be explained that millions in the West swallowed all this, and swallowed it voluntarily, in self-imposed discipline, with no Gestapo or G.P.U. to back it up?

Such unconditional surrender of the critical faculties always indicates the presence of a factor which is *a priori* beyond the reach of reasoning. One might be tempted to call it a neurotic complex but for the fact that the true Believer (whether in the Christian or the Soviet myth) is, as a rule, happier and more balanced than the atheist or the trotskyite. Deep-rooted, archetypal beliefs lead only to neurosis when doubt provokes a conflict. To keep doubt away, a system of elastic defences is established. The outer defences are provided by the Catholic Index, the banning of 'trotskyite' literature, avoidance of contacts with heretics and suspects. They produce a characteristic sectarian intolerance, which, coming as it often does from otherwise good-natured people, manifests itself in surprisingly violent forms.

The inner defences are unconscious. They consist in a kind of magic aura which the mind builds around its cherished belief. Arguments which penetrate into the magic aura are not dealt with rationally but by a specific type of pseudo-reasoning. Absurdities and contradictions which outside the magic aura would be rejected at once are made acceptable by specious rationalizations. The higher developed the mental faculties of the person, the subtler the patterns of pseudo-reasoning which he develops. Scholasticism, talmudism, alchemy are amazing in their ingeniousness and inner consistency. The magic or 'thalamic' systems of reasoning have a kind of non-euclidian geometry, an inherent logical curvature. The curvature is provided by certain axioms and dogmas; in the case of the Communist believer the operative formula is that a statement might be mechanically correct but dialectically false'.

As the gulf between Soviet myth and reality widened, the dialectical curvature in the believer's mind increased, until he found it quite natural to see Ribbentrop decorated with the Order of Lenin, to call a millionaire a proletarian and a table a duckpond. To go through the editorial leaders of the *Daily Worker* during the last ten years makes one feel like Malice in Wonderland.

EXPLORATIONS

Under these circumstances almost every discussion with myth-addicts, whether public or private, is doomed to failure. The debate is from the beginning removed from the level of objectivity; arguments are not considered on their merit, but by whether they fit into the system, and if not, how they can be made to fit. It is a type of approach to reality similar to that of the infant who examines any object which falls into his hands from the sole angle of whether it can be eaten or not, whether it is goody-goody or dirty-dirty. If, for instance, you happen to mention that Trotsky created the Red Army you have not stated an historical fact, but said something that is dirty-dirty, and you have to be prepared for the appropriate reaction.

The affective element does not necessarily manifest itself in outward agitation. The defence mechanism often works as a smooth, well-oiled machinery. If in danger of being pinned down, the machinery automatically reverts to question-begging and circular argument. Thus it often happens that the opponent loses his temper while the addict preserves his calm — the smiling superiority of the fanatic and the priest.

The opponent has still other difficulties to contend with. He is embarrassed by undesirable allies, by approval from the reactionary camp, their triumphant I-always-told-you-so. They were proved right with all their wrong reasons, and in his heart he is with the addict who is wrong for the right reasons. But at the same time he is exasperated by the foolish addict, for nothing makes one more impatient than to see another person stubbornly cling to the errors of one's own past; that is why adolescents get so much on one's nerves. In some this exasperation turns into hatred — the Trotskyite attitude of the betrayed lover who proclaims to all and sundry that his sweetheart is a whore and yet foams with rage at each new proof of it. The loss of an illusion has the same un-balancing effect as a libidinous disturbance.

And finally there is the danger of swinging to the other extreme, the warning example of the Lavals and Doriots, both one-time members of the French Communist Party; the fear of sliding down the slope polished by the broad behinds of the long procession of idealists turned into traitors. It is a difficult job to hang on in the middle of the slope, and a rather lonely one.

VIII

The magic aura of the Soviet myth affects not only the Communist Party-membership but, in a more blurred way, Socialists, Liberals, progressive intellectuals, enlightened clergymen. In the wretched decades between the two wars, when the Left lived in an atmosphere of constant defeats and betrayals, when inflation, unemployment, Fascism swept over country after country, Russia was the only thing to live and die for. She was the only hope in an age of hopelessness, the only promise for the tired and disillusioned. On the surface the attitude of the 'Sympathizers' was more critical, but deeper down they were all affected by the myth. Not bound by the vows of orthodoxy, they could permit themselves heresies, even frivolous jokes; their critical objections did not destroy their beliefs, because it was vaguer and therefore more elastic. But there was a solid and untouchable core to it, a magic formula which amounted to something like: 'In spite of all Russia is "the real thing"; "the only pointer to the future"; "the last hope" '; and so on. Even frightened stockbrokers and enlightened business men discover in times of depression that 'after all there may be something in it' — much like the atheist on his death-bed taking the Last Sacrament.

Though vaguer and woollier, this belief is as unconsciously and jealously guarded as the doctrine of the orthodox. The *New Statesman and Nation*'s interpretations of Stalinite policy display all the ingeniousness of the official Apologist, though with a somewhat more elegant logical curvature. The sympathizer enjoys the apparent superiority of the broad-minded Theist over the doctrinaire Catholic; but the roots of one belief are as irrational as the other's.

The attempt to break down the addict's defences by bringing these irrational roots into his consciousness is practically hopeless. As with all firmly embedded beliefs, the unconscious resistance against this operation, which threatens its very foundations, is enormous. This resistance itself is rationalized in the Communist rejection of 'bourgeois psychology' as a 'diversion from the class-struggle'; psycho-analysis is officially banned in Soviet Russia. Communist psychology is based on the hypothetical notion of a 'class-consciousness' which is supposed to reflect a person's position in the process of Production, and which has never been demonstrated by a psychologist on a living individual. Thus an axiomatic belief is defended by the equally axiomatic rejection of the means to analyse it; a process familiar both to psycho-therapeutists and historians of the Church.

And as in the case of the Church, the process of weaning is dependent on two factors: the gradual attrition caused by the ever-widening gulf between reality and myth; and the emergence of a new creed of equal emotional power and in better harmony with reality.

II

SOVIET MYTH AND REALITY

I

THE previous essay dealt with the psychological aspects of the Soviet myth. The subject of the present essay is Soviet reality. Its aim is to investigate, within the limits of available space and information, the question whether the Soviet system is socialistic (in fact or tendency), or whether it is not.

Such an inquiry has to work its way through a series of obstacles which surround the truth in concentric rings. The outer defence consists in a deafening propaganda-barrage concentrated on some topical subject — a polar expedition, stratosphere flight, or the building of the Moscow underground — which in itself has no bearing on the question of socialism but creates the impression that it has. The latest of these propaganda-barrages may be summarized as follows:

1. The Soviet people, and particularly the defenders of Stalingrad, defeated the Germans because they 'knew what they were fighting for'; the Russian victories prove the excellence of the Stalinite system and give the lie to its critics.

If this kind of topical argument is found to be too superficial to withstand serious inquiry, the inner defences come into action. They are:

2. *Camouflage or denial of facts* (which are sometimes later admitted); e.g. the famine of 1932-33.
3. *The doctrine of 'esoteric' and 'exoteric' truth.* Official statements which sound too fantastic to the Western mind are justified as being aimed at home consumption only, with a reference to the backwardness of the Russian masses; e.g. Zinoviev, an agent of the British Intelligence Service.
4. *Distinction between socialist strategy and tactics.* All reactionary

measures of the Soviet regime are justified as 'temporary expedients'; e.g. capital punishment for strikers.

5. *The End justifies the Means.* Means which are damnable if employed by a capitalist state automatically become commendable if they serve the cause of the Soviet state; e.g. Stalin-Hitler pact.

6. *The doctrine of the unshaken foundations.* This is the last line of defence of the sophisticated apologist. It is also the tie which links dissenters — Trotskyites, Socialists, critical fellow-travellers — to the Soviet myth. Weaknesses, failures, even crimes of the Soviet bureaucracy are admitted but claimed to be mere surface-symptoms which do not affect the fundamentally progressive nature of the Soviet Union, guaranteed by the nationalization of the means of production and the abolition of the profit-motive. It is argued that as long as these foundations survive, Russia is still to be regarded as a socialist country and hence the special concern of the Left all over the world.

Though the line of Soviet Apologetics is subject to frequent changes, the particular arguments used can always be reduced to one of the six headings above. We now have to examine these in greater detail.

II

Owing to peculiarities of war-time psychology, argument No. 1 though logically the weakest, is emotionally the most powerful, and not only among political illiterates. The success of the Red Army released an irresistible wave of enthusiasm for Russia among the common people of Europe, and cowed its critics into uneasy silence.

It would be absurd to belittle the fighting quality of the Russians or the efficiency of the Soviet war machinery. The defeat of the German Army was an historic performance of the first magnitude, though by no means a miracle. The population of Soviet Russia is more than twice that of Germany; her industrial potential in 1939 was, according to Soviet statistics, equal to Germany's; her enormous arid spaces and her climate are invaluable assets against any invader. Thus *a priori* there was no earthly reason why the Russians should be defeated by the Germans, even if we leave the British Empire and the United States completely out of the picture.

The endurance and fatalism of the Russian soldier are proverbial. In 1815 they defeated Napoleon. In 1914 Russia's industrial potential was less than one fifth of Germany's; during the famous Brussilov offensives the first Russian line went into battle with rifles and boots, the second line only with boots, the third line without rifles and without boots; they had to pick them up from their dead comrades. Nevertheless they fought on for more than four years, first for the Tsar, then for Kerensky, finally for the Bolsheviks. The revolution, as in Germany, came only after the exhaustion of the military and supply machine.

If, as Soviet propaganda assures us, the success of the Russian armies in 1944 is a proof of the excellence of Stalinism and its superiority to other social systems, then we may also assume that the victory of 1815 proved the excellence of the Tsarist system and the superiority of serfdom over the principles of the French Revolution. The same analogy may be applied to any nation fighting in this war. No army can compete with the Japanese suicidal devotion to his flag; *ergo* the heroic defenders of Salamaua who died to the last man, and were mostly simple workers and peasants like those of Stalingrad, proved by their supreme sacrifice that the reign of the Mikado is the most progressive on earth. I know that this is blasphemy in pious ears; but we are talking of the permissibility of logical deductions and not of sentiments. Nobody will deny that the German army fought outstandingly; is that a proof that Nazism is right and that those who denounce the horrors of the Gestapo were slanderers and must keep silent? The Chinese fought for almost a decade alone against the superior Japanese aggressor; is that a reason for the working classes of the West to imitate the Chinese social system?

The logical fallacy is obvious; and yet the emotional power of the Soviet myth is such that even intellectuals unquestioningly accept the formula that the Russians fight well *because they know* what they are fighting for, whereas the misguided and fanatical Germans, Japanese, etc. fight well *because they don't know* what they are fighting for. If the morale of the German soldier does not prove the desirability of Nazism, then the morale of the Russian soldier cannot prove the desirability of Stalinism, *except* by taking *a priori* for granted that Stalinism is good, Nazism bad; that is, by substituting the premise for the conclusion.

All historical evidence goes to show that the morale of an army depends on a series of factors, among which the rational content of the Cause for which it is alleged to fight is only one, and usually one of secondary importance. People have fought and died with equal fervour for stupid or enlightened, progressive or reactionary causes; for causes often unconnected with and sometimes diametrically opposed to their personal interest. Rational self-interest, economical and social, is a conscious factor only in the wars of (a) primitive nomadic people (conquest of pastures), or (b) when a civilized society reverts to the primitive stage by the collapse of its accepted values and structures, that is, in revolutionary civil wars. Otherwise the connection between the real interest of the individual fighting man and the alleged Cause is dependent on a series of intermediary links, formed by emotional conditioning; a chain so involved that people will often fight to maintain their own status of slavery. Any direct conclusion from emotional morale to the value of a Cause is a fallacy.

One of the most powerful emotional factors is xenophobia, from its totemistic tribal form to modern nationalism. This factor, too, is largely independent of real self-interest; thus the socialist workers of Warsaw took arms against the Russian Revolutionary Army in 1920; thus the Arabs of Palestine took arms against Jewish infiltration which economically brought them enormous benefits. In the present war wherever Nationalism conflicted with social ideology, Nationalism won. Fascist Greece under Metaxas fought the Italian Fascist invader; democratic

Britain courted Fascist Spain; Japanese feudalism found a *modus vivendi* with Russian Bolshevism; in other words, all the political Isms might as well not have existed, and the grouping of the belligerent Powers would have been much the same. Under the façade of high-sounding ideologies the real content remained that of a war of Nations, for purely national interests, for conquest and in self-defence against the invader, and with all the emotional fervour which Nationalism commands. From the point of view of the Left it was a war against the greatest Fascist power, and hence worth fighting; but the Allied governments and the great majority of politically indifferent people did not fight for or against any Ism, but for national survival and the traditional values of the last century.

The Communist argument under discussion is based on the assumption that whereas this is true for the capitalist countries, Russia is an exception. What evidence is there for this distinction? Even if the Russian armies were fighting under internationalist slogans, it would be open to doubt whether the real emotional force which drives them was derived from these official slogans, or from the primary desire to throw the murderous invader out of their country. But, as it happens, the official slogans have dropped all ideological pretence and have completely reverted to the traditional pre-revolutionary symbols. The 'Internationale' was replaced by a new national anthem, the revolutionary army-oath replaced by a new nationalistic oath, all equalitarianism in the army was abolished, revolutionary discipline replaced by authoritarian discipline, old Tsarist generals who had fought the French Revolution were reinstated as national idols, and the blessing of God dispensed by the reborn Orthodox Church. We shall speak about these developments in greater detail later on.

Thus the upshot of argument No. 1 is that the warlike prowess of any nation allows no direct conclusions as to the progressive or regressive character of its regime, but seems mainly dependent on emotional driving forces of a traditional, conservative nature; that the Soviet regime has adapted its slogans to these traditionalist driving forces and eliminated precisely those slogans which previously distinguished it from conservative countries; and that, if the argument by itself is to prove anything, it can only prove that the Russian soldier who always fought well in the name of God, country and Government, continues to fight well in the name of God, country and Government.

This does not exclude the possibility of Russia being after all a socialist country; but that would have to be proved by more valid arguments. On the strength of the Russian way of waging war alone, all we can say is that if she *is* a socialist country, this fact has been carefully hidden both from the outside world and her own soldiers and citizens.

III

Denial of facts about Soviet-reality may be conscious or unconscious. If it is conscious, it falls under the next heading. But mostly it is unconscious, based on ignorance.

Ignorance of Soviet reality among the addicts of the Soviet myth is stupendous. Nine out of ten are shocked and incredulous when told, for instance, that the workers' right to strike is abolished in Russia, and that striking, or the incitement to it, is punishable by capital punishment; or that the Soviet electorate's only function is to vote 'yes' or 'no' to a single list of officially appointed candidates. This ignorance is partly due to the difficulty of obtaining factual information, partly to an unconscious fear of disappointment   One could almost say that the more importance people attach to Russia the more reluctant they seem to find out the facts. To believe entails no desire to know; everybody reads the Bible but who reads Flavius Josephus?

Given the Left's unconscious willingness to be deceived, Soviet propaganda could achieve feats unparalleled in history. Their achievements were mainly based on two methods: (*a*) the indirect method of suppression of facts, and (*b*) direct methods of propaganda. We shall treat the two separately.

THE YOGI AND THE COMMISSAR

(a) *Suppression of Facts*

Foreign newspapers were and are forbidden in Russia. The Soviet Press is controlled to a degree which Nazism could never achieve. Each town in the Union, Moscow included, has two morning papers: a government organ and a party organ. All government papers throughout the country appear every morning with one uniform leader, distributed by radio and telegraph: the leader of the Moscow *Izvestia*. All Party papers all over the country appear with the leader from the Moscow *Pravda*. Both foreign and home news are similarly distributed by the official TASS agency. Local news consists of official hand-outs.

The effect of this total centralization of news in a country with vast distances is that the great mass of people are not only kept in ignorance of events abroad, but also of events outside their immediate neighbourhood. Here is one example of how the system works:

I spent the winter of 1932-33 mainly in Kharkov, then capital of the Ukraine. It was the catastrophic winter after the first wave of collectivization of the land; the peasants had killed their cattle, burned or hidden their crops and were dying of starvation and typhoid; the number of deaths in the Ukraine alone is estimated at about two millions. Travelling through the countryside was like running the gauntlet; the stations were lined with begging peasants with swollen hands and feet, the women holding up to the carriage-windows horrible infants with enormous wobbling heads, stick-like limbs, swollen, pointed bellies. You could swop a loaf of bread for Ukrainian embroidered kerchiefs, national costumes and bedcovers; foreigners could sleep with practically any girl except party-members for a pair of shoes or stockings. Under my hotel-room window in Kharkov funeral processions marched past all day. The electricity supply in Kharkov had broken down; there was no light in the town, and the trams functioned only for an hour or so a day to take workers to the factories and back. There was also no fuel or petrol in the town and the winter was hard even for the Ukraine, with temperatures of 30 degrees below zero. Life seemed to have come to a standstill, the whole machinery was on the verge of collapse.

These were the conditions which drove the old Bolshevik guard into opposition against Stalin, to their half-hearted conspiracy of despair; they were the real background of the purges and trials. To-day, the catastrophe of 1932-33 is more or less frankly admitted in Soviet circles; but at the time not the slightest allusion to real conditions was allowed to appear in the Soviet press, including the newspapers of the Ukraine itself. Each morning when I read the Kharkov *Kommunist* I learned about plan-figures reached and over-reached, about competitions between factory shock brigades, awards of the Red Banner, new giant combines in the Urals, and so on; the photographs were either of young people, always laughing and always carrying a banner in their hands, or of some picturesque elder in Usbekistan, always smiling and always learning the alphabet. Not one word about the local famine, epidemics, the dying out of whole villages; even the fact that there was no electricity in Kharkov was not once mentioned in the Kharkov newspaper. It gave one a feeling of dream-like unreality; the paper seemed to talk about some quite different country which had no point of contact with the daily life we led; and the same applies to the radio.

The consequence of all this was that the vast majority of people in Moscow had no idea of what went on in Kharkov, and even less of what went on in Tashkent, or Archangel or Vladivostok — twelve days' train journey away, in a country where travelling was reserved for government officials; and these travellers were not of a talkative nature. The enormous land was covered by a blanket of silence, and nobody outside the small circle of initiated could form a comprehensive picture of the situation.

A second belt of silence isolated the country from contacts with the outside world. Foreign missions and newspaper correspondents were concentrated in Moscow. The capital had priority in everything, from food and fuel to industrial goods, toothbrushes, lipsticks, contraceptives and other luxuries unknown in the rest of the country; its living standard was entirely unrepresentative. If the average citizen of Moscow was to a large extent ignorant of what was going on in remoter parts of his own country, the foreigner's ignorance was unbounded. He could only travel chaperoned by Security officials performing the various functions of interpreters, guides, car-drivers, chance acquaintances and even amorous conquests. His contacts were restricted to Soviet officials; to the ordinary Soviet citizen social intercourse with foreigners meant running the risk of being accused of espionage or treason. In addition to the difficulty of obtaining factual information, the foreign correspondent was faced with the problem of passing it on. To smuggle out news vetoed by the censor meant expulsion; a risk which both journalists and their employers will take only reluctantly, and only when vital issues are at stake. But 'vital issue' is an elastic term, and the practical result of continuous pressure was that even conscientious newspapermen evolved a routine of compromise; they cabled no lies, but *nolens volens* confined themselves to official dope and expressed such comment or criticism as they dared 'between the lines' by some subtle qualifying adjective or nuance — which naturally passed unobserved by anybody but the initiated reader.[1] The cumulative effect of all this was a picture distorted by half-truths and systematic omissions. This was the foundation on which direct Soviet propaganda could build.

(b) *Direct Propaganda*

Soviet propaganda abroad employs two devices with complementary effect. The first consists in emphasizing the statistical framework and leaving out the human detail; the second, in emphasizing one untypical detail and filling the whole frame with it.

The first method appeals to our Americanized imaginations by means of the statistical stunt. A barrage of figures on production, building, education, transport, top-wages, etc. is laid down in

[1] I am talking of course of progressive and neutral papers; if the red scare campaign of the reactionary press had any influence on the Left at all, it was to increase their loyalty to the Soviet Union.

front of the spectator; behind the noise and smoke the realities of the human factor, of Soviet everyday life, are hidden away.

That Russia went through an industrial revolution nobody of course will deny. So did England, Germany, America and Japan in the eighteenth and nineteenth centuries. In Russia industrialization came *after* the proletarian revolution: this serves Soviet propaganda as a justification to represent the building of factories and railways as a 'unique triumph of socialism'. This dialectical sleight-of-hand has a history; it goes back to Lenin's famous phrase: 'Socialism is Soviets plus Electrification'. Lenin meant by it that Socialism is only possible in a modern, highly industrialized country with a predominance of the industrial worker over the backward rural population; in other words, industrialization is a *precondition* for the establishment of a socialist society. This elementary truth has been twisted round by Stalinite propaganda until the masses were made to believe that the mere building of factories was *identical* with Socialism. The Dnieper Dam, the Turk-Sib railway, the White Sea canal and the Moscow underground, etc., were thus seen not as respectable technical achievements comparable to similar achievements in England and America, but as something unique the world has never seen, the very essence and flower and fulfilment of Socialism itself. The majority of the Russian masses actually believe that Moscow is the only town in the world to have an underground railway.

The hypnotic effect of the propaganda equation 'Socialism — Industrialization' was such that it was accepted not only at home but by the sympathizers in the old industrial countries abroad. For the addict of the Soviet myth Dnieper Dam and underground, Soviet stratosphere flights and Polar expeditions, Soviet aviation and Soviet flame-throwers, assumed the fetish-character of a lock from the hair of the beloved. The apotheosis of this cult was reached in the hysterical ballyhoo during the show-tour of the Socialist Woman Sniper Ludmilla Pawlitchenko who had shot 137 Germans with Socialist Marksmanship and described the process to the bourgeois Press with Socialist Realism. The capitalized expressions are quotations from the Soviet press.

The second method, generalization from the, untypical detail, is the more obvious one. Tourists, journalists and photographers are shown model factories, model crèches, model workers' clubs and sanatoria. These benefit perhaps one per cent of the population; the other ninety-nine never enter the picture. Before the war, tourists could travel unrestrictedly inside any civilized country in the world once they obtained a visa on their passports; this was true even for Fascist Italy and Nazi Germany. In Russia alone were their movements restricted to approved sites.

Soviet officials became very indignant when accused of using showroom technique with the deliberate intention to mislead. The obvious and logical way of refuting this accusation would have been to abolish those restrictions on which the accusation was based and to tell the world: Come and see for yourself. This was declared to be impossible as every foreigner might be a saboteur or a spy. Sympathizers accepted this excuse as something quite reasonable. Its absurdity becomes obvious when we remember that Germany had at least as much reason to fear spies in the period of her secret rearming from 1933 to 1936. But the Germans knew as well as the Russians that military secrets and even the crasser forms of political persecution are easy to hide from the traveller by normal police methods, especially in a country under dictatorship. The secret which the Soviet Union so jealously guarded was not of a military nature; it was the average living conditions of her citizens. Behind the fireworks of statistics, symbols and tokens lay the vast land of Soviet reality in darkness and silence. This reality, the everyday life of people in Kazan and Saratov, Ashkabad and Tomsk, even in the very suburbs of Moscow — not to speak of the Forced Labour Camps on the White Sea, of the exiled and deported millions in Siberia and Central Asia — is as remote from the Western observer as the dark side of the moon from the star-gazer's telescope.

EXPLORATIONS

IV. ESOTERIC AND EXOTERIC TRUTH

For a whole generation Russia has been separated from the rest of the world by a new Chinese Wall which threw its shadow on both sides: the Soviet people's ignorance of conditions in the capitalist world was even greater than the other way round. The only consolation they had amidst their hardships was the conviction that life under Capitalism was even worse; they might live in purgatory, but those abroad lived in hell. In films, radio, press and literature the world beyond Negoreloye appeared populated by fat bankers wearing toppers and tails at every hour of the day, bourgeois with fixed cynical smirks and starved proletarians conspiring in cellars. It was a world full of the naive horrors of old Russian fairy-tales.

In 1933 in Moscow I saw a film in which a German scientist was flogged in the vaults of a Catholic monastery by monks in black cowls, reinforced by Nazi storm troopers. The film was prefaced by Lunatcharsky, former People's Commissar for Education. It was a film for home consumption, a category sharply distinguished from the early masterpieces designed for propaganda abroad.

I remember with equal vividness another episode. A popular Ukrainian writer asked me for advice: he was writing a short story with the action in London and had got stuck on a scene in which a worker, walking through the streets on a Sunday morning, is pushed off the pavement by a policeman. What would the policeman say, what colloquialism or curse would he use?

'The question is', I said, 'why does the policeman push him off?'

'Why', said the Ukrainian colleague, 'I told you he is a workman. He wears no collar or tie.'

He was honestly convinced that in capitalist London policemen walk about on Sunday mornings pushing proletarians off the pavement. And he was not illiterate, but a young man educated in a Soviet university and with a growing literary reputation. The Russian's idea of Capitalism was the counterpart of the *Daily Mail* reader's idea of Bolshevism.

The same black-and-white technique was applied to the inner-

Russian opposition. The dictatorial regime, committed to its own infallibility, could not afford to let the masses realize that in political matters there was scope for different opinions within the same camp. Hence the accused in the Moscow trials had to belong to the 'black' side; they could not appear as bona fide politicians at variance with the government, but had to play the role of counter-revolutionary agents of foreign Powers who had acted not out of conviction but for pay and some undefined satanic motives.

The victims lent themselves to this game for reasons which varied according to their personality. Men like Bukharin who shared their accusers' philosophy acted their role voluntarily in the conviction that this was the last service they could render to the Party after they had been politically defeated and had, according to the all-or-nothing law of totalitarian politics, forsaken their lives. Others, worn out by a life-long struggle, hoped to save if not their own, at least the lives of their families held as hostages (cf. Kamenev's references to his son during the second trial). Others, still on a lower level, had been broken down by physical or mental torture alternating with promises of mercy to which they clung against better reason; and finally there were the *agents provocateurs* who had nothing to lose. The confessions of the Moscow trials only appear mysterious to those who look for one uniform explanation of the behaviour of men prompted by heterogeneous reasons.

The method of gross over-simplifications in Soviet home propaganda led to the tradition that the accused in a political trial must confess lustily and voluntarily his alleged crimes; and once this tradition became established there was no going back. Hence the curious phenomenon that during the Kharkov trial of German war criminals in December 1943 the accused German officers and N.C.O.s were made to behave like characters from Dostoievsky. One of them at the trial told of his own accord how during a mass execution of Russians he took a tommy-gun from a soldier and shot a mother with a child in her arms. For the foreign observer the Kharkov trial (which was filmed and publicly shown in London) gave the same impression of unreality as the Moscow trials, the accused reciting their parts in stilted phrases which they had obviously learned by heart, sometimes taking the wrong cue from the State Prosecutor and then coming back to the same point again. There is no doubt that the Germans committed bestialities in Russia which surpass the imagination of the Western mind, but that those particular Germans committed those particular crimes was proved by no other evidence than their own confession. This does not extenuate the horrible guilt of Nazism, but it shows that the methods of Soviet Justice, subordinated to the needs of home-propaganda, have lost the faculty of making even the truth appear credible.

A judiciary which functions as an auxiliary to propaganda must produce absurd results. According to the findings of the Moscow trials Trotsky was already a foreign agent at the time when he commanded the Red Army and defeated foreign intervention; and the men who made the Russian revolution were, with the exception of Stalin and those who died in time, all agents of the British, German or Japanese Secret Services. They poisoned Gorki with arsenic, tried to poison the chief of the G.P.U. (who later turned out to be one of their accomplices) with quicksilver vapours, spent their time throwing spanners into machines, selling the country piecemeal to dirty foreigners, trying to kill Little Father Stalin, and generally behaving like the characters in Chesterton's *The Man who was Thursday*. If these absurdities and contradictions are pointed out to the apologist, he will at first try to deny them; but if he happens to be confronted with the official verbatim reports of the trials issued in Moscow, he will say that those exaggerations were the 'exoteric' type of truth, meant to satisfy the mentality of the 'backward Russian masses'.

Actually the Russian masses are politically the most advanced or most backward in the world, according to the needs of the moment. The effects which twenty years of exoteric truth had on them we shall discuss in the next section.

V. ENDS AND MEANS

... The British Government has announced that its aim in the war with Germany is nothing more nor less than the 'destruction of Hitlerism'. This means, that the British and the French have declared something in the nature of an 'ideological war' on Germany, reminiscent of the religious wars of olden times ... There is absolutely no justification for a war of this kind. One may accept or reject the ideology of Hitlerism as well as any other ideological system, that is a matter of political views. But everybody should understand that an ideology cannot be destroyed by force, that it cannot be eliminated by war. It is therefore not only senseless but criminal to wage such a war for the 'destruction of Hitlerism', camouflaged as a fight for 'democracy'. . . .

Thus Molotov, People's Commissar for Foreign Affairs, speaking on October 31st, 1939, at a meeting of the Supreme Council of the U.S.S.R.

The Soviet-apologist, confronted with the text of this and similar speeches and with the Russian record of 1939-41, will answer at once with a knowing smile that all this was an emergency expedient to gain time; it comes under the heading 'revolutionary tactics'. The Stalin-Hitler pact was a tactical measure to appease Germany until Russia was ready for war; just as the dissolution of the Comintern and Earl Browder's statements in favour of Capitalism are tactical measures to appease the Allies until the stage is set for a new revolutionary wave. The same argument is used to defend any reactionary measures, decrees, speeches, etc., inside Russia or on the international stage.

This argument involves the age-old problem whether the End justifies the Means — all means. I shall not here go into the ethical aspect of the question.[1] From a purely realistic point of view the ruthless application of Macchiavellian tactics may have benefited Soviet Russia but at the price of corrupting, warping

---

[1] cf. 'The Yogi and the Commissar'—II, below, p. 227.

and finally destroying the international revolutionary movement and sacrificing the best elements of the European working class. Acts like the hoisting of the Swastika on the Moscow airfield for Ribbentrop's reception, and the playing of the Nazi anthem by the Red Army band — such symbolical acts may be passed over as cynical opportunism if committed by capitalist countries, but have a different effect if committed by the Fatherland of the Workers and Peasants. The advantages thus gained cannot be weighed on a scale against the damage done to socialist morale; such acts are not justifiable by cool mathematical calculation because their consequences are unpredictable; both sides of the equation consist of unknown terms. It has been too quickly forgotten that the collapse of France in 1940 was not exclusively the work of Fifth Columnists of the Right; the Communist slogan of the 'rich men's war' which was 'no business of the working class' played a decisive role in the demoralization of the French army. Who can say whether the profit which Soviet Russia derived from this policy balanced the loss of the First Front of the war? From 1939 to 1941 the Press and apparatus of the Comintern took up an openly anti-Ally attitude to please Hitler. Two years later the Comintern was disbanded, allegedly to please Churchill and Roosevelt. But one cannot sack a workers' International like a useless servant and to-morrow engage a new one; the reactions of millions of people of all nationalities, their idealism and self-sacrifice cannot be manipulated like a bookkeeper's account.

The same applies to the masses inside Russia itself. Admittedly political education is a basic requirement for the realization of Socialism. Admittedly the Russian masses are so backward that propaganda for home consumption must be couched in over-simplified terms. What effect, then, can be expected from a succession of all-out propaganda campaigns each in total contradiction to the previous one? Obviously this: that the masses, bewildered by the contradictions vaguely sensed behind the fiery exhortations, resign themselves to the fact that the mysteries of politics are impenetrable, unconditionally surrender their critical faculties to their leaders, and fall back into the mental state from which they started twenty-five years ago.

There are, however, emotional compensations for the masses. Deprived of the right to judge, they are encouraged to condemn; scapegoats are provided to canalize unease and discontent; a new and unique political vocabulary, including 'mad dogs', 'devils', 'hyenas' and 'syphilitics', replaces the distinctions for political dissent of former days.

The apotheosis of this process of socialist re-education was reached in the revival of public hangings as a mass festival. A crowd of thirty to forty thousand people watched the hanging after the Kharkov trial; the proceedings were filmed in detail, including close-ups of the actual process of strangulation, and shown all over Russia and even abroad. The event was described by the Special Correspondent of *The Times* (December 31st, 1943) in terms of obvious approval and sympathy which are worth quoting:

> ... The trial itself was an important phase in the educational process. It not only satisfied a burning desire for justice in its sternest form, but revealed to the huge crowds that thronged the market-place — the centre of German-inspired speculation and corruption — and to the country people, who for three days after the execution saw the swinging bodies, the vulnerability of the enemy and the fundamental weakness of the Fascist character ... When the vehicles on which the condemned men stood were moved away, causing their bodies to drop slowly and initiating the strangling process, there went up from the great crowd a hoarse, low growl of deep satisfaction. There were some who showed their scorn of the dying men by adding whistles to the sound of their gasps. Others applauded. ...

This description was headed by the caption 'RE-EDUCATION', which was by no means meant to be ironical.

History is not squeamish. Our argument was not that we are horrified by the Means employed (which we are) but that their outcome is unpredictable. It follows that they cannot be justified *a priori* by logical calculation; but it also follows that there remains a doubt in us whether they will not, after all, be justified *a posteriori*. We may shudder at the ruthless sacrifice of millions both inside and outside Russia, at the damage done to the socialist movement and the corruption of its moral climate — and yet, *as long as we take it for granted* that Russia moves towards Socialism, however slowly and by however devious routes, the question must remain open. But what evidence is there that this assumption is still valid, that the basic trend of Russia is still toward Socialism whereas all the disturbing phenomena are merely ripples on the surface? This is the real core of the problem.

If I start on a journey from London to Edinburgh and, waking up in my compartment in the night, find that my train is moving south instead of northward, I shall be a little puzzled, but then I shall explain to myself that we are probably in the mountains where the track has to run in a serpentine. But if, the next morning, I wake up to find myself in Bournemouth; and if the engine-driver maintains that the shortest road from London to Scotland *does* lead through Bournemouth, then I shall be entitled to have some doubts about his truthfulness.

Detours on the road are unavoidable, and the only means to decide the broad direction of a movement is to watch it over a reasonable stretch of time and then draw the average curve of its oscillations. Subjective statements of its leaders are of no interest, and the question of their bona fides is historically meaningless. The only valid criterion is the cumulative effect of its achievements in various spheres. The following sections contain a short survey of the relevant trends of development in the social structure of Russia.

VI. THE INHERITANCE OF PRIVILEGE

(i) *Inheritance of Money*

One of the first tenets of Socialism is that each child born into this world should have equal opportunities of education and career. Accordingly inheritance through Relationship, Last Will, or Life Insurance were abolished shortly after the revolution.

1. Heritage both by law or by will (Testament) is abolished. After the death of a person his property (mobile or immobile) becomes State property of the R.S.F.S.R.

2. Up to the passing of the decree concerning general social insurance for those in need, the directly descendent relatives of the deceased, brothers and sisters, the wife or the husband who are unable to work, will receive a subsidy out of the property left.

3. If the property does not exceed 10,000 roubles, and in particular if it consists of land, household goods, tools or implements, it is placed at the temporary disposition of and administration by the husband, wife or relatives as per Art. II of this decree.

Decree of April 27th (14) 1918 V.Ts.I.K.[1]

On November 18th, 1919, all insurance for life, capital and income, was abolished. (Code of Laws, 56-542.) Old people, invalids and minors affected by the abolition of inheritance and life insurance were entirely at the charge of the State.

The new Constitution of 1936 re-established inequality from birth. Inheritance was made legal again and the right of un-restricted disposal of property by Last Will guaranteed to each individual citizen.[2] Life insurance was also reinstated. Well-to-do citizens are encouraged by advertisements of the State Insurance Trust (GOSSTRAKH) to contract policies; the mini-mum premium is fixed at 5000 roubles; it is paid out in case of death to the heirs (e.g. advertisement in *Litteratura i Isskustvo* of October 9th, 1943).

Complete equality at birth must of course have remained rather theoretical as long as inequality of income of the parents remained. This was unavoidable for the period of transition from the 'First Stage of Socialism' ('everybody to work according to his capacity and be rewarded according to his *work*') to the Second Stage

[1] V.Ts.I.K. — All-Union Central Executive Committee.
[2] Soviet Constitution, Article 10.

(everybody to work according to his capacity and be rewarded according to his *needs* — i.e. number of children, preferred recreation, etc.). Not even the most purist critic could expect a sudden jump to total equalitarianism. But one was entitled to expect from a regime moving, however slowly, towards a socialist goal, that it should make efforts to minimize the effects on the child of the unavoidable inequality among the parents, i.e. to prevent the emergence of privilege from the cradle. Soviet policy took exactly the opposite course. Inheritance was revived, life insurance encouraged; moreover, the children of prominent people were endowed with special money grants from the State until their coming of age. I quote only one example:

(at the) death of the outstanding aircraft designer, Comrade N. M. Polikarpov, Hero of Socialist Labour, Deputy of the Supreme Soviet of the U.S.S.R., following a serious illness, the Soviet Government has decided to assign a grant of 100,000 roubles to Polikarpov's wife and daughter, and pensions of 1000 roubles a month to his wife for life, 500 roubles a month to his daughter until she completes her education, and 400 roubles a month to his sister for life.[1]

Young Miss Polikarpov will thus grow up in a household which between three members has an unearned monthly income of over 3000 roubles plus a capital of 100,000 roubles to fall back upon. Assuming that she had been born in an ordinary Russian working-

Old Age Pensions (per month) as per Decree of Jan. 8th, 1938[2]		
	With 1 non-earning member of the family	With 2 or more
	Roubles	*Roubles*
Miners and workers in dangerous industries	60	75
Workers in heavy industry and railways	50	60
Others	30	40

[1] *Soviet War News*, August 2nd, 1944. [2] *Coll. of Laws*, 1939, No. 1-1.

class family and her father had been disabled by old age or accident, then she would grow up in a household with a monthly income of 30 to 75 roubles, instead of 3000. See Table on p. 155.

(ii) *Inequality of Education*

Thus inequality is not restricted to grown-up wage-earners, but carried straight into the nursery by a deliberate policy of the regime. Children in Soviet Russia grow up rich and poor as in capitalist countries. The first bulwark against inherited privilege fell when the new constitution sanctioned the inheritance of property; the second and more important bulwark fell when free education was abolished by the introduction of fees for higher education.

The decree of October 2nd, 1940[1] fixed the tuition fee for Secondary Schools (technical, normal, agricultural, medical, etc.) at 150-200 roubles per year, for universities at 300 to 500 roubles. The fees for the first term had to be paid within one month from the promulgation of the new law; 600,000 students from poor families who couldn't pay the fee had to leave school.[2]

Thus higher education (from the 15th year onward) became a privilege of the children of parents who could afford it; i.e. bureaucracy, technocracy and the new intelligentsia. This development had started long before the introduction of direct fees. Up to 1932 a minimum of 65 per cent of the students in Engineering Colleges and Technical Schools had to be manual workers or their children (*Pravda*, July 13th, 1928). By this policy of the 'Educational Cadres' (also called the principle of the 'Workers Nucleus') a crowding out of the poor by the rich in the higher schools was effectively prevented. In the decree of September 19th, 1932, the 'Workers Nucleus' principle was tacitly abandoned. The following statistics show the decline of the percentage of manual workers and their children in higher education:[3]

[1] *Izvestia*, October 3rd, 1940.

[2] Peter Meyer, 'The Soviet Union: A New Class Society', *Politics*, April 1944, New York, p. 83.

[3] From *Sozialisticheskoie Stroitel'stvo SSSR* ('Socialist Construction in the USSR') Moscow 1934, p. 410, and 1936, p. 576, and *Kul'turnoie Stroitel'stvo SSSR* ('Cultural Construction in the USSR') Moscow 1940, p. 114; quoted by Schwarz 'Heads of Russian Factories' *Social Research*, Sept. 1942, New York.

	1933 %	1935 %	1938 %
Universities	50.3	45.0	33.9
Secondary Schools	41.5	31.7	27.1

The most revealing figures are those for Industrial Colleges — the gateway to the managerial key-positions in the Soviet State. They were for 1938:[1]

	%
Manual workers and their children	43.5
Peasants and their children	9.6
Bureaucracy, specialists and their children	45.4

The introduction of school fees in 1940 was followed by the creation of cadet schools ('Suvorov military academies') with special entrance facilities for officers' sons (decree of August 23rd, 1943). There are also special schools reserved for the children of the bureaucracy. At the same time children whose parents cannot afford the fees for Secondary education are conscripted on leaving school to four years' compulsory labour service. (Decree of October 2nd, 1940). They are given 'vocational training' lasting from six months to two years, and are obliged for a further four years to work wherever directed. The upshot of the whole development is that on the average the children of manual workers and peasants remain manual workers and peasants, whereas the children of the upper strata are automatically put on the road to jobs in the upper strata.

There are, of course, scholarships for the poor, but their conditions are harsher than in most capitalist countries: two-thirds 'excellent' marks and the remainder 'good' on the examination paper. The very fact that the child of poor parents has to show special gifts to be granted the benefits of education which the son of rich parents obtains as a matter of course indicates the presence of a class barrier, a filter through which only the exception can pass.

[1] From Solomon Schwarz. 'Heads of Russian Factories', *Social Research*, Sept. 1942, New York, p. 324.

The whole development can be summarized in two stages. First, the population became stratified according to income-classes, which was unavoidable; secondly, this economic division is transferred to the following generation from the cradle, by deliberate government policy. A hereditary bureaucracy, technocracy and military caste emerges in the framework of a new type of class-society, based no longer on the ownership of the means of production but on control of the levers of the State, and following the same trend towards self-perpetuation which characterizes all stable class-rule in history.

It is hard to see how the series of decrees which conditioned this development could be explained as 'temporary expedients' or 'emergency measures'. The restoration of inheritance is embodied in the Constitution which was certainly not meant as a temporary expedient. The abolition of the Workers Nucleus policy in 1932 can hardly be explained as a gesture of appeasement towards Roosevelt or Churchill, nor could the introduction of school fees be expected to speed up the opening of the Second Front.

If there were only one single decree in the realm of education issued during the last ten years which pointed in a progressive direction, one could accord the Soviet regime the benefit of the doubt regarding its intentions. I challenge the indignant myth-addicts among my readers to produce such a decree.

The same applies to methods and contents of teaching, and the atmosphere in the schools. Everything fresh, experimental, and promising in the methods of Soviet education has been abolished. Co-education has been abolished; boys and girls are again segregated at the age of twelve. Competitions between pupils and teachers are abolished. Pedology, an American educational theory adapted in the early years of the revolution, which aimed at the tapping of the child's own sources of curiosity and initiative, has been abandoned as a 'false science . . . full of injurious anti-Marxist tendencies'; and the true 'Marxist tendency' was restored by proclaiming principles such as:

The Headmaster is the sole master of the school . . . the

teacher should not only be unafraid of giving orders to the
pupils, but where necessary punish them. . . .[1]
Practical experience of the best teachers long ago refuted all
the talk that compulsion or punishment was harmful.
Reasonable severity is more effective than persuasion.[2]
Persuasion . . . only hinders the training of disciplined
people . . . The corrupting and nihilistic influences of schools
which pay no sufficient attention to the training of patriotic
spirit. . . .[3]
And so on. All perfectly honourable principles for an English
Public School of the more conservative type.

VII. PAUPERS AND PROLETARIAN MILLIONAIRES

I have emphasized that inequality in earnings is inevitable
during a considerable transition period and as such cannot be
the object of criticism of the present Soviet regime. But criticism
becomes legitimate when we inquire into the degree of this
inequality and into its tendency to increase or decrease.

The starting-point of the whole development is Lenin's principle, laid down in *State and Revolution*, of the 'Maximum Income' —
viz., that no member of the State Bureaucracy up to the President
of the Republic should receive a higher salary than a qualified
worker. It was one of the three fundamental principles to protect
the Dictatorship of the Proletariat against bureaucratic degenera-
tion (the other two being the unification of executive and legis-
lative power, and the electorate's right to recall any State official
at any time from his post).

Equalitarianism was taken so literally in the first revolutionary
period that Lenin himself during the Civil War had to order that
leaders responsible for the life and welfare of their comrades

[1] Commissar for Education, Potemkin, at the All-Russian Educational Conference, August 1943. *Uchitelskaya Gazeta*, August 7th, 1943.
[2] *Pravda*, August 2nd, 1943.
[3] Commissar for Education, Potemkin, at the All-Russian Educational Conference, August 1943. *Uchitelskaya Gazeta*, August 7th, 1943.

should be granted priority in the basic necessities — meaning that Troop-Commanders in the chaotic conditions of the war should get food, sleep and if possible a quiet corner to work on their maps. It was a concession dictated by absolute necessity, a real 'emergency expedient' — but it was a seed which bore unexpected and exotic fruit. Henceforth 'Priority for the responsible leaders' became an accepted principle in every walk of life, from exclusive recreation homes in the Crimea to private summer houses, from hospitals reserved for 'responsibles' to 'closed co-operatives', restaurants and canteens.

However, these were privileges in the form of goods and social services, not in cash. The Maximum Income (of about 400 roubles per month) remained in force for Party members, and those who earned more — NEP men, Russian and foreign 'non-party specialists'—were regarded with contempt as a necessary evil. During the first Five Year Plan contrasts in earnings became more prominent, but the basic and radical change came with Stalin's famous six-point speech in June 1931. It was a declaration of war against 'Uravnilovka', or equality of pay.

Equalitarianism in wages was to cease once and for all, since it was 'alien and detrimental to socialist production'. Equalitarianism became a 'petty-bourgeois deviation', a crime against the State, a bogy-word like 'Counter-revolution' and 'Trotskism'. Stalin's speech was followed by the usual nation-wide propaganda campaign, a holy crusade against 'Uravnilovka', with the effect that the majority among the people became honestly convinced that inequality of pay was a fundamental principle of Socialism.

The motives behind the new line were the difficulties which the first Five Year Plan encountered. The tremendous wave of enthusiasm which in 1927 had been created by the promise to 'reach and surpass' the capitalist countries had worn off as the standard of living, instead of rising, had fallen below pre-revolutionary level.[1] A new incentive had to be found at all costs to increase production and the quality of output; it was found in the temporary expedient of differentiating salaries and wages to an

[1] See p. 164.

extent which soon 'reached and surpassed' the inequality of income under capitalism, as we shall presently see. It should be noted that the new policy was not presented as a transitory measure or necessary evil, but as a triumph of socialist ethics.

An equally urgent necessity for the young Soviet industry was rationalization, i.e. the switching from individual methods of production to extreme division of labour, the assembly-belt system and graduated piecework rates. This was made palatable to the masses under the romantic guise of 'Stakhanovism', one of the most curious propaganda stunts in modern history.

On the night of August 30th, 1933, Alexei Stakhanov, a young coalminer of the Donetz Basin, cut during his six-hour shift 102 tons of coal instead of the usual 7 tons — about fourteen times the average norm.[1] A few days later he beat his own record 'by hewing first 175 tons and then 227 tons of coal in one shift' — i.e. thirty-two times the average norm.[2]

The radio, newspapers and public speakers of the whole Soviet Union echoed the miraculous achievements of young Stakhanov with an excitement only comparable to the effect of the apparitions of Bernadette of Lourdes. Soon other miracles began to happen: the miner Dyukanov cut 125 tons on a shift; the weavers E. Vinogradova and M. Vinogradova from the Nogin textile mills, instead of tending 16 to 24 looms, went over to tend 144 and 150 respectively; *Pravda* mentioned a milling worker performing the work of 63 planers, 55 fitters, 15 millers, etc. Each factory soon had 200-per centers, 500-, 1000- and even 2000-per centers.

The clue to these miracles was given by Stakhanov himself in his speech at the first 'Stakhanovites Conference'. He had

> observed that he and his fellow hewers used their pneumatic drill for a part only of the shift, because when they had cut out some coal they had to interrupt the cutting to clear it away from the working face and again to interrupt this work to return to the cutting.

[1] *Labour in the Land of Socialism; Stakhanovites in Conference*, Moscow, 1936.
[2] Ibid.

Stakhanov thus

> came to the conclusion that a team would achieve better results if one man cut the coal and the others performed the subsidiary work.

In other words, a division of labour was achieved which has for decades been a matter of course in the rationalized mining industry of the West — which, however, meant the end of the old-fashioned and comfortable methods of work from which the Russian miner was loth to part, and which had to be forced upon him under the naively-romantic guise of Stakhanovism.

Rationalization *as such* was of course inevitable — just as differentiation of income *as such* was inevitable. But just as inequality of income was carried beyond capitalistic standards, so the hardships for the workers entailed by rationalization were driven ruthlessly beyond any reasonable limit by disguising a sober necessity as a socialist imperative:

'The Stakhanovite movement is something specifically Soviet, something specifically Socialist', the Commissar for Heavy Industry, Ordshonikidse, assured the Stakhanovite Conference.[1] And Molotov explained: '. . . it is not a question . . . of overstrain . . . Counting minutes and seconds during one's work means introducing a rhythm . . . means introducing culture in one's work. It is therefore not a question of *overstrain* on the part of the worker but of a *cultured* attitude towards work.'[2] (Molotov's emphasis.)

Culture in this new interpretation made rapid progress in Soviet industry. 'Stakhanovites' — that is team-leaders; foremen in capitalist terminology — had separate dining-rooms in factories and were paid up to twenty times the average. To take an example: according to the Moscow paper *Trud* (Jan. 20th, 1936) sixty employees of a Donetz mine earned monthly wages of 1000-2500 roubles per head; seventy-five employees earned 800-1000 roubles per head; four hundred earned 500-800 roubles per head and the remaining thousand *averaged* 125 roubles. The top wages in this

[1] *Labour in the Land of Socialism; Stakhanovites in Conference*, Moscow, 1936.
[2] Ibid.

average mine were about thirty times higher than the minimum wages. But the director of a mine of 1500 employees belongs only to the medium stratum of the technocracy; the salaries of directors, chief engineers and administrators in the top stratum are up to one hundred times higher than the average wage and up to three hundred times higher than the minimum wage. In 1943 the appearance of the first 'Proletarian Millionaires', enthusiastically welcomed by the Soviet Press, completed the development.

The apologist may argue that, regrettably unequal as Soviet incomes may be, they still represent *salaries* and not *profits* as in capitalist countries. The theoretical implications of this argument form part of the doctrine of the 'unshaken foundations' with which we shall deal later. But from a practical point of view it makes little difference whether Comrade Berdyebekov, the Director of a State Farm in Kasakstan who became the first officially proclaimed Soviet millionaire, owns the farm or merely directs it. His powers over the employees under the present labour-legislation (see below) are actually greater than the powers of ownership in capitalist countries; his children will be privileged by wealth, educational and social opportunities. Their income will be just as 'unearned' as that of any capitalist millionaire offspring's. The only difference is that Berdyebekov cannot buy land or a factory of his own; but who wants to *buy* a factory if he can enjoy all the benefits of ownership without the financial risks?

The true significance of the Proletarian Millionaires can be appreciated only when set against the background of the living conditions of the Proletarian Paupers. The Soviet Union is the only great country in the world which publishes no standard-of-living index, no statistics about the distribution of income-groups and spending. Russian statistics make a deafening noise with their figures of industrial production; about the consumer they are silent. Individual reports about the dismal living conditions of the masses by people who lived among them and had both the chance to get abroad and the courage to speak up — e.g. Ciliga, Sedov, Yvon, Serge — are dismissed as Trotskyite slander. There are, nevertheless, methods to establish the truth by careful analysis of official Soviet sources which are *ex hypothesi* beyond doubt. Thus, for example, *Planovoie Khoziaistvo* ('Planned Economy'), an official Soviet periodical, published in 1938 some figures about the food consumption of an average family of St. Petersburg textile workers under Tsarism.[1] Using these as a basis, Hubbard arrives at the following figures:[2]

		1913	1929	1937
Cost of 1 week's food	Roubles	3.40	5.90	49.60
Index of food prices	Per cent	100	172	1449
Average Money Wages	Roubles	25	66	245
Index of Real Wages	Per cent	100	154	68

Thus the average standard of living had risen from the Revolution to 1929 by 54 per cent and had by 1937 dropped to a level 32 per cent lower than the pre-revolutionary standard.

The same result was obtained by different methods by F. Forest, based on official Soviet sources and a survey of prices in Moscow retail stores by the American Embassy, endorsed by the Soviet Press. His figures are:[3]

	1913	1928	1940
Index of Prices	100	187	2248
Index of Money Wages	100	233	1383
Index of Real Wages	100	125	62

Again the same result was obtained by Colin Clark (*Critique of Russian Statistics*) based exclusively on official Soviet figures. Clark estimates that the food consumption per head has fallen from 1913 to 1934 by 30 per cent (from a value of 49.6 pence per week in English prices of 1934 to a value of 38 pence). This figure, according to Polanyi, stands 30 per cent below that found by Sir John Orr for the worst-fed 10 per cent of the British population.

To the best of my knowledge, no Soviet or Communist authority has so far attempted either to refute these figures or to publish

[1] Peter Meyer: 'The Soviet Union: A New Class Society', *Politics*, New York, March, 1944.
[2] Hubbard, *Soviet Labour and Industry*, London, 1942, p. 164.
[3] F. Forest: 'An Analysis of Russian Economy', *New International*, January-February, 1943.

different standard-of-living estimates. This would in any case be a difficult undertaking as the results were obtained by calculation based on official Soviet figures for food production, average money wages, population census, etc.

Income differentiation in *agriculture* began with Stalin's famous 'enrichissez vous' to the peasants in February 1933. How to abolish 'the curse of equalitarianism' after the land had been collectivized with all peasants holding equal shares in the communal acre seemed at first an insoluble problem, but an ingenious remedy was soon found. The produce of the land was not distributed equally between the members of the Kolkhos, but according to the 'working days' which each member contributed; and the definition of a 'working day' again varied according to the nature of the job performed. Thus for a day's work a labourer is credited with half a 'working day', a tractor driver with five, the administrative personnel with five and even ten 'working days'. Translated into capitalist terminology, the farmers became wage earners, with the same widely varying wage scales as the factory workers, and with Kolkhos Managers, Sovkhoz Directors, 'Brigadiers', etc. as equivalents to technocracy, Stakhanovites and foremen. As already mentioned, the millionaire Berdyebekov is actually Director of a State Farm in Kasakstan, one of the notoriously poorest districts of the U.S.S.R.

Workers, peasants and soldiers being the three pillars of the Soviet State, the Army could not lag behind industry and agriculture in the socialist struggle against 'petit-bourgeois Equalitarianism' (Stalin). The private in the Red Army to-day is paid 10 roubles per month, a lieutenant 1000 roubles, a colonel 2400 roubles.[1] The ratio of a private's to a subaltern's pay in the British Army is approximately 1 : 4, in the American Army 1 : 3, in the Soviet Army 1 : 100. It may be of some interest to hear what the Soviet apologist has to say about this phenomenon. In *Soviet Millionaires*, a pamphlet issued in 1943 in the communist 'Russia To-day' series, written by Reg. Bishop, we read:

[1] *The Economist*, July 3rd, 1943.

Another item on which there has been a great deal of mis-understanding concerns army remuneration, the fact that whereas a private soldier gets a mere pittance, Red Army officers receive relatively high pay — a lieutenant gets approximately 1000 roubles a month, a colonel something over 2000 roubles, and so on for the higher grades.

Obviously, Soviet millionaires are not going to develop on the pay of a ranker, but equally obviously this is no question of class differentiation, but one of sound socialist policy, in line with the general wages policy of the U.S.S.R.

Every male citizen is liable to military service in the U.S.S.R.; for a limited period of time he gives his services to the State, receiving in return a pocket-money allowance. At the end of that time he returns to civil life, usually better equipped for his vocation than when he was called up. Although his remuneration in the Army has been tiny, he has had so many free services — postage, travel, cleaning materials (!), enter-tainment, smokes, etc. — that he has been at least as well off as soldiers in the armies of other countries.

One wonders what the British soldier would say if his pay were cut down by the War Office to approximately eighteen pence a week and Sir James Grigg defended this measure by the argu-ment that each soldier can travel gratis to the front and gets the benefits of two free postage-stamps, eighteen fags a week, free blanco, and free ENSA shows.

VIII. LABOUR CONDITIONS AND THE TRADE UNIONS

Labour legislation, designed to teach the masses, in Molotov's terms, a cultured attitude to work, attained rigours which sur-passed those imposed upon the workers in both Fascist Italy and Nazi Germany. Foremen and factory managers were invested with the power to discharge without notice workers for being more than 20 minutes late at work, for leaving work before time, for 'idling', 'unsatisfactory output', etc.[1] Dismissal for idleness entailed loss of one's ration card (as long as rationing was in force) and of the right to dwelling space. In 1939 each salaried person was issued with a Labour Book which remained in the hands of the personnel management and was endorsed by it with remarks on the worker's conduct, offences committed, his zeal or idleness, etc. To employ a man who did not produce his book was made a criminal offence.

However, no threats and victimization sufficed to stop large-scale migrations of discontented workers. Hence from 1938 onwards measures were taken to tie the workers down to their working place. Since 1940 unauthorized quitting of one's job and even lateness, 'idling', etc., are punished with Forced Labour; each offence has to be tried within five days by a single judge (instead of, as previously, by a judge and two lay advisers); judges and managers are threatened with heavy penalties for showing any leniency.[2] Health Insurance and other insurance benefits were made dependent on the length of employment in one job. Thus workers get no sickness allowance during the first six months of work in a new job, then the allowance rises gradually to reach the full amount only after ten years of service at the same working place. A change of employment means starting again at the botton of the scale.[3]

At the same time the six-day week and seven-hour day were abolished, piece rates cut and norms of output raised, so that despite a 15 per cent increase in working time the average monthly wage remained the same, with deductions imposed on workers unable to fulfil their individual production quota — which 32 per cent of the workers were unable to fulfil.[4] Protective legislation in favour of women and adolescents (preventing their employment on night work and overtime) was abolished. It should be emphasized that all this refers to pre-war days; since

[1] Decree of December 29th, 1939.
[2] Decrees of June 26th and July 24th, 1940.
[3] *International Labour Review*, Vol. 38, 1938.
[4] Statement by Shvernik, head of Soviet Trade Unions, April 16th, 1941 (quoted by Meyer).

December 1941 all branches of Soviet industry and transport directly or indirectly connected with the war were placed under martial law;[1] Absenteeism, Idling and Carelessness became capital offences.

At this point the question arises how such debasement of the workers' legal status, the abolition of their elementary rights, the lowering of their living standard under pre-revolutionary level with the simultaneous rise of a new luxury class, could remain unopposed in a country nominally under the dictatorship of the proletariat.

In capitalist democracies the working masses have two channels to influence government decisions: the electoral machinery, and their Trade Unions.

The first channel is obviously non-existent in a country run by the one-party system. The Soviet elector has the right to vote for or against the single list of candidates appointed from above; to vote against entails considerable risks as in most rural areas the candidates are elected in open meeting 'per acclamationem', and is besides pointless, as there is no alternative. There is no legal opposition, and no independent Press; there are no means whatsoever to convey the pressure of public opinion to the Executive; the only course open to discontents is political conspiracy by cliques.

The second, economic, channel is the Trade Unions. The singular function of the Soviet Trade Unions is practically unknown among Soviet-sympathizers in the West. During the Civil War and the ensuing period the Trade Unions through their Factory Committees and Control Commissions exercised factual control over the country's economic resources and saved it from chaos and collapse. During the NEP they lost their key-position in the State economy, but remained the watchdogs of the workers' immediate interests. The crystallization of the Stalinite bureaucracy in the second half of the 'twenties brought a radical change

[1] Margaret Miller: *Labour in the U.S.S.R.*, Brit. Assn. for Labour Legislation, 1942, pp. 19-21.

in the function of the Trade Unions. With the beginning of the first Five Year Plan they became integrated in the State bureaucracy; their task was no longer to protect the interests of the workers but to strengthen labour discipline and to promote maximum efficiency. From an organ of the working class they had changed into an instrument of coercion of the working class. Accordingly most of the decrees quoted in this chapter about the penalties for infringement on labour discipline, the 'Labour Books', the lengthening of working hours, etc. etc., were passed officially on recommendation by the Trade Unions and carry the formal preamble: 'In accordance with Suggestions of the All-Union Central Council of the Trade Unions, the Presidium of the Supreme Council of the U.S.S.R. decrees that . . .'

The Soviet Trade Unions are organized on the Corporative pattern according to production branches, and embrace the whole staff of the concern 'whether director, manager or charwoman'; elections are carried out in factory meetings with lists presented by the Executive of the District Council, Regional Council, etc., and decided by the raising of hands *en bloc*. Their programme can best be summarized in the words of two of their prominent leaders:

> The fixing of wage-scales must be left entirely in the hands of the heads of industry. They must establish the norm (Andreiev in *Pravda*, Dec. 29th, 1935).[1]
>
> The proper determination of wages and the regulation of labour demand that the industrial heads and the technical directors be immediately charged with responsibility in this matter. This is also dictated by the necessity of establishing a single authority and ensuring economy in the management of concerns . . . [The workers] must not defend themselves against their government. That is absolutely wrong. That is supplanting the administrative organs. That is Left opportunistic perversion, the annihilation of individual authority and interference in the administrative department . . . (Weinberg in *Trud*, July 8th, 1933).[2]

[1] Quoted by Meyer, *Politics*, New York, March, 1944.
[2] Ibid.

To sum up, we have again to ask: what motives prompted the Soviet regime to take the course described in this and the previous chapter? To suspect them of subjective mala fides or 'counter-revolutionary deviations' would obviously be on the sterile level of communist polemics. If we want to arrive at objective conclusions, we have to assume that the regime acted bona fide by falling back on 'temporary expedients' which, because of propagandistic necessities, were camouflaged as something else. The main factors that led to these temporary expedients were obviously: the insufficiency of ideological incentives to increase production and their replacement by the money incentive; the insufficiency of voluntary labour discipline and its replacement by enforced discipline.

Neither of these two motives can justify the carrying of the remedy to the excesses described. But even more serious for a historic evaluation of the Soviet experiment is the fact itself that the incentives which form the basis of socialist theory have broken down. I shall try to draw the conclusions later on.

IX. ASPECTS OF SOVIET LEGISLATION

After the devastations of the Civil War and the famine, tens of thousands of children had become tramps, members of juvenile criminal gangs, a plague to the citizen and a thorny social problem to the regime. The official term for them was 'Besprisorny' — Waifs and Strays.

The Besprisorny played during the 'twenties an important role in Soviet propaganda abroad. The aims of this propaganda were twofold: to evoke sympathy with the terrible sufferings of the Russian people, and admiration for the modern paedagogical methods of tackling the problems. One of the most admirable of the great Soviet films of that period was Ekk's *The Road to Life*. It showed the rehabilitation of a gang of hardened juvenile criminals under strict avoidance of coercion, authority and punishment, by methods of occupational therapy, persuasion and communal life. The film, which had a triumphant success all over the world, symbolized the socialist attitude to criminology, based on environmental psychology. The concepts of Punishment, Retribution and Intimidation had been discarded and replaced by measures of social protection and social therapy. These indeed were fundamental principles of early Soviet legislation, and cornerstones of socialist philosophy. If they are taken away, the whole system collapses. For if the social defaulter, warped by his environment, cannot be reformed by changing that environment, then there can be no hope of reforming our warped society by any change of political institutions. In that case the Conservatives are right, human nature is unchangeable, and will never be capable of developing such unselfish and responsible traits as are required for a socialist society. These are elementary tenets of socialist theory, and it would be unnecessary to repeat them had not Soviet dialectics succeeded in almost completely obscuring the fundamentals.

The Besprisornis thus became a test case for the regime. However poor a country may be, given a healthy social development, it must be possible to lead those juvenile tramps back on the 'Road to Life', to re-integrate them into the national community. It must be remembered that they were by no means criminals of a pathological heredity, but orphans whose parents had perished in the Civil War, representing an average cross-section of the population. In 1934 the test case was decided. All pretence of social therapy, etc. was abandoned and by the decree of April 7th, 1935 capital punishment was extended to children down to the age of twelve.

This happened eighteen years after the revolution. By then the Waifs and Strays of the Civil War had become grown-up men and a new generation of juvenile criminals had sprung up, born under the new regime and apparently so far beyond hope that instead of by teacher and governess they had to be dealt with by the firing squad.

The existence of this decree has frequently been denied by apologists. Here is the full text, translated from the Soviet Code of Laws (1935, 19-155):

On Measures to Combat Criminality among Minors
Decree of April 7th, 1935. C.E.C. and S.N.K.
With the aim of the quickest liquidation of criminality amongst minors, C.E.C. and S.N.K. decree:

1. Young people from 12 years of age caught at theft, violence, infliction of bodily injury, mutilation, homicide or attempts at homicide, are to be brought before the criminal law courts and punished in accordance with all measures of the criminal code.

2. People caught inciting minors or inviting them to take part in various crimes, or forcing minors to indulge in speculation, prostitution, beggary, etc., are liable to imprisonment for not less than five years.

A law which treats a child of twelve as a grown-up in the Criminal Court has no parallel in the legislation of any civilized country — or, for that matter, any uncivilized one.

Another law, equally unprecedented in the legislation of any country, decrees the deportation for five years 'to the remote regions of Siberia' of all the dependants of a man who escapes military service by deserting abroad, *if they did not know about his crime*. If they did know about it, the penalty is five to ten years of imprisonment and confiscation of property. Paragraph 3 of the decree of June 8th, 1934 (published in *Izvestia*, June 9th, 1934), runs:

3. In the event of flight or escape abroad of a military person, the adult members of his family, if they have in any way assisted the preparations or the commitment of the act of treason, or even if they have known about it without bringing it to the knowledge of the authorities, will be punished with five to ten years imprisonment with confiscation of their property.

   The other adult members of the traitor's family, living with him or being his dependants at the time of treason, are deprived of their electoral rights and deported for five years to the remote regions of Siberia.

EXPLORATIONS

The decree revives the primitive conception of the collective responsibility of the family or clan (blood-guilt). Since 1935 the routine of deporting relatives of arrested people has been extended to all forms of High Treason and Counter-Revolutionary Activity — terms which cover practically any offence: political dissent, 'wrecking', absenteeism. What it amounts to in practice is that every individual has to regard his whole family as potential hostages for his conduct. Hence the current practice on the part of women whose husbands have been arrested to rush to the registrar and obtain divorce by unilateral declaration; a measure regarded as a mere formality which does not affect the personal relationship between those concerned.[1]

Commenting on the new terror-decrees, the People's Commissar for Justice, Krylenko, explained (*Izvestia*, No. 37, Feb. 12th, 1936):

> In the opinion of Liberals and of opportunists of all kinds . . . the stronger a country is, the more lenient it can be towards its opponents. No, and again no! The stronger the country is, the mightier it is, the stronger the ties which unite Party and Government with the toiling masses . . . and the greater our indignation and revolt against those who disturb our Socialist construction and the more justified are we in taking stern measures against them. . . .

By that time any pretence of socialist principles in judicature had been dropped. The new Soviet Text-book of Law restored the term 'Punishment' for 'Measure of Social Defence', and retribution, intimidation and the spreading of fear became its officially avowed aims. The victims of the purges, high and humble, were no more called 'Social defaulters' but 'mad dogs, rats, vermin, hyenas, dung and scum'. For if the criminal was a product of his environment as Marx taught, what sort of environment was it which turned the whole old bolshevik guard into traitors and mad dogs? It was an awkward question to answer, but a question which automatically cropped up in every marxistic-

[1] This possibility is now barred by the new divorce laws of 1944.

173

ally trained mind. To avoid it was only possible by discarding the very foundations of socialist thought.

This tendency permeates the new laws and decrees regulating every aspect of public and private life: marriage, divorce, sexual relations, travel, religion and military training. I shall touch upon only a few aspects of them.

Both Socialists and Communists on the Continent had fought ardent campaigns against laws in capitalist countries penalizing homosexuality and making abortion a crime. The arguments about homosexuality are too well known to need repetition. If it is a crime, half the writers, painters and musicians from Plato through Leonardo to Proust would have had to spend their lives in gaol. As to abortion, the socialist argument can be shortly summarized as follows: The average woman if unwilling to have a child will practise birth control. If a woman has decided to undergo an abortion she must have serious reasons of a psychological or economic nature. In *both* cases it is socially preferable that the unwanted child should not be born. If a woman is determined to get rid of her pregnancy she will attempt it regardless of the law. (In the Weimar Republic the average yearly number of hospital admissions after illegal abortion attempts was over 500,000 — and this figure only comprises cases where hospitalization became necessary!) Hence the only practical effect of outlawing abortion is that the rich have their illegal operations performed in relative hygiene and comfort, whereas the poor are driven into the squalor and dangers of self-damaging manipulations and quacks.

The decree banning abortions was the only law in the history of the Soviet Union which was submitted to public discussion before its promulgation. A plebiscite was promised and test votes were taken in a number of factories and meetings. They showed a majority against the law; whereupon the plebiscite was called off and the law promulgated by decree of December 27th, 1936 (Code of Laws 1936, Nos. 34-309). The dangerous counter-revolutionary experiment of public discussion has never since been repeated. Moreover, the medical indications required by the new law to legalize an abortion, and the administrative procedure to obtain legalization, are more severe than the corresponding regulations in Germany, Great Britain and the United States.

The last remark also applies to the new divorce laws of July 1944. The procedure laid down for divorce amounts to an equivalent of the medieval pillory. The notice of bringing in a divorce action has to be advertised in the local newspaper at his or her own cost by the man or woman seeking divorce (Art. 24, Sect. c.). What that means will be appreciated by anybody who has ever seen a Russian small town or village. Compulsory entries have to be made in the home-passports of man and woman, giving full details of marriage and divorce — and Soviet home-passports have to be produced on every occasion, whether to obtain bread-rations, employment or permission to travel on a local train. The proceedings take place in open court, the People's Court — whose only function is to try to reconcile the couple. If a reconciliation does not take place, there the matter ends as far as the People's Court is concerned — it has no competence to pronounce a divorce. However, 'the claimant has the right to apply for dissolution of the marriage in a higher court' (Art. 25). The next higher, Regional Court may or may not dissolve the marriage — this is entirely left to the Judge's discretion, as the law gives no indication whatsoever of valid grounds for a divorce. As the officially avowed tendency of the new law is to counteract divorce, a Judge under the prevailing conditions must indeed possess exemplary courage to dissolve a marriage. The claimant, if not yet tired, may then work his way up to the Territorial, District, Town and Supreme Courts — a matter of a few years and of a fortune. For the fee for divorce which hitherto was 50 roubles is henceforth 500-2000 roubles, not including lawyers' fees and other expenses (Art. 27). Including the latter, we arrive at 3000 roubles as a modest estimate for a case decided on the lowest, i.e. the Regional Court, level. The average monthly earnings of the Soviet citizen was 289 roubles according to the last official figures, published in 1938. Taking taxes and wage deductions into account, we find that the cost of the simplest case of divorce represents slightly more than the average citizen's net earnings in a year. In other words, from the financial angle alone divorce is made impossible for anybody under the income level of chief engineers, directors and higher bureaucracy. But, as we saw, the financial aspect is not even the decisive one. In August 1944 the Press reported that during the first month following the promulgation of the new law (July 8th, 1944) not a single petition for divorce had been filed throughout the whole U.S.S.R.

What the law amounts to is the pure and simple abolition of divorce for all but the privileged upper stratum. That is its avowed intention, and the Soviet regime has never stopped at half measures. In theory each Soviet Republic has the right of secession from the Union; henceforth the Soviet citizen's chance of secession from his spouse will be about equal to the Ukraine's chance to declare her independence.

The Soviet woman, once married, is tied down for her life to the job of breeding. The same decree which bans divorce imposes a special tax on bachelors, spinsters and *families with less than three children* (decree of July 8th, Arts. 16-18); whereas mothers with three or more children receive a money grant, with four or more children a monthly allowance, with five to six children the Motherhood Medal, with seven to nine children the order of 'Motherhood Glory', and with ten children or over the title of 'Heroine Mother'. The panegyrics of the Soviet Press about the new law surpassed even the usual scales of hysteria. *Pravda's* editorial on the day following the decree asserted:

> With us, *for the first time in the history* of peoples and countries, motherhood became a matter of solicitude on the part of the State ...

— an assertion of unusual stupidity even for home consumption, given the fact that in England, for instance, family allowances under the National Insurance scheme will start with the second, not with the fourth child; and the further fact that when Nazi Germany began its birthrate drive some years ago, with bachelor tax, money premiums and all the rest, the Soviet Press echoed with justified derision about the 'debasement of womanhood to the role of prize brood-mares'. Without being of a particularly vindictive nature, one may wish that all leader-writers of the Soviet Press should be compulsorily married to Mother Heroines.

The history of Soviet legislation since Lenin's death is the history of a gradual freezing of individual liberties in every realm of life, right down to the liberty of movement in space. The decree of Dec. 27th, 1932 (Code o.L. 1932, 84-516), introducing the compulsory Home-Passport system, deprived the Soviet citizen of the right to travel freely in his own country. Special permission is needed to enter all the bigger industrial towns and the surrounding areas varying in radius from 20 to 100 kilometres; absence from home even of twenty-four hours has to be reported to the police. Again we look in vain for a parallel in the peace-time regulations of any other modern country.

Travel abroad is banned except on government missions. Illegal attempts to reach a foreign country are punishable by death. To be sent abroad on an official mission is regarded as a danger — a person who has been abroad will on his return automatically fall under suspicion of having been 'contaminated'. To keep the country free from contamination, i.e. the knowledge of conditions of life abroad, to maintain the hermetic wall which has surrounded Russia for the past twenty-five years, is a vital issue for the regime to which all other considerations have to be subordinated. Hence Russia's refusal to admit refugees from Nazi Germany which led to the breakdown of the Evian Conference in 1938 and of all attempts at an international solution of the problem; hence the refusal to admit the survivors of the International Brigades interned in French concentration camps; hence also the handing over of German anti-Fascists to Nazi Germany after the Stalin-Hitler pact — evidence of which, including names, is available in this country.

Once more we have to ask: what were the probable motives behind these developments? And once more the only possible answer is: the breakdown of the incentives for self-imposed discipline foreseen by the socialist theory, and their replacement by coercion and intimidation; with the additional necessity to prevent all knowledge of and comparison with conditions of life in countries under parliamentary-democratic regimes.

X. THE NEW RULING CLASS

The nucleus of power in the Soviet Union is the Party. The radical changes both in leadership and membership which the Bolshevik Party underwent during the last decade are of fundamental importance for the understanding of the new regime; they give in a nutshell the significance of Stalinism.

First, the changes in leadership. I shall not repeat the names of the revolutionary leaders who were liquidated during the purges; it is sufficiently known that among the great figures of Lenin's period Stalin alone survives. It is, however, commonly assumed that the massacre by trial affected only the top stratum; that it was a kind of Olympian battle, a showdown among the leaders, in which Stalin rid himself of all rival personalities and rival policies to gain a free hand and thus be able to pursue his own line of subtle manœuvring and temporizing — which alone, it is asserted, could assure Russia's survival in the years of external and internal crisis. If this were so, the purges would represent merely a political crisis, solved with the ruthlessness which is in the tradition both of Russia and the Bolshevik Party, but nevertheless restricted to professional politicians, and not affecting the foundations of the revolutionary State. Such a crisis, except for the methods of its solution, would still be comparable to a cabinet crisis in democratic countries; it would not amount to a counter-revolution or 'Thermidor'.

But this interpretation of the purges is demonstrably wrong. They were not an affair of the top-layer and the politicians, but affected the whole Party from top to bottom and completely changed its character. The following official figures will prove this.

EXPLORATIONS

The 17th Congress of the All-Soviet Bolshevik Party was held in January-February 1934, before the purges.

The 18th Party Congress was held in March 1939, just after the purges.

At the 17th Congress 22.6 per cent of the delegates had been party members since before 1917, that is since before the Revolution.

At the 18th Congress the corresponding figure was 2.4 per cent. In other words, only one-tenth of them had survived the party purge.[1]

At the 17th Congress 17.7 per cent had been party members since 1917, that is had joined during the year of the Revolution.

At the 18th Congress the corresponding figure was 2.6 per cent.

In round figures at the 17th Congress 40 per cent of the delegates dated their membership from before the Civil War; at the 18th Congress only 5 per cent.

The comparison becomes even more impressive if we take 1919 as the test year. At the 17th Congress 80 per cent of the delegates were 'old party members' (since 1919 or before); at the 18th Congress the corresponding figure was 14.8 per cent.

In absolute figures the Party had at the time of the 18th Congress 1,588,852 members. Out of these only about 20,000 — that is, 1.3 per cent — were 'old Bolsheviks' belonging to the Party since 1917 or earlier. But in 1918 the Party had numbered 260,000 to 270,000 members, the majority of them young people. What had happened to them? Schwartz assumes that roughly one-fourth were killed during the Civil War — a rather high estimate. That would still leave 200,000 survivors at the time of the 18th Congress. But only 20,000 remained in the Party — nine-tenths had disappeared, as the reports of the Mandatory Commissions show, between 1934 and 1939. And these were not leaders, not even Party delegates; they are the ordinary rank-and-file, the workers and peasants who had made the Revolution and fought in the Civil War.

---

[1] These and all following figures are taken from the official Reports of the Mandate Commissions of the 17th and 18th Party Congresses, quoted by Schwartz: 'Heads of Russian Factories' (*Social Research*, New York, September, 1942).

The Bolshevik Party had emerged from the purges as a completely new body, which had with the Party of the heroic days of the Revolution only the name and 1.3 per cent of its members in common.

But still, the apologist will perhaps say, it has remained a Party of workers and peasants. Has it? Again the official figures speak for themselves. According to the report of the Mandatory Commission at the 17th Congress, 9.3 per cent of the delegates were 'workers from production', that is actual, not former, manual workers. At the 18th Congress the Mandatory Commission for the first time gave no figures as to the percentage of the workers among the delegates. The reason for this became clear during the Congress itself, which, with the usual unanimity, changed the statutes of the Party by eliminating those clauses which safeguarded the proletarian character of the Party — the clauses referring to the Party candidates' social origins. The Communist Party of Russia had thus, both in theory and in practice, ceased to be a Party of the Working Class. To make this the more obvious, not one of the famous Stakhanov workers who were paraded among the delegates of the 18th Congress was elected into the Central Committee of the Party, a large body consisting of 139 persons.

Who, then, is the Party, the all-powerful body of a million and a half people who occupy all responsible positions and administer the country? Who are the 90.7 per cent among the delegates who were already in 1934 *not* 'workers from production'? The Soviet State knows only one great class of people besides them: the administrators of economy and State apparatus — bureaucracy and technocracy. About one-third of the Soviet Government consists of engineers; the rest of administrators. We have seen in previous sections how this new 'managerial' ruling class became more and more segregated from the masses, how it succeeded in creating a new framework for the inheritance of privilege, so as to approach the criteria of a hereditary caste (similar to the old Russian administrative aristocracy), and how it gradually closed its ranks against newcomers from below by legislation, differentiation of income, educational restrictions, and the abandonment of the 'workers' nucleus' principle in the higher schools. The purging and 'taking over' of the Party by the Bureaucracy was the decisive step from the Dictatorship of the Proletariat to the stabilization of the new ruling class.

XI. FORCED LABOUR—A PARENTHESIS

There is one question connected with the political changes during the past two decades which cannot be satisfactorily answered: the number of Soviet citizens who in connection with these changes lost life or liberty. The wall of silence around Russia which so effectively prevents information even regarding relatively trivial matters from leaking through is at its densest where this question is concerned. It has been officially admitted by the Soviet Government that the White Sea Canal was built entirely, and the Turk-Sib Railway partly, by Forced-Labour Brigades; gigantic enterprises which involved the labour of about a million men. But here official information ends; no figures were published and no outsider was ever permitted to visit those camps.

Indirect indications may be gained from Soviet population statistics — or rather the lack of such statistics. In 1930 the Statistical Bureaux were purged and it was announced that 'Statistics were a weapon in the fight for Communism'. They were certainly a silent weapon for, as we saw, the Soviet Union is the only great country in the world which has for years published no standard-of-living index. Likewise, no population census was published between 1926 and 1940. A census was taken in January 1937 but the results were not published because, according to an official statement, they contained 'grave mistakes owing to the activities of enemies of the People' (*Izvestia* March 26th, 1939). So the Statistical Bureau was once more purged and a new census was undertaken in January 1939. Its results gave the total population of the U.S.S.R. as 170,126,000 souls — roughly 15 millions less than statistical expectation (Census of December 1926: 147,000,000; official government estimate of 1930: 157,500,000;

average yearly increase according to Stalin's statement on October 1st, 1935: 3,000,000; minimum estimate for 1939: 185,000,000). What happened to those at least 15 million 'lost souls'? They were not the victims of a sudden increase of birth-control, for contraceptives were practically unobtainable throughout Russia during the whole period. Some millions may have perished during the famine of 1932-33; the number of miscarriages and child mortality may have increased owing to malnutrition; the others may have perished in the Forced Labour Brigades, where eye-witnesses put the mortality among the prisoners at 30 per cent per annum. But all this is guesswork. The only certainty is that roughly 10 per cent of the Soviet population is statistically missing.

So far, I have relied entirely on official Soviet sources. As to conditions in the Forced-Labour Brigades and the total number of the disfranchised people in Russia, only private sources are available — the publications of Ciliga, Trotsky, Victor Serge, etc. Among several eye-witness reports of more recent origin in my possession I wish to quote one, the testimony of Lucien Blit, a leading member of the Bund (the Jewish Socialist Party of Poland). The following facts are based partly on a confidential report delivered by Blit to the 'Group of Inter-allied Socialist Friends' on April 9th, 1943, and partly on details related by him to myself.

After the fall of Poland in 1939 Blit, who had taken an active part in organizing the defence of Warsaw, escaped to Vilna, then under Lithuanian rule. From Vilna he was sent by his Party in March 1940 back to Warsaw as a delegate to the Warsaw underground movement. He had a passport issued under the assumed name of Wiscinsky, a Polish accountant. On his way from Vilna to Warsaw he had to cross a stretch of Russian-occupied Polish territory. He was caught by the Russian frontier-guards on May 30th, 1940. Arrested, he did not disclose his identity and mission, as the Bund, being a section of the Second International, is illegal in Russia. In those days of chaos, tens of thousands of Poles were escaping from the Germans to the Russian occupied parts of Poland. Blit pretended to be one of them and shared the average fate of Polish refugees to Russia.

He was brought to the prison of Lomza and kept there for ten months — from May 30th, 1940 to March 30th, 1941. His cell — No. 81 on the third floor — measured 4.8 square yards, contained one bed and was intended for one prisoner; he shared it for ten months with *seven* others. The first ten minutes' exercise for these eight men took place on January 22nd, 1941 — after 236 days of confinement; the next a month later, on February 22nd. They were not permitted to read, to write or to communicate with the outside world. Disciplinary punishment — inflicted for speaking too loudly, opening the window, making chessmen out of breadcrumbs, etc. — consisted in standing for forty-eight hours against a wall in the icy cellar clothed only in a shirt; in more serious cases standing for forty-eight hours in cold water up to the belt. The latter punishment frequently ended in paralysis, insanity or death. Questioning was usually done at night time and as a rule accompanied by beating and threats of execution. Beating was also applied to women, particularly to girls accused of being members of Polish patriotic student organizations.

Cases of insanity and suicide were frequent. In B.'s cell 'One night a powerfully built peasant from the region of Kolno woke us up to tell us that he was Jesus Christ and that it was time they took him down from the cross. He was raving for five days, but the wardens only took him away on the sixth . . . A Jewish boy who had escaped from Nazi-occupied to Soviet territory shouted day and night for a week: ' "I am not Trotsky".'

If the investigation revealed no specific political charge against the prisoner, his case was dismissed and he received the administrative routine sentence of three to eight years' deportation to 'Correctional' Labour Camps for unauthorized entry into Soviet territory. This fate was shared by all Poles who had sought refuge from the Germans in the Soviet Union. In B.'s case the proceedings took the following form:

In the night of February 26th, 1941, I was ordered to collect my belongings and was taken downstairs. After some time I was led with some others into a big dark room. Without any explanations we were each given a slip of paper to sign. The slip contained three typewritten lines to the effect that the OSOBOY SOWYESCENIE (the Special Commission) of the OGPU in Lomza decreed that for the illegal crossing of the State frontier M. Wiszynsky was sentenced in accordance with Art. 120 of the Penal Code of the White Russian Republic to three years in a 'Correctional' Labour Camp. The only thing left for me to do was to sign, which I did. Later on the Governor of the prison — who was at the same time Chairman of the Special Commission — told me that there were no specific charges against me; that was why I had got away with such a short sentence. Many others, former soldiers of the Polish Army, got five years. A Jew whose name I cannot recall and who had been driven over the frontier to Kolno by the Germans got as much as eight years. The Special Commission had the right to inflict sentences up to eight years only. There was no appeal against their decision.

On April 4th, 1941, Blit arrived in the Labour Camp of Pleseck on the river Onega. It contained about 35,000 prisoners. In the sub-polar climate where the temperature even in June dropped under zero point Fahrenheit, the men and women had to work twelve to thirteen hours per day, felling trees in the snow-covered Arctic forest. Their food consisted of bread plus two hot soups between 4-5 a.m. and between 8-9 p.m.; in between, nothing but hot water. Sugar, fruit and vegetables were unknown and in consequence all prisoners were attacked by scurvy; within the first few months they lost their teeth. No clothing, mattresses or blankets were provided; after a couple of weeks suits were reduced to rags, wet on return from work, frozen stiff during the night. Each man or woman was assigned the task of cutting 6 cubic metres (8 cubic yards) of wood per day.

A man of average strength could not do much more than half of it; to the women, the same norms applied; and the weight

184

of the bread ration depended on the amount of wood cut. To fall below half the norm meant direct starvation. The younger women supplemented their rations by prostituting themselves to the guards; their price was a pound of bread a time. Prostitution, theft, graft, denunciations, accompanied the struggle for survival. In the August of 1941 out of four hundred and fifty Poles in my section a hundred and twenty had swollen bodies and were unable to get up from the barrack-floor. The mortality in the camp was 30 per cent per annum. We worked without respite. Sunday was also a working day; even the first of May was a working day. The majority of the Brigades in my camp had had no rest-day throughout the five months which I spent there.

The camp population consisted of criminals and political prisoners. The latter were divided into two groups: 'Spies and traitors' and 'socially dangerous elements'. The second group consisted mainly of people from the national minorities. In my camp, for instance, there were four hundred Greeks, old inhabitants of Kiercz in the Crimea, who had all been arrested on one day in 1938 and collectively sentenced to five years of Forced Labour.

They will never leave the camp. In the U.S.S.R. release after a sentence served is not automatic, but subject to a special decision of the OGPU. For political prisoners this decision never arrives, or arrives in the form of a prolongation of the sentence for a further five years.

Blit was released, together with other Poles, after the German attack on Russia in 1941 and the subsequent signing of the Stalin-Sikorsky treaty. He joined the Polish Army, then under formation in Alma-Ata. For the Soviet citizen no such happy event is possible. Once sent to one of the Arctic Labour Camps he never returns, doomed to perish in the cold inferno of the Polar night.

How many of them? There is no means of ascertaining; but estimates by people who have peeped behind the Soviet scene suggest about 10 per cent of the total population. This is not so fantastic as it seems, since the five million Kulaks officially deported in the years of Collectivization already represent a solid core of $3\frac{1}{2}$ per cent. Then came the crushing of the various oppositions of Left and Right — Trotskyites, Bukarinites, etc., culminating in the purges. And opposition cannot have vanished since, in a people with a great revolutionary tradition, subjected to such sudden and mortal shocks as the arrival of Ribbentrop in Moscow out of the blue sky of an August day in 1939. It would be a miracle if among the 170 million people of the U.S.S.R. there had not been a few hundred thousand who carelessly betrayed their disgust and despair. It is difficult for the Western mind to visualize in a concrete way conditions of life in a country where dissent is officially identified with crime. Once this point is established, the steady trickle of 'socially dangerous elements' into the pool of the Forced-Labour Battalions and the maintenance of this pool at a level of about 10 per cent appears as a logical and inevitable phenomenon.

'I have lived with a number of Russian families', Blit says at the end of his narrative, 'and there was not a single case in which at least one member among the relatives or friends of the family was not "absent". When I spoke to a well-known Soviet journalist in Kuibishev he emphasized, with some pride in his voice, that there were not more than 18 million of them; everything else was exaggeration. Officials of the regime grew very angry at estimates over 20 million; up to that figure their attitude was one of tacit admission.'

This is one first-hand report among many, whose authors are personally known to me as reliable and responsible persons. I am fully aware, however, that to the Soviet addict, and also to many uninformed sympathizers, this report will sound like a tale from the moon. One is generally prepared to accept a correction of one's ideas by, say, 10 per cent; a correction by a thousand per cent is beyond one's capacity of immediate adaptation. Through the cumulative effect of two decades, the gulf between myth and reality has become so great that it requires an equally great mental effort to take the jump and part with one's most cherished illusion.

That is why I have called this section a 'parenthesis'. It is the only part of this survey whose contents are based on private, not on official, data. The indignant reader is at liberty to disbelieve them, to call me a Trotskyite agent, a menshevik counter-revolutionary, a Japanese spy, a howling hyena or any other name applied to critics of Russia. But he won't be able to take the same attitude towards the official Soviet sources, Soviet laws, decrees, statistics, etc., quoted in the rest of this work. I have selected Blit's testimony as an illustration. The reader may discard the illustration without affecting the text.

XII. THE DOCTRINE OF THE UNSHAKEN FOUNDATIONS

We have now arrived at a point where a summing up of the argument is required.

Soviet policy during the past two decades allows theoretically of two interpretations. *Either* Russia has abandoned its socialist aspirations, in which case its policy both in the international field and at home presents no mysteries, but forms a coherent picture of power politics carried out with admirable cunning and efficiency by the leaders of a young, expanding nation. This is the interpretation of realists from Lord Beaverbrook to the late Wendell Willkie, who understood the necessity of doing business, both in politics and economy, with this newest arrival in the international arena. *Or* Russia still moves on the road to Socialism, in which case the phenomena which we described have to be understood as temporary expedients. But a survey of the relevant trends of development contradicts the alleged temporariness of those expedients and reveals a continuous and coherent movement in a direction opposed to fundamental principles of Socialism. Moreover, we find that even the theoretical formulations of these principles have been abandoned and replaced by a new ideology which we still have to define.

And yet, before deciding in favour of the first alternative, we have to examine one more argument of the Soviet apologist — his last line of defence as it were. It may be formulated as follows:

Admittedly something has gone wrong in Russia. Admittedly certain policies and decrees have gone beyond the scope of temporary expedients and indicate a serious danger for the future of the U.S.S.R. But as long as the economic foundation of the Soviet State remains untouched — that is, State ownership of the means of production and the abolition of the profit-system — Russia remains fundamentally sane in the socialist sense, and sooner or later the new economic order will automatically rectify the warped political and cultural superstructure.

This statement contains two quite different assertions under the guise of one. The first is that the economic structure of Russia is historically progressive compared with private capitalistic economy. The second is that such nationalized economy is in itself a sufficient guarantee for the eventual emergence of a healthier and happier socialist society.

I believe the first assertion to be true, the second a fallacy.

Economically the Soviet Union represents State Capitalism. The State owns the means of production and controls the production and distribution of goods. The distinction between State Capitalism and State Socialism is from the Economist's point of view meaningless. The difference between the two lies in the political and social structure of the country, in the question 'The State controls everything, but who controls the State?' We have seen that the Soviet masses have no means to control either through elections or through Trade Unions, through political or economic pressure, the decisions of the State. The workers of the coal mines in the Urals have less influence on their wages, their working hours, their living conditions than the miners in Britain or the U.S.A. They cannot strike, they cannot elect their Union delegates, they cannot start a row in parliament, in the Press or in the streets. The Soviet workers 'are not owners of their factories any more than the British citizen is the owner of the British Navy' (Polanyi).

Russian State-ownership and planning is economically progressive compared with private capitalism, in the same sense as Schacht's export-control and clearing system, as Nazi economic planning was superior to, and economically progressive compared with, Western *laisser-faire*. Hitlerite Germany before and during the war was rapidly moving towards State Capitalism. The power of the Junkers and industry magnates had been broken; industrialists had to produce what they were told, pay the wages they were told and sell their produce at the price they were told. If they nominally still remained owners of their factories, their real control over them was limited much in the same way as the Director's of a Soviet factory; and their income, though nominally still 'profit', was fixed by the State just as the Soviet Director's salary is. An analysis of the intricate term of 'ownership' is to be found in Burnham's *Managerial Revolution* which, though questionable in many details, gives the gist of the matter. There is little doubt that Nazi economy moved along the road towards State Capitalism, and that even the half-way house they achieved was more efficient and more progressive in the economic sense, than *laisser-faire* capitalism. Shall we therefore conclude that Nazism was on the road to Socialism, towards a happier society? The man of the Left will indignantly reject this inference. Yet the same man of the Left will automatically base his claim that Russia is socialist on the same inference from economical to political structure.

This is the point where we have to part company with Trotsky-ites and other dissident communist sects, who maintain that, despite the 'malignant growth' of Stalinite bureaucracy, Russia, because of its nationalized economy, is still 'basically' a socialist country. Without entering into Marxian scholastics, it is worth while to recall that Marx and Engels themselves, in spite of their numerous dialectical ambiguities, opposed the view that national-ization alone guaranteed Socialism — cf. Engels' remark that if this were so, the first socialist institution must have been the regimental tailor. *Historical evidence of the last decades proves that nationalization and planning are a necessary but not a sufficient condition for the creation of a socialist society.* Nationalization and planning may lead to Socialism *or* Fascism — it depends on the political and ethical context. The Leftist contention that Soviet economy (i.e. nationalization) *is* Socialism is as spurious as the Rightist contention that state-controls and planning *are* Fascism.

A planned, state-controlled economy is the inevitable next step of historical evolution, and thus 'progressive' in the same sense as industrialization, rationalization, air-transport and artificial manure. We have seen how official Soviet demagogy identified Socialism with the building of factories and power stations. But power stations, artificial manure, state-control or planning are as such neither 'Left' nor 'Right'; they are 'progressive' in a purely mechanical sense — they represent progress in time, not on any social and ethical plane. A nationalized economy may serve any master, Fascist, Democratic or Socialist.

We thus come to the conclusion that the political, cultural, ethical conditions of a country are not, as a degenerated socialist doctrine wants us to believe, mere 'superstructures' automatically determined by the economic foundation, but are factors of primary importance which decide to what use the economic machinery is put. This does not mean to underrate the importance of the economic factor: as long as private ownership of means of production prevails Socialism is impossible; and we may as well write the italicized phrase of the previous page the other way round: 'Nationalization, though not a sufficient, is a necessary condition of Socialism.'

But the hope, cherished by Marxists with arrested development: the hope that socialization of the means of production is a sufficient guarantee for the emergence of a new world — this hope we shall have to discard for ever, after the lessons of the last decades.

XIII. OBJECTIVE FACTORS AND SUBJECTIVE
•   RESPONSIBILITY

Is it possible to determine at what point the first socialist experiment in history began to go wrong, why it went wrong, and whether its going wrong was inevitable?

I do not believe that a conclusive answer is possible except at a greater historical distance; but at least a rough outline of the main factors involved has already become discernible. The Russian experiment neither proves nor disproves the possibility of Socialism; it was an experiment carried out under the most unsuitable laboratory conditions and hence inconclusive. The conditions were unsuitable because socialist theory is based on the assumption that the working class will first attain power in industrial countries where the masses have attained a high degree of political maturity — whereas Tsarist Russia was proverbially the most backward country of Europe, with Asiatic traditions, a rural population ten times outnumbering the industrial proletariat and with illiterates numbering about 80 per cent. It is obvious that, put to the test in an advanced country — say Germany or the United States — Socialism would have produced quite different results.[1]

But even under these given conditions was the development in Russia inevitable or was it all 'Stalin's fault'? This leads, of course, to the great question of historical determinism and of the role of the so-called Subjective Factor (hazards, exceptional personalities) in history; a question upon which we can only touch very briefly.

The most evident hypothesis at our present state of knowledge is that the movements of history are determined by laws of a statistical nature, analagous to the physical laws of probability. A great mass of people exposed for a long time to certain forms of pressure — climatic, economic, etc. — will sooner or later react in certain roughly predictable ways. The emphasis is on the 'sooner or later' and on 'roughly'; they provide the margin within which the Subjective Factors of chance and leadership can exert their influence. However, if we survey history in big time units — centuries instead of decades — the importance of the Subjective Factor becomes negligible and statistical probabilities become certainties. Thus we may confidently predict that the increased

---

[1] It is the tragedy of the European Left that the second great social experiment – the coalition between the working classes and the progressive bourgeoisie known as Popular Front – was first tried out in the most backward country of the West, Spain, with equally inconclusive results.

speed of transportation will inevitably lead to a unified Europe; if Hitler didn't succeed Stalin may, and if Stalin doesn't somebody else will do it within a century or two. History resembles a river and the Subjective Factor a boulder thrown into its bed. A mile further down the water will flow in its broad bed designed by the general structure of the terrain as if the boulder had never existed. But for a short stretch of say a hundred yards or years, the shape of the boulder does make a considerable difference.

Now politics do not count in units of centuries but of years, thus leaving a margin of freedom and subjective responsibility to the leaders. It is not an abstract responsibility to history, but an ethical responsibility to their contemporaries. *Historically* it makes little difference whether Hitler unifies Europe or some future figure. For within a century or two the rough edges of Nazism would have become polished down, race-theory and Jew-baiting would have shrunk to episodes of the past, and the lasting result would have been a unified Europe which, round about A.D. 2500, would have displayed much the same general features as the one which Hitler's successor will create. But *politically*, that is, counted in short time units, the difference is enormous both as regards the amount of human suffering involved and the painful detour forced upon the river's course. The same applies to the Stalinite regime. It cannot invoke historical inevitability any more than Hitler or Marshal Pétain as an excuse.

There are at least half a dozen nodal points in the history of Soviet Russia during the past two decades where the regime had the choice between two equally possible alternative courses which were in no way 'historically determined'. Such crossroads were, to quote only a few examples, the China Policy of 1927; the agrarian Policy of 1929-30 (i.e. the error, later indirectly admitted by Stalin of rapid enforced collectivization which drove the peasants into killing their cattle and burning their crops, and thus led to the famine, the purges, the terror); the Prussian policy of 1929 (collaboration between Communists and National-Socialists against the Social Democratic government of Prussia); and finally the policy of 1939 (Stalin-Hitler pact). At none of these crossroads could historical inevitability or fatality serve as an excuse; in each case the regime assumed full subjective responsibility by crushing fractional inner-party opposition advocating the alternative course. The objectively unfavourable starting conditions for the Soviet experiment were thus capped by subjective errors of the regime.

What were the common denominators of these errors, the motives which propelled Stalin's regime on its course? In the sphere of foreign policy we have already mentioned the ruthless subordination of the European working class to the interests of Russia, based on the doctrine of Socialism in One Country, which led to Socialism in no country at all. To this we have to add the gross ignorance of European conditions among the Russian leaders, caused by artificial isolation; the fanatical hatred of rival movements of the Left, rooted in the traditions of Russian Party history; finally, both the extreme rigidity and the sudden, abrupt changes in policy which reflected the zig-zag course of an autocratic regime deprived of the balancing effects of legal opposition and public opinion.

In internal policy we have distinguished two main factors which led to the gradual elimination of Socialist principles: the tendency to self-perpetuation of the new ruling caste, and the breakdown of the revolutionary incentives. Among all these threads it is the last one which dominates the pattern and decides the failure of the Soviet experiment.

XIV. THE BREAKDOWN OF THE NEW INCENTIVES

Capitalism had replaced the religious incentives of medieval Feudalism by economic competition; without it Capitalism would not exist. Socialism has to replace Capitalist competition by new incentives; without them a socialist society cannot come into being.

The Revolution of 1917 abolished the profit-motive and financial competition. The shopkeeper became an employee of the

State Trust, that is, a civil servant whose pay remained independent of his turnover; the farmer gradually became a wage earner partly paid in natural products but with no intimate proprietory feeling toward the field or the cattle; the worker, in the days of the Factory-Committees, had no fear of being punished or sacked; the schoolboy learned only what he was interested in; the soldier fought without officers, people married without priests and were divorced by simply stating their intention.

The new revolutionary incentives were: collectivism to replace individual competition; voluntary discipline instead of economic and legal coercion; the consciousness of responsibility towards the community; international class-solidarity to replace chauvinism; the dignity of labour to replace dignity of birth or position; a spirit of fraternity among equals to replace the paternity of God and Leader; reform instead of retribution; persuasion instead of compulsion; in general a new spiritual climate permeated with the feelings of brotherliness, equality, solidarity — 'All for one and one for all.'

All this sounds to-day like bitter irony. The words 'utopianism', 'romantics', 'sentimentality', automatically present themselves, even in the minds of convinced communists. Twenty-five years of Soviet reality have turned them into unconscious cynics; and because they want to believe that Russia means Socialism they have forgotten what Socialism really means. Without the creation of new human incentives the abolition of the capitalist incentives leaves a vacuum in which the social body becomes paralysed. A society with no incentives and ethical values will, whatever its economical structure, either dissolve into chaos and anarchy, or become a dumb mass under the whip.

It was not to be expected that the new spirit of 1917 would triumph without great transitional difficulties and setbacks. But the history of the Soviet Union is not one of advances alternating with retreats. The curve of development ascends during the first decade roughly until the middle 'twenties, and from then onwards shows a continuous and uninterrupted fall until, a generation after the experiment started, the new incentives have been replaced without exception and in all walks of life by the old, abandoned ones.

The war has accelerated this development and brought it to its completion. The crowning of the Orthodox Metropolitan Sergius in Moscow Cathedral and his official recognition as Patriarch of all Russians on September 12th, 1943 was a symbolic act in more than one respect; it was a confession of the Soviet regime's failure to create a new human creed, new ethical values, a new faith for which to live and die. If the apologist objects that one generation is too short a time for the creation of a new spiritual climate, he should read the history of the Reformation, the history of Islam, or of the Renaissance. Genuine spiritual revolutions have at all times spread with the speed of spring-tides — the emotional forces they released swamped the withered traditional beliefs. And yet neither Luther nor Mohammed nor Galileo had the means of a monopolized Press and Radio at their disposal. In modern history the Nazi movement has shown what climatic changes can be achieved in a great nation in much less time: within ten years Christianity and Humanism were superseded by the national-socialist mystique.

It is argued by apologists that one of the reasons for the revival of the Orthodox Church was to attract the people of the Balkans. This is very likely true, but it only proves our point. It signifies that the regime, in its appeals for support abroad and at home, had to fall back upon religious incentives, precisely because the kind of Socialism practised in Russia has no sufficient spiritual attraction. This is borne out by the revival of yet another ghost of the past: Panslavism.

Pan-Slavic Congresses[1] were held in Moscow yearly since 1941, with delegates representing Poland, Czechoslovakia, Bulgaria, Yugo-Slavia, Montenegro, etc. The speeches held at these Congresses would have sounded reactionary even in 1910. The Fatherland of the Workers had once more become the Leader of the Slavs: the adversary was no longer the capitalist order, but

---

[1] To avoid the provocative terms of Panslavism they are now officially called 'All-Slavic' Congresses.

the 'eternal enemy of the Slav races, the Teutonic invader'. (General Berling at the Fourth All-Slavic Congress).

Addicts to the Soviet myth who get enraged by the term Pan-Germanism often retain a soft spot for Pan-Slavism; it reminds them of Russian shirts and balalaikas, which, as we know, are integral parts of Socialism. Yet in the world of facts Pan-Slavism is a racialist movement, which served the expansionist tendencies of Russian Imperialism. Its historic aims were the Dardanelles and outlets to the Baltic, Aegean and Adriatic Seas — and are still the same to-day. To disband the Comintern and replace it by the instruments of Orthodoxy and Panslavism signifies the final switch from Socialist to Imperialist policy.

A new militarist spirit and a wave of jingoism accompanied the change. The Army oath was changed. The Soviet recruit who formerly swore to

> pledge all my deeds and thoughts to the great aim of the emancipation of the workers and to fight for the Soviet Union, for Socialism and the brotherhood of all peoples,

swears since 1939:

> to serve to my last breath my Fatherland and Government...

The 'International' as a national anthem was abolished on March 15th, 1944 and replaced by a new anthem extolling 'Russia the Great' which forged the 'Union of free Republics', omitting any internationalistic reference.

Military Academies, officially described as 'of the type of the old Cadet Corps' were established on August 23rd, 1943. Political Commissars in the Army were finally abolished on October 10th, 1943. The title 'Guard Regiment' was re-established in the winter of 1941-42. The Order of Lenin and the Order of the Red Banner were superseded by the new Orders of Suvorov, Kutuzov and Alexander Nevsky on July 29th, 1942. Officers' messes and clubs, batmen, saluting, etc. were gradually re-established since 1935. Finally the decree of January 6th, 1943, re-established the epaulettes worn by the officers of the Tsarist

Army. It would have been easy to devise new types of distinctions; the intention of the decree was òbviously to emphasize in a symbolical and provocative way that the last relics of revolutionary nonsense were liquidated for good.

To comply with the new spirit, school books, history books and even encyclopedias had to be pulped and rewritten. Up to the beginning of the purges the leading Soviet Historian was Pokrovsky, who had viewed history in Marxist terms and fought chauvinism and hero-worship in all its disguises. In 1934 Pokrovsky was liquidated and succeeded first by Shestakov and later by Eugen Tarlé. Shestakov's prize history text-book was introduced into all public schools in 1936 and bore the motto: 'We love our country. We must know its wonderful history.' Under his successor, Tarlé, the revaluation of history assumed grotesque forms. Up to the purges the leaders of the great popular revolts of the seventeenth and eighteenth centuries; Bulavin, Stenka Razin and Emelyan Pugachov, were officially and correctly regarded as forerunners of the Proletarian revolution. But Bulavin had rebelled against Stalin's hero Peter the Great; Pugachov, leader of serfs and Ural miners, had been defeated by Prince Suvorov in whose honour Stalin created the Suvorov Order; and in any case they were rebels against Authority and hence in the wrong. Accordingly the leading official Historian of the Soviet Union decreed that those revolutionary leaders of the past had not been serious politicians because 'their movements had contained bandit elements'. On the strength of this dictum all revolutionary history from Spartacus to Danton and Lenin, whose movements had all contained 'bandit elements', can be wiped out with one stroke.

In his famous speech on the 24th anniversary of the Soviet Revolution, November 7th, 1941, which started the new hero-cult, Stalin said: 'May you be inspired in this war by the manly images of our great forefathers: Alexander Newsky, Dimitri Donskoi, Kuzma Minin, Dimitri Pozharsky, Alexander Suvorov, Mikhail Kutuzov.' The usual barrage of propaganda has since promoted these six to patron-saints of Russia in succession to Marx, Engels, and the revolutionary martyrs of the past. Among these six figures of the new Soviet Pantheon four were Princes, one a Saint, and not one stood for a socially progressive cause. About Kuzma Minin the Soviet Encyclopedia (pulped) of 1930 remarks: 'Bourgeois historians idealized him as a classless fighter for "Holy Mother Russia" and tried to make a national hero of him.' Prince Pozharsky led the Russians against the Poles in 1611; Prince Suvorov fought the French Revolution, Pugachov's proletarian rebellion and the Poles; Prince Kutuzov quelled a peasant rising, defeated Napoleon and the Poles; while Prince Donskoi fought the Mongols in the fourteenth century and is a Saint of the Orthodox Church.

Literature and the arts had to follow in the wake. Soviet painters paint heroic battle-pictures of past and present Russian campaigns; Soviet poets extol once more the Sacred Soil of Mother Russia; Soviet novelists hack out biographies of national heroes of the past. The four Stalin Prize-winning novels of 1942 were: Borodin's biography of Prince Dimitri Donskoi (see above) Antonovsky's *Great Muravi* (who was a national hero of Stalin's Georgia); Yan's *Ghenghis Khan* and Ehrenburg's *Fall of Paris*. The Stalin Prize for Lyrical poetry of the same year went to Gusev, whose most celebrated poem starts:

> I am a Russian man, Moscow's son, the heir of Russian glory, etc.

A prize-winning play in the same year was Korneichuk's *Front* in which an old Bolshevik leader of the days of the Civil War is featured as practically an idiot who has to be sacked from his post. In the same year Alexey Tolstoi went one better on his *Peter the Great* and wrote a play on Ivan the Terrible. The play was filmed by Eisenstein. 'Eisenstein', writes Kolarz in his *Stalin and Eternal Russia*, 'regarded most of Ivan's atrocities as inventions or exaggerations on the part of his enemies inside and outside Russia. In producing the film, he was guided by the idea that Ivan the Terrible, the founder of a strong and united Russia and of a regular Russian army, acted at the dictate of historical necessities. . . .'

Thus Eisenstein in an interview given to *Trud*. The revaluation of Russia's Caligula, the defence of his reign of Terror by 'historical necessity' are too obvious to need comment. It is a long way from *Battleship Potemkin* to *Ivan the Terrible* — and one which symbolizes the spiritual evolution of the Soviet Union.

The Soviet government had watched with benevolent neutrality the Nazi conquest of practically the whole of Europe. It officially sneered at the idea of an ideological war. It opened no Second Front when France was invaded and the Allies were on the verge of defeat. It only fought when directly attacked, a war of national survival, under nationalistic slogans. The necessity for the Soviet regime to fight in the name of Suvorov instead of Marx, with a national instead of an international anthem, with Tsarist epaulettes, Pan-Slav slogans and under the blessing of bearded Orthodox priests, is the final proof of the breakdown of socialist incentives. The new springs of action which the revolution of 1917 had planted into the hearts and brains of the masses have worn out in the corroding climate of insincerity which the Stalinite regime created. They were new and precarious psychological forces which needed constant encouragement, a warm and fraternal human climate to grow and become stable, and finally to transform the whole habitus of man, to create the new type of *Homo Sapiens liber*. The regime, grown from the roots of nineteenth century materialism and economism, never recognized the decisive importance of the spiritual factor. Based on the axiom that the end justified the means, quickly tired of the inertia and dumbness of the peasant-masses, they treated the living people as raw-material in a laboratory experiment, working on the tender malleable mass with hammers, chisels, acids, and showers of propaganda-rays of ever varying wave-length. For the superficial observer the method worked. The people apparently believed all that was said to them, hailed their leaders, worked like robots, died like heroes — like the robots and heroes which the Germans or Japanese produced. But inside them the new springs had snapped and had to be replaced by the old ones, fetched from the dusty shelves of the lumber room.

THE YOGI AND THE COMMISSAR

The Russian revolution has failed in its aim to create a new type of human society in a new moral climate. The ultimate reason for its failure was the arid nineteenth century materialism of its doctrine. It had to fall back on the old opiates because it did not recognize man's need for spiritual nourishment.

EXPLORATIONS

III

THE END OF AN ILLUSION

One swift blow to Poland, first by the German Army and then by the Red Army, and nothing was left of this ugly offspring of the Versailles Treaty which had existed by oppressing non-Polish nationalities. Everybody realizes that there can be no question of restoring old Poland.

MOLOTOV on October 31st, 1939

I always wanted a strong and independent Poland.

STALIN, repeatedly in 1944

I. METHODS OF RUSSIAN POWER POLITICS

I

THE results of our inquiry[1] can be summed up as follows:

Soviet Russia is a State-Capitalistic totalitarian autocracy. It is progressive in its economic structure and regressive in every other respect. Politically, culturally, in the relations between rulers and ruled, it is reactionary compared with most Capitalist democracies. It pursues an expansionist policy which, though operating with new methods, reflects the old historic aims of Imperial Russia.

To the working classes and the progressive forces in other parts of the world Russia has no more specific significance than any other great power. She is neither a menace to the Right nor a concern of the Left. Her attitude to the Right and Left parties in other countries is exclusively determined by the momentary interests of her power politics. In future as in the past she will choose and drop her allies regardless of their political philosophy according to the demands of the moment.

This, however, requires two qualifications. Firstly, there is a difference between the power politics of Russia and other states. Power politics are necessarily opportunist and cynical; in critical situations ethical principles are always sacrificed to expediency.

---

[1] See the previous essay 'Soviet Myth and Reality'.

But there are differences in the degree of cynicism and immorality. Public opinion in democratic countries has little positive influence on Foreign Policy, but in certain cases it can prevent the worst by a kind of veto of the street — e.g. the Hoare-Laval pact. This veto is rarely exercised, but it exerts a latent pressure on the rulers; they have to count to a certain degree with the electorate, with a relatively independent Press, and even more with parliamentary opposition — however timid, dim and half-hearted these are. The importance of these democratic factors is usually over-stated by hypocritical eulogies; but it is equally under-estimated by the extreme Left. The fact is, that under the influence of these correcting and balancing factors the policy of powers like Great Britain and the U.S.A. may still move in sickeningly wavy curves, but never in the wild zig-zag of the U.S.S.R.

Democracies may appease dictators or back Darlans; but it is impossible for them to change fronts in twenty-four hours or to tear up treaties before the ink is dry. The leaders of Soviet Russia and Nazi Germany are completely unhampered by such limiting factors; they rule in a vacuum and can perform any sudden volte face, can spring any surprise on their partners in the international field. This gives Russia a great advantage in the coming diplomatical struggles: the advantage of complete unpredictability of the next move. A country which sails without ethical ballast is much more manœuvrable than those hampered by traditions. Statesmen of the Western school break treaties only when they have no other choice — and even then with a bad conscience. Statesmen of the Russian school on the other hand double-cross their Capitalist partners with glee and a perfectly clean conscience; they have learnt to scorn 'bourgeois ethics' and besides still have a dim feeling that they serve an Idea, though they have forgotten what exactly the Idea was about.

It will take some time for the statesmen of the West who still live in the traditions of the nineteenth century, to get accustomed to the new game — that diplomatic shock-treatment of which they have so far only had a faint foretaste. Meanwhile Russia will reap all the benefits, as Nazi Germany did in the Munich years.

The second difference between Russian and other power politics is derived from the old rivalry between the Bolshevik Party and other parties of the Left. It originated in a quarrel of doctrines which has long since become obsolete, but, as usual, spite and vengefulness survive their own cause. Few Soviet admirers are aware of the fact that the European Sections of the Second International — the British Labour Party, the French S.F.I.O., Italian, Polish, Austrian, Spanish socialists and their leaders, are in Russian terminology still called 'counter-revolutionary mensheviks'. How strong and virulent this hatred is has been proved by Moscow's persistent refusal to make common cause with Socialists on the Continent against the growing Fascist menace — until it was too late. In Hitler's concentration camps Communist and Socialist workers were killed side by side, and yet the former still abused the latter as 'social fascists'. The Popular Front policy of 1934, dictated by necessities of Russian foreign policy (the military alliance with France and Czechoslovakia and Russia's joining the League of Nations) brought no real change of heart towards the parties of the Left; behind the façade of Popular-Front Committees, anti-Fascist and peace campaigns, the air was thick with Comintern-intrigue and fractional conspiracy. They reached a murderous peak during the Spanish Civil War, when behind the front-line the Russian 'apparatchiks' waged their private war of liquidation against the rival parties of the Left — Syndicalists, POUM, independent Socialists. Communist policy is variable to the extreme; its only constant factor is intolerance against dissenters.

During the last few years Communist parties have formed alliances with Prussian junkers, Austrian Monarchists, Croat Ustachis, Italian Catholics; they have crowned Orthodox patriarchs and negotiated with the Vatican; they have promised to 'help American capitalism work' by backing alternatively Republicans and Democrats;[1] they have, all within two years, abused British Labour for supporting the War and for not suffi-

[1] Earl Browder, leader of the American Communist Party, in his speech on January 10th, 1944.

ciently supporting the War; for being anti-German and for being opposed to the dismemberment of Germany; they have called the Labour Party any invective contained in the vocabulary of a fish-wife or a Soviet State prosecutor and they have asked for affiliation into the same Labour Party. They have eaten their words and spat them out and swallowed them again. Communist parties have proved themselves capable of every transformation but one: to collaborate sincerely with other parties of the working class.

This inherent, structural incapacity is rooted in the traditions of the Russian party. The split into Bolsheviki (majority fraction) and Mensheviki (minority fraction) dates back to the London Conference of 1903 and has never been healed. The Bolsheviki were revolutionary centralists, the Mensheviki reformist democrats. In the years to follow the Leninist movement extended the use of the term 'menshevik' from the Russian to all reformist wings of socialist parties, and after the foundation of the Communist International (1919) 'Mensheviks' became synonymous with Socialists. During the last decade Socialist parties have frequently taken up a revolutionary attitude while the corresponding sections of the Comintern preached appeasement, so that the position between the two rivals became reversed. But while the divergence in doctrines had lost all meaning, the irrational hatred of 'counter-revolutionary menshevism' survived — like a tribal vendetta whose original cause has been forgotten generations ago. Political movements of a sectarian character are as capable of preserving traditional hatreds as clans, religious sects and nations.

But there is a second, more rational reason for the Russian attitude. The Soviet leaders realize that collaboration is easier with capitalist powers and interest groups than with independent working-class movements. The former type of collaboration is based on coolly calculated mutual interest, whereas the latter type inevitably contains an ethical and ideological element, which implies a moral obligation and deprives Soviet policy of its manœuvrability. Had an alliance existed between the British C.P. and the Labour Party, it would have inevitably broken down in September 1939 by the latter's refusal to endorse the Stalin-

Hitler pact; had later on an alliance existed with the I.L.P. it would have broken down by the latter's refusal to become pro-war in 1941. Even the Communist International, ruled by blind obedience, became a clog on Kremlin diplomacy; how much more of a nuisance are independent Left parties and movements! The Russian leaders know that one can do business with the stranger, but not in one's own family. Idealistic individuals and movements are unmanœuvrable. Hence the liquidation of the old party-membership and the favouring of 'non-party specialists' inside Russia; hence the analagous preference for dealings with Beaver-brook[1] and Willkie rather than with Labour Ministers, in the international field.[2]

The existence of independent socialist movements is thus a problem of the first order for the Russian regime, which officially still pretends to hold the monopoly of Socialism. A solution of the problem would logically only be possible if either the rival move-ments surrendered their independence and subordinated their doctrine to the changing necessities of Russian power politics; or if Russia officially dropped the pretence of being a socialist state and thus forsook her most powerful lever on international policy. Neither of these being practically possible, the only course open to the Soviet regime is persecution and defamation of the rival socialist movements and leaders. It is the continuation of the method successfully applied in home politics against Social Revolutionaries, Mensheviks, Anarchists, Trotskyites and Old Bolsheviks. As in inner-Russian use, the terms 'Trotskyite' and 'Menshevik' are elastically stretched out to cover everybody unwilling to become a blind instrument of the regime; and like Hitler's Judaic World Conspiracy they represent a mixture of calculated deception and genuine persecution mania.

Since the purges, the Soviet rulers have come to regard as the greatest danger to their international aspirations, not the cynics

---

[1] The first foreign politicians to be decorated with Soviet Orders since Ribben-trop were Sir Oliver Lyttelton and Lord Beaverbrook.

[2] Hence also the significant refusal to participate in the activities of the Inter-national Labour Office – which would have entailed the exposing of Russian Labour conditions and Labour legislation to public scrutiny.

and reactionaries, but the politically conscious Left abroad. With cynics one can always find a *modus vivendi*; idealists are intransigent, a nuisance and a danger. This goes for individuals as for movements. Consequently the first preoccupation of the expanding Soviet state was the liquidation of the Left in occupied Poland and the Baltic States.

III

Mass deportations on a scale hitherto unknown in history were the main administrative method of Sovietization in Eastern Europe during the two years from the Russian invasion of Poland to the German invasion of Russia. They were carried out in four great waves: February 1940, April 1940, June 1940 and June 1941. The number of persons actually deported from Eastern Poland amounted to roughly one million, but the number earmarked according to the categories of the deportation plan was considerably greater; the execution of the plan had to be interrupted — or rather postponed — owing to the Russo-German war. According to their fate the deportees fell into three categories: (*a*) Those sentenced to 3-8 years of work in Forced Labour Brigades, mainly in the Sub-Arctic camps, and employed on timber-felling, mining, dangerous industries and other public works; (*b*) families settled in unpopulated areas and employed under G.P.U. supervision on forestry work, in saw-mills, on road-building, etc.; (*c*) families settled in Central Asia (mainly Kasakstan and the Kirghiz and Yakuts Republics) and employed by the native kolkhoses under conditions of nominal freedom except for restrictions of movement.[1]

Mass deportations from the Baltic States were on a similar scale. An administrative decree issued by Gusevitius, People's Commissar

---

[1] The Polish-Soviet pact signed in London on July 30th, 1941 provided for the release of Polish deportees of all categories. The Polish Government, aided by the Red Cross and Anglo-American relief organizations, succeeded in locating roughly 500,000 citizens, i.e. about half of the deportees. A considerable number of these, including the Polish Army formed on Russian territory, were evacuated via Teheran. Those who remained in Russia were, after the Russo-Polish diplomatic break in 1943, considered by the Russian authorities as Soviet citizens and treated accordingly. About 20 per cent of the deportees are estimated to have died in the Arctic camps or on the journey to their destination.

for the Interior of Soviet-Lithuania (No. 0054, November 28th, 1940) defines 14 categories of Lithuanian citizens liable for deportation. Category No. 1 comprises 'members of the Russian pre-revolutionary Parties: Social-Revolutionaries, Mensheviks, D.D.; Trotskyites and Anarchists.' Categories 2 to 6 comprise active members of other Lithuanian Parties (Valdemarasites, Christian-Democrats, Patriotic Students' Organizations, Shaulisists); also Police Officers, Gendarmerie and Prison staffs, Officers of the former Tsarist and White Russian Armies and of the Polish and Lithuanian armies. Category 7 are 'Persons expelled from the Communist Party'. Category 8: 'Political émigrés and re-émigrés and contraband-runners'; Category 9: Citizens of foreign states and representatives of foreign firms; Category 10: 'Persons who have travelled abroad or are in contact with foreign diplomatic missions; Esperantists and Philatelists'; Category 11: Officials of Lithuanian ministries; Category 12: 'The staff of the Polish Red Cross and Refugees from Poland'; Categories 13 and 14: Clergymen, aristocrats, landowners, bankers, industrialists, wealthy merchants, hotel and restaurant proprietors.

Analysis of these categories shows that they are designed to amputate from the national body

(a) all politically conscious and active elements, first of all those of the Left except the Communists;

(b) the top-layers and the administrative apparatus of the ancient regime;

(c) all cosmopolitan elements.

In Eastern Poland this process of amputation included also the intelligentsia (teachers, lawyers, journalists, etc.) regardless of their political views. Characteristically the fourth deportation wave (June 1941) already included a considerable proportion of members of the Communist Party itself — mainly organizers of the revolutionary 'Local Committees' who had taken over during the days of chaos before the arrival of the Soviet administrators, and members of the Workers Militia.

As a rule the deportation affected the whole family of those concerned; small children were sent to orphanages. The mass-exodus was operated without voluntary sadism and cruelty, but under such appalling conditions — journeys up to three weeks in sealed cattle-trucks — that a considerable proportion died on the roads. The deportees were called for at night by the so-called 'Executive Troikas' of the N.K.V.D.[1] according to pre-arranged lists and had only an hour or so for packing their things; the maximum luggage allowed per family was 200 pounds. The trains departed before dawn with doors and windows blocked up except for apertures for the elimination of excrement and the handing in of food; they were not opened again before arrival at destination — in the Polar region or Central Asia.

The aims of this policy were to deprive the newly absorbed regions of those elements which in Soviet terminology are called 'Activists' — meaning the politically conscious strata of Left and Right, the leaders and organizers of intellectual, economical, social life, the nuclei of independent thought and action.[2] A nation thus deprived of her backbone and nervous centres becomes a kind of amorphous jelly, reduced to the degree of malleability necessary to adapt herself to the conditions of Soviet Dictatorship. For one has to bear in mind that these millions of new citizens of the U.S.S.R. have to learn to live without parliament, without public criticism, under new laws which restrict their personal liberty of movement, of speech, of reading, of work, and confine their whole range of existence between hard and narrow limits undreamt of even under the semi-dictatorial Polish or Lithuanian regimes. The greater the difference between the cultural levels (and standards of living), the more radical this softening process has to be, to make the conquered nation digestible by the Russian regime.

[1] Commissariat for Internal Affairs, which has taken over the functions of the OGPU. In current usage N.K.V.D. and G.P.U. are synonymous.
[2] The same purpose was served by Russia's malevolent passivity during the crushing of the Warsaw revolt by the Germans in the summer of 1944. This method of getting rid of troublesome allies has an historic precedent in the Russian attitude to Armenia during the first World War, when the Tzarist Government had called on the Armenians to revolt against their Turkish oppressors and then let those Armenians who had followed the call be massacred by the Turks under the nose of the Russian armies who performed a series of advances and retreats ('the Russian Quadrille') and barred the surviving Armenians from entering Russian-occupied territory.

EXPLORATIONS

IV

A comparison between Soviet and Nazi Policy in Eastern Europe shows both similarities and contrasts. There is similarity in the methods of reducing the conquered nation to a terrorized herd deprived of purpose and leadership; but there the parallel ends.

The Germans wanted space in the East for purposes of colonization, and their policy in parts of Poland and the Ukraine was clearly aimed at a gradual extermination of a considerable proportion of the native populations by mass killings, undernourishment, segregation of the male population; while the surviving natives were, according to their position in the racial hierarchy, to be reduced to the status of helots.

Russia on the other hand with her enormous under-populated spaces and constant shortage of manpower pursues quite different aims. She needs mobile labour for the gigantic tasks of industrial reconstruction, road-building, public works; and she needs colonists for the unexploited remote regions of Siberia and Central Asia. In a country inhabited by over two hundred different nationalities, some of them living in curious ethnical enclaves like the Germans of the Ukraine and the Volga Republic, the Jews of Birobeidshan or the old tribes of the Caucasus, the idea of shifting and re-settling national minorities on a large scale is by no means paradoxical or utopical. Before the war several million Ukrainians had been deported to Siberia; during the war practically the whole of the German Volga Republic has been deported. The categories of the deportation plan for Lithuania involved about 700,000 persons out of a total population of 3 millions; the plan for Eastern Poland, 3 to 4 millions out of a total population of 13 millions. The German invasion interrupted their execution at an early stage. After the war, when Russia will have uncontested mastery in Eastern and South-Eastern Europe, the world may witness, among other surprises, mass dislocations and forced migrations on an unprecedented scale, carried through with the efficiency, and total disregard of the human factor which characterizes the Soviet regime's treatment of its own people.

II. THE PERSPECTIVES OF SOVIET EXPANSION

I

Before the war, the European field was dominated by the triangle Great Britain — Germany — Russia. Each of the three protagonists tried to manœuvre in such a way as to split the other two and, in case of war, to remain the laughing third.

If we abstain from wishful thinking and look into the future beyond the short period of elations and illusions which victory will bring, we see a similar triangle on a larger scale design itself: the triangle Britain — U.S.A. — U.S.S.R. Already the tensions along the three sides make themselves felt: economic and financial tensions across the Atlantic, political across the Pacific and along the Arctic; political and territorial across Europe and the Middle East.

Of the three powers, Britain will obviously be on the defensive, intent, in Churchill's words, to 'hold what we have'. To neutralize the centrifugal tendencies within the Empire, the ties with the Dominions will probably have to become even more elastic and the Colonies will have to be given more rope. This inevitable loosening of the Empire's texture will invite pressure on the more vulnerable points by her competitors. Among these, the United States will be mainly interested in economic expansion and in securing strategical bases on nodal points. The second tendency need not lead to conflict with Great Britain, as the U.S.A. does not seek new living spaces but rather a series of strategic footholds. Economic competition, however, will probably prevent the formation of a really stable Anglo-Saxon bloc and give the third partner ample scope for triangular manœuvring.

Russia, among the three, represents the most vigorous expansive force. As a world power it arrives on the stage young and full of ruthless dynamism. With its nationalized economy, centralized power, and totalitarian methods, the U.S.S.R. presents an aspect of massive compactness compared with the loosely-knit, extended and decentralized British Empire — rather like a giant battering ram facing the long, crumbling walls and moats of an ancient fortress. This does not mean that the ram will actually attack the wall; it only means that the men behind the ram and the men behind the moat, however amicable their relations, both know at the back of their minds the potentialities of the situation. And these potentialities must inevitably translate themselves into latent pressure.

According to the laws of least resistance, this pressure will be the stronger the more exposed and vulnerable the point of attack: that is, in the Middle East, the Mediterranean and on the Continent of Europe. Expressed by a polite euphemism, the aim of this pressure is to procure 'zones of influence'. But the definition of this term depends entirely on the balance of forces. Where the balance is nearly equal, such zones merely mean trading facilities and political treaties, e.g.: Britain and Portugal. A tilt of the scales, and the same term means the use of airfields and strategic bases; the zone of influence has become a satellite country. One further tilt and we get puppet governments and all but official incorporation into the bigger state: e.g.: Japan and Manchukuo. Finally direct incorporation either by military conquest or by terror-referendum: e.g. Eastern Poland and the Baltic States.

When people talk of 'expansion', even the politically educated are apt to think in static and antiquated terms. The Nazis spoke of the Russians as 'Asiatic hordes' and tried to scare us with the anachronistic picture of Stalin-Ghenghis Khan riding with his Cossacks to Boulogne; in Conservative clubland the German conquest of Czechoslovakia is conceived of in the old-fashioned terms of straight forward military conquest. Hence the general incredulity regarding the real perspectives of Russian expansion on the Continent. The possibilities of modern political warfare by internal disruption and vassalization, were by no means exhausted by Hitler and are not yet appreciated in their true significance.

The structure of the Soviet Federation, comprising nationalities as wildly different as Eskimos from Ukrainians and Estonians from Turkmenes, has a far greater capacity to absorb new countries than the racially homogeneous German Empire. For the Reich swallowing Czechoslovakia meant swallowing a foreign body under danger of choking; for the U.S.S.R., the incorporation of a new 'autonomous Republic' means merely the addition of a new stone to its racial mosaic. The constitutional reform of 1943, by granting a greater semblance of autonomy to members of the Federation, considerably improved the absorbing capacity of the framework. The gates are wide open to receive any newcomer, be it the Hungarian, Slovakian or Saxonian Autonomous Soviet Republic. Needless to say that in each case there would be gradual transitions of varying duration, and that each final adhesion would have the appearance of a voluntary act.

The question 'how far Stalin intends to go' is naive and meaningless. The expansion of great Empires follows certain dynamic laws. A great power surrounded by a political vacuum will expand its zones of influence until it feels a growing pressure of resistance. The greater density of communications, higher industrialization and living standard of the countries West of Russia exert the pull; the desire for more and more security and power provide the push; the traditions of Pan-Slavism and the centenary aspirations to hegemony over Poland, the Balkans and Constantinople provide the historical background. The drive for access to the world trade lines through the Mediterranean, the Baltic and North Atlantic must inevitably follow. There is no possibility of saturation in a vacuum.

On the other hand, each new increase in power means an increase in attraction towards the small states, unable to maintain their independence without outside aid. They have to become protégés of the big neighbour, to be gradually transformed into satellites and knit closer and closer into his framework. Within fifty years from the first appearance of railways in Europe the three-hundred odd independent German principalities became unified in the Reich. The same process of amalgamation is now inevitable on the European scale; the anachronistic jig-saw puzzle of dwarf states cannot outlast the age of aviation by more than a few decades. Germany became unified by the most militant, autocratic and spartan of its states. The Soviets occupy to-day the same position towards Eastern and Central Europe as Prussia did towards the other German states in the middle of the last century.

II

Politicians thinking in nineteenth-century terms counter this perspective by two arguments. First, that after the war Russia will need a prolonged period of peace; secondly, that she will depend on Anglo-American economic help to reconstruct her devastated country.

Of course Russia will need peace — so will Great Britain. But the extension of zones of influence by treaties of friendship and mutual aid — as for instance the Benesch-Molotov treaty—has always a peaceful rather than a bellicose appearance. And the tightening of the noose within these zones, from the stage of friendly collaboration to vassalization can be done by a series of equally discreet steps, none of which presents a neat *casus belli*. Who will expect Britain to declare war on Soviet Russia because of, say, a change in the Rumanian government, accompanied by certain measures against the opposition? Or because the government of Poland decides to merge all parties into one of National Unity and to conclude a Customs Union with the Ukrainian and White Russian Soviet Republic? Though the experts of the Foreign Office may realize the significance of the event and the inevitable next step to follow, the *New Statesman and Nation* will find the appropriate explanations; and only a lunatic can imagine the starting of a new world war on such a flimsy pretext.

The same applies to economic help. The question whether the popular referendum in which 98.5 per cent of the Hungarian people express their desire to join the great Union of free republics was genuine or faked, will not make the American machine-tool industry decide to stop executing their export agreements with Russia — just as Japanese aggression against China did not stop Anglo-American oil supplies to Japan, and the Versailles treaty did not stop Anglo-American firms from re-arming Germany. Even assuming the unlikely development of some sort of public control over the armament industry, exports for the needs of peaceful reconstruction would remain unaffected, and Russia's primary needs are not for arms. The Soviet Union will be the greatest and most attractive market in the world; and world-trade will obey its own laws and not the niceties of ethical considerations. Up to 1932 old-fashioned politicians argued that Hitler will never dare to implement his threats against the Jews for fear of America withdrawing her short-term credits to German industry; the results are known. The naive hope of dominating Soviet policy by economic levers rests on two premises: (a) the elimination of commercial competition between Britain and the U.S.A. and a rigidly co-ordinated trade policy; (b) absolute control by the Foreign Office and State Department of every single business-firm in the two countries. (Export licence control would obviously be insufficient, for the State would have to compensate firms for breaches of contracts imposed on them, find them alternative markets and thus fulfil the functions both of policeman and wet nurse.)

In other words the conditions of such a policy could only be fulfilled by the abolition of private capitalism in both Britain and the U.S.A.

It should be emphasized that we are discussing the future perspectives for Europe in terms of decades rather than in years. The Soviet bid for European domination will take shape only gradually, both in the intensification of her hold over her zones of influence and in expanding these zones. Most of the intermediary steps will be camouflaged as internal developments within the small nations concerned. The technique of vassalization will be perfected, and the speed and rhythm of events adapted to the patient's pulse. A series of quick, brisk surprise blows may be followed by prolonged lulls of idyllic tranquillity, diplomatic shock treatment by soothing periods of convalescence, spread over several years. *Faits accomplis* will alternate with tokens of goodwill, tensions with relief and new pressure. All this sounds like rather sinister prophecy, whereas it is simply the projection of past experiences in power politics into the future.

III

For centuries Central and Eastern Europe were under Germanic domination. The break-up of the Austrian Empire disturbed the balance and created a vacuum. The treaty of Versailles replaced one of the great European power centres by an unstable mosaic of small states, each of them an ethnical mosaic in itself, without the capacity for economic and political independence. The Balkans and the Danube Basin were crowded with potential satellites in search of a sun.

Three great powers made their bids for including them in their zone of influence: Russia through the Comintern; France through the Little Entente; Germany through the barter-trade system and through fifth column tactics. Germany succeeded — only to be broken up in turn by military defeat; thus the unstable situation created in 1918 was re-established on an even larger scale. Europe east of the Alps is atomized and in a state of political, economical, ideological chaos as never before. But this time Russia stands without a rival as a great power on the Continent. She has a crushing superiority in every respect over the next single competitor, France. Never since the days of Charles V has the European balance been so profoundly tilted in favour of one single power.

The outstanding feature in this situation is the collapse of Germanic hegemony over the eastern half of Europe. One may object that Germany lost the last war too and yet recovered. But this time conditions are radically different. After the last war Germany's eastern neighbours, Poland and Russia, were fighting each other, while her western neighbour France, with only half the population of Germany and a much weaker industrial potential, could never dream of permanently dominating the

215

bigger neighbour. But this time Germany's victorious neighbour is the Russian giant; her industry is a shambles, her territory will for the first time suffer total occupation and partial dismemberment. East Prussia beyond Koenigsburg will go to Russia; West Prussia, Pomerania and Silesia along the line Stettin-Breslau will probably go to Poland which will be no longer Russia's rival but her satellite. The boundary of the Russian zone of influence will thus run about fifty miles east of Berlin. But temporarily it will extend much further to the west, about half-way between Berlin and the Rhine, where the Russian zone of occupation ends.

How long this occupation will last we do not know; but we may rest assured that if and when it ends, the occupied country and people will have undergone profound and irremediable changes. The probabilities are that the temporary partitioning of Germany into zones of occupation will lead to a permanent break-up; 'red Saxony' for example with its strong revolutionary traditions may have a communist government and vote itself into the Soviet federation, while the Catholic Rhineland with its easy-going, civilized and liberal traditions may become a French-sponsored autonomous republic. The details of this development during the next five years are difficult to foresee; further south however the process is both quicker and clearer in its outlines.

Great Britain's hopes to redress the balance by the creation of an Eastern European Federation collapsed with Benesch's journey to Moscow and the signing of the Soviet-Czechoslovak alliance. By the time of writing — September 1944 — the Soviet conquest of the Balkans is in full swing and Russia's intentions towards Poland have become visible even to the politically snow-blind. Instead of arguing about Stalin's intentions we should endorse the facts; and the facts are that *the demarcation line between the Russian and Western zones of influence has already shifted from the Vistula to the Elbe; from the Black Sea to the Adriatic and Mediterranean, from east of Warsaw to west of Prague.*

EXPLORATIONS

III. THE WEANING OF THE LEFT

I

How far will Russian expansion go? The only possible answer is that it will continue until the European balance, upset by the fall of the two great Germanic empires and the weakening of France, is restored.

But the potential forces which may one day restore the balance are chaotic and confused compared to Russia's compact dynamism. They may be divided for the sake of convenience into conservative and progressive forces, though there is no sharp dividing line between them.

The weakness of the conservative position is obvious. Its only aim is to maintain somehow the *status quo*, to prolong the nineteenth century beyond the twentieth, to counter dynamism by inertia. It holds no promise for the victors and has no plan for the vanquished. It is both grotesque and sad to watch the perplexity of Western statesmen when faced with the problem of the future of eighty million human beings of the German race. They sneer at the idea of re-educating them, because they feel that they have no philosophy to teach; they complain about the self-destroying fanaticism of German boys of sixteen and offer them no alternative of survival; they ask the beleaguered fortress to surrender without telling them what will happen if they do. They have no guiding idea about the future of Europe or the world, no banner and no programme. The ink on the Atlantic Charter has faded before it even dried.

And yet there were not often moments in history which offered so much scope for the revival of traditionalist values. Under the threat of totalitarian ideologies, a threat which is by no means ended with Hitler's fall, these decaying values of the West appear in a new, nostalgically attractive light. Human rights and moral traditions which fifty years ago we took for granted, are abolished in large parts of the world and in the process of abolition in others. *Habeas corpus*, freedom of speech, civil law, respect for the individual life, the unwritten codes of certain minimum decencies of conduct — how stale and ridiculous all these appeared at a time when utopia seemed at hand, and how desperately important they are now, when we stand with our backs to the wall! The tragedy is that only those realize what oxygen means who have known the torture of suffocation; only those who have shared the life of the ordinary native in Nazi Germany or Stalinite Russia for at least a year know that disintegration of the human substance which befalls people deprived of our basic liberties. But how many of us are capable of drawing comparisons? The English dockyard worker has not experienced the difference between risking, for the same negligence, a cut in pay or death as a saboteur. The English journalist does not know the difference between a limited freedom of expression and the status of a human teleprinter. The English highbrow, fed up with a statesman's cigar or a general's photo-mania, has no idea of the abject idiocy of regimented byzantine leader-worship. The English public, disgruntled but secure within the law, does not know the shivering insecurity, the naked horror of an autocratic police state. They only know their own frustrations. The atmosphere of democracy has become a stale fug, and those who breathe it cannot be expected to be grateful for the air which it contains. The predicament of Western civilization is that it has ceased to be aware of the values which it is in peril of losing.

How can these values be revived? How can the European vacuum be filled with new contents? A mere political alliance of Great Britain, France and other countries of Western Europe is not enough. It is true that those countries of the West which went through the public school of Roman colonization have a great tradition in common, and that two thousand years of judeo-christian ethics and a century of western liberalism have left in them a sediment which is not easily washed away by political storms on the surface. But deep and lasting though this moral substratum is, it is buried by layers of rubble. No inspiration can be derived from it until the rubble is cleared away. In other words, the traditional values can only be revived by the forces of progress.

To become equal to this task, the Left has to shed its illusions and regain its ideals.

This is a twofold process. Its negative half can be expressed as a process of weaning. The Left is an infant which was at first fed on the breasts of patriotism and later on the Russian bottle. The British Labour Party never grew out of the first stage, as her toothless leaders so touchingly demonstrate. The Communists became addicted to the bottle, and the evil smell of their diapers bears witness to the indigestibility of its contents. It is a painful metaphor, but who, looking at Europe a century after the birth of the Communist Manifesto, can deny its truth?

The first weaning was a failure because of a psychologically wrong approach. That famous sentence in the Communist Manifesto 'The workers have no fatherland' is inhuman and untrue. The farm-labourer, miner or road-sweeper is bound to his native village or street, to the traditions of language and habit, by emotional ties as strong as those of the rich. To go against these ties is to go against human nature — as doctrinaire Socialism with its materialist roots so often did. Weaning consists not in the denial of a human need, but in its transformation. The transition from a nationalistic to a cosmopolitan outlook can only be achieved by making people emotionally richer, not poorer. The traveller, who after a long absence visits his native village will still feel devoted to it; but his attitude will be very different from the narrow intolerance of those who have never left it. The aim of socialist education is to bring about a similar change in people's attitude to their country; the fraternity of the poor and humble of this earth must become a live reality of the mind.[1] This seems rather utopian to-day; but without a spiritual renaissance the socialist movement will continue on the road of bureaucratic ossification to the bitter end.

[1] One of the first tasks of a truly international socialist movement would be the organization on a large scale of workers' holidays abroad, with private billeting on an exchange basis.

The second weaning of the Left is a task not less difficult. We have seen to what deep, archetypal craving the Soviet myth responded. It is no accident that the revolutionary wing of the working class which broke its allegiance to its own country became the most addicted to the Proletarian motherland substitute. Russia became the kingdom of heaven for those who most keenly felt that paradise was lost.

Particularly tragic in this respect is the situation of the revolutionary underground movements in formerly German-occupied territories. They have witnessed the failure and treachery of their own ruling class, and their hatred against the invader fused with the resolution never to go back to the old system. They have come under the sway of that revolutionary mood which rejects the past but has no clear conception of the future; a state of mind which Juenger once described as 'that anti-capitalistic nostalgia'. It is a mood at the same time violent and vague; it is a craving for something radically new, a total change and regeneration. This is the mood out of which true revolutions are born — or ghastly pseudo-revolutions; it depends on the historical constellation. History has a few glorious examples of the first, and abounds in illustrations of the second course. Again and again the revolutionary masses, having shaken off the fetters of an outworn regime, carried a new tyranny into power. Thus Hitler was carried into power by the anti-capitalistic nostalgia of the impoverished German middle-classes; thus the revolutionary maquis of Eastern Europe may become a tool of Russian expansion. To them, who had lived cut off from the world in darkness and despair, the Soviet myth had appeared in even more radiant colours than to sympathizers in the West. Russia was their only hope; and the more German propaganda vilified it, the more immaculate her image became. The absence of a true and healthy socialist movement has driven the best revolutionary elements into an emotional trap; and by the time they awake from their happy dream to a nightmarish reality of purges, deportations and liquidations, the trap will be closed.

The Western proletariat, we may hope at least, will escape this tragedy. The next few years will bring a gradual awakening to Soviet reality. Russia's advance to the footlights of the European stage will make it increasingly difficult for her to deceive the world about her interior regime, though she will do her best to isolate newly-conquered territories as thoroughly as Poland and the Baltic states were isolated after the first conquest in 1939-41. The truth will filter through, but only slowly and gradually; it is well to remember how the Nazi regime succeeded in keeping the majority of the British and French in ignorance about the German terror for six whole years from 1933 to 1939, although Germany was wide open to tourist traffic and much nearer than Russia. Those who knew the truth about Germany and kept on shouting it into the ears of the deaf were accused of war- and atrocity-mongering; to tell the truth about Russia is to-day an equally ungrateful and equally necessary task. Had the Cassandras of 1933-38 been listened to — or had they been endowed with a more powerful voice — the war might have been avoided; the Cassandras of to-day are faced with a similar situation but this time the men of Munich are of the Left.

The attitude of the Left and Liberal press in the Russian-Polish conflict was an uncanny replica of the Conservative attitude in the German-Czech conflict of 1939. The same flimsy arguments about ethnic minorities (Sudetan-Germans in the first, Ukrainians and Belorussians in the second case) were invoked to mollify an act of conquest by terror and military might; there was the same impatience with the annoying victim who refuses to be murdered in silence, and the same desire not to antagonize the aggressor; there were the same symptoms of uneasy conscience and the same veiled admissions that small nations and big principles have sometimes to be sacrificed in the interests of peace between the great powers.

How convincingly the Left columnists proved during the days of Munich that appeasement leads not to peace but to war — and how thoroughly they have forgotten the sermons which they preached! In the case of Russia as in that of Germany, appeasement is based on the logical fallacy that an expanding power, if left alone, will automatically reach a state of saturation. But history proves the contrary. A yielding environment acts as a vacuum, a constant incentive to further expansion, and gives the aggressor no indication how far he can go without risking a major conflict; it is a direct invitation to him to overplay his hand and stumble into war by sheer miscalculation. Both world wars actually arose from such miscalculations. Appeasement transforms the field of international politics from a chess board into a poker table: in the first case both partners know where they are, in the second they don't. Thus the opposite of appeasement is not bellicosity, but a clearly outlined, firmly principled policy which leaves the partner in no doubt how far he can go. It does not eliminate the possibility of war but prevents the danger of stumbling blindly into it; and that is as much as political wisdom can achieve. It is highly unlikely that any great power will commit an act of aggression against a small nation if it is clearly and definitely understood by all concerned that a new world war will be the inevitable consequence. In other words: the point of saturation of an expanding power depends not on its own appetites which are unlimited, but on the forces of potential resistance in the environment.

The balance of Europe can only be restored through a revival of the values on which Western civilization is based. But this is a task beyond the powers of the conservative rearguard, and can only be achieved if the socialist movement sheds its illusions and regains its vigour and independence, both in the national and international sphere. Whether or not Labour will exert a direct or indirect influence on the government of post-war Britain, its foreign policy must be based on the realization that Soviet Russia is a power pursuing its own aims like any other great power, and no more concerned about the fate of the workers, the peasants or the dentists than any other country. Unless this fact is clearly and definitely realized, the Left will be heading for one more disaster.

The gradual decline of the Soviet myth will lead to new developments among socialists in Western Europe, particularly in the liberated countries. The radical wing will probably split into a new independent revolutionary movement and into faithful partisans of Russia. The former are the greatest and perhaps only hope for a socialist renaissance, though as yet entirely hypothetical. The latter, the incurable addicts, are in for a particularly tragic fate. Russian foreign policy being unconnected with any socialist principle, its partisans abroad will imperceptibly change from militants of the Third International into members of a Third Column, from defenders of the revolutionary fatherland into agents of a foreign power pure and simple. A minority of professional party-bureaucrats has already undergone this change with conscious cynicism. The majority, the rank and file, will continue to slide blindly down the slope. They will go down in the history of the socialist movement as a fanatical and degenerate sect, of the type which abounds in the history of religious movements. They will continue to live and die according to their strange laws and twisted logics, suffer willingly prison and death, and joyously sacrifice themselves in the name of Socialism for the Orthodox Church, for Panslavism, red millionaires, and the glorified traditions of Ivan the Terrible and Peter the Great.

They have to be written off as a tragic loss — the more tragic as they once represented the bravest and most virile elements of the working class.

III

Nothing is more sad than the death of an illusion. The Soviet devotee, even if only a fellow-traveller, had trained himself to trust the Soviet Union implicitly, and a breach of loyalty on his part appears to him as a moral betrayal, regardless of any breach of covenant committed by the other side. Even when forced to admit that Russia to-day is not a socialist country he will find comfort in the hope that she may still become one — perhaps 'after the death of Stalin', or 'when the power of the bureaucracy is broken'.

Now Russia may of course at some distant day go socialist — so may Portugal or the United States. But all we can say at present is that the U.S.S.R., despite her nationalized economy, is no nearer to this aim than, for instance, New Zealand or even Great Britain. The curve of evolution in Russia since 1917 has moved not towards but away from Socialism, whereas the curve of England shows a slow and oscillating, but nevertheless distinct tendency towards an improvement of social institutions, a crumbling of class-barriers and a considerable rise in both the relative and absolute living standard of the proletariat. There may come severe setbacks and periods of reaction; but England would have to go a long way down the slope before sinking to the political level of Russian autocracy.

If we apply Marxist criteria in weighing the chances of Socialism in Russia and in England, the odds are in favour of the latter. One of the basic teachings of Marxism is the importance for the proletariat of preserving certain democratic liberties in the State. Capitalist democracy is a sham democracy and the capitalist state is essentially an instrument of the ruling class; but the democratic institutions within the State — parliament, freedom of speech and assembly, etc. — enable the working class to build up her organizations, to concentrate and develop her powers. Under a dictatorial regime this task becomes infinitely more difficult.

We have seen that the one legal party in Russia ceased to be an instrument of the working class and became identified with the ruling bureaucracy; the same applies to the trade unions. Russia is not a dictatorship of the proletariat, but the dictatorship of a bureaucracy, which clings as tenaciously to power as any other ruling class. Never in history has a ruling class or caste voluntarily relinquished its privileges and power; and least of all has such tendency been shown by a ruling class which is young and vigorous, and has only just established herself. Individual members of a ruling class may have an enlightened philosophy; the class as such is fatally bound to obey the rules of the struggle for power.

Socialism in England is only possible if the power of the Conservatives is broken; Socialism in Russia is only possible if the power of the Bureaucracy is broken. The British Labour Party in its present state is a lame duck; but the legal and constitutional facilities for the rise of a truly Socialist movement are given in Britain, while they are absent in Russia. Moreover, the constitutional framework of British democracy provides at least a chance for a relatively smooth transition to Socialism, whereas the rigid crust of a dictatorship can only be broken by violence. But a revolution which is not prepared by a strong, organized party with clearly defined aims may take any course; and as under the conditions of the Russian dictatorship such a party cannot develop, a new Russian revolution would be a chaotic and horrible affair, the opposite of the revolution of 1917, without any guarantee of a change for the better.

The conclusion towards which all our arguments converge is that the spreading of Russian pseudo-communism over Europe can be stopped only by a true socialist movement. The antidote to Eastern Byzantinism is Western revolutionary humanism.

None of the old Parties of the Left seems at present adequate to this task. Whether a new international movement will arise in time to prevent the next cataclysm is an open question. If it does, the past errors and sacrifices of the Left will appear as a small price paid for the service rendered to humanity. If not, we and the next few generations after us, are in for a bad time, and the decline of the West may become historic reality.

The paramount lesson which we have to draw from the failure of the Russian experiment is that economic factors are important, but not all-important. The regimental tailor is not a socialist institution, and a nationalized economy may become an instrument of tyranny and reaction. By concentrating all her attention on the economic issue, the Left became deaf to the strange and changing moods of the People. Their religious nostalgia turned into free valencies of the soul, apt to fuse into the wrong compounds of chauvinism, mysticism, addiction to new myths.

The weaning of the Left, the breaking up of the false emotional compounds, is one half of the task. The other half is the creation of a new fraternity in a new spiritual climate, whose leaders are tied by a vow of poverty to share the life of the masses, and debarred by the laws of the fraternity from attaining unchecked power. If this seems utopian, then Socialism is utopia.

The age of enlightenment has destroyed faith in personal survival; the scars of this operation have never healed. There is a vacancy in every living soul, a deep thirst in all of us. If the Socialist idea cannot fill this vacancy and quench our thirst, then it has failed in our time. In this case the whole development of the Socialist idea since the French revolution has been merely the end of a chapter in history, and not the beginning of a new one.

EXPLORATIONS

I V

THE YOGI AND THE COMMISSAR—II

'Science is a vast and impressive tautology.'
c. c. pratt, *The Logic of Modern Psychology*

I

It is now six o'clock in the evening; I have just had a drink and I feel a strong temptation to have a couple more and then go and dine out instead of writing this essay. I have fought myself over this issue for the last quarter of an hour and finally I have locked the gin and the vermouth in the cupboard and settled down to my desk, feeling very satisfied with myself. From a scientific point of view this satisfaction is entirely spurious, since the issue was already settled before I started fighting myself; it was also settled that I should feel this spurious satisfaction and write what I write. Of course in my heart of hearts I do not believe that this is so, and I certainly did not believe it a quarter of an hour ago. Had I believed it, the process which I call 'inner struggle' would not have taken place, and fatality would have served me as a perfect excuse for going on drinking. Thus my disbelief in determinism must be contained in the set of factors which determine my behaviour; one of the conditions for fulfilling the prearranged pattern is that I should not believe that it is prearranged. Destiny can only have its way by forcing me to disbelieve in it. Thus the very concept of determinism implies a split between thinking and doing; it condemns man to live in a world where the rules of conduct are based on *As If-s* and the rules of logic on *Becauses*.

This paradox is not confined to scientific determinism; the Moslem, living in a world of religious determinism, displays the same mental split. Though he believes, in the words of the Koran, that 'every man's destiny is fastened on his neck', yet he curses his enemy, and himself when he blunders, as if all were masters of their choice. He behaves on his own level exactly like old Karl Marx who taught that man's mental make-up is a product of his environment, yet showered invectives on everybody who, in obedience to his environmental conditioning, couldn't help disagreeing with him.

Destiny versus freedom (or explanation versus volition) is an eternal duality in man's mental structure. Both concepts are derived from fundamental instincts, though in different periods they are expressed in different forms. The idea of destiny responds to the need to find some organizing principle, a universal order behind the threatening chaos of the natural world. Its instinctual root is probably the feeling of insecurity, a cosmic anxiety, which craves for reassurance by 'explanation', that is, the reduction of the strange and threatening to the familiar. In primitive religion this is achieved by explaining the forces of nature through animism and personification. However choleric or arbitrary those deities are, they are moved by familiar impulses, and everything that befalls us is thus satisfactorily explained.

About A.D. 1600 the character of destiny underwent a change. A new method of explanation arose in the measurements of the quantitative aspects of things and the formulation of their rules of interaction. Many phenomena which had appeared different in kind proved to be explainable in differences of degree — colours, sounds, heat and cold, above and below, animal and man. The success of this method meant that the organizing principle of the universe could now be more satisfactorily explained in terms of these quantities and relations. Deity, whose human passions had gradually decreased with increasing wisdom, now became entirely de-personalized. The idea of an enforced order 'fastened around man's neck' remained untouched, but the seat of the organizing power had been shifted. The gods had been supermen, extrapolations on an ascending scale; atoms and electrons were subhuman, extrapolations on a descending scale. Destiny which had operated from above now operated from below.

Volition, destiny's antagonist, we shall define as the psychological aspect or projection of the interplay of impulses and inhibitions. If this interplay takes place on the conscious level it is experienced as a not-enforced, not-inevitable process of choice. This subjective experience of freedom is the stronger the closer the process to the focus of attention. Actions resulting from processes on the pre-conscious fringes are experienced as 'absent-minded' semi-automatic doings, and from extra-conscious processes as fully automatic.

The experience of freedom resulting from processes in the focus of attention is probably synonymous with consciousness itself. Its essential characteristic is that the process is experienced as working from inside outwards instead of from outwards in; it seems determined from the subject's core and not by outward environment. On the psychological plane the experience of freedom is as much a given datum or 'reality' as are sense-perceptions or the feeling of pain. The abolition of the experience of free volition leads to collapse of the individual's whole mental structure, observable in certain forms of insanity (de-personalization). The concept of free choice is implicit in all systems of moral values and ethical imperatives.

Thus both the beliefs in determinism and freedom are rooted in primary instincts: the first in the need for protection by a universal order which 'explains' and thus tames the threatening forces of nature; the second in any drive for action — which, when balanced by inhibition and focused by attention, gives rise to the experience of free choice. We have seen, however, that the two beliefs stand in a reciprocal relation. Each progress in explanation draws the net of cognized objective relations tighter and narrows the scope of subjective choice. Thus the mind is driven to deny its own experience of freedom.

It is important to notice that this conflict is originally *not* (as it appears to-day) a conflict between objective thought and subjective feeling. The 'explanations' of animism and deism are just as affective, irrational and pre-logical as the experience of free volition. The conflict between freedom and determinism is a conflict between two instinctual beliefs, experienced in alternation and with equal intensity.

II

The Primitive's life is a series of rites to influence the spirits which govern his destiny. He believes that he has a free choice to perform those rites or not, and to perform them well or badly, which means that at those times he is *not* subject to destiny; more-over under certain conditions he may be able to force his will on the spirits, and thus completely reverse the situation. The Primitive is not conscious of this paradox, because his deities are still very human and imperfect. They in turn would need super-deities to impose order upon their conduct, and so on, through a receding series, to a completely de-personalized, ubiquitous and all-knowing godhead.

The Primitive, however, is satisfied with a rather coarse determinism of the first degree. As the human mind develops, more complete explanations are needed, the determining network becomes tighter and the divinity which operates it more perfected. At this point the paradox of destiny and volition becomes con-scious; the contradiction between divine omnipotence and human striving expresses itself with unparalleled dramatic force in mythology. Eve eats the fruit of knowledge of good and evil against the will of the Lord; Prometheus steals the fire from the gods; Jacob fights the angel; the tower of Babel is built and destroyed. The two instincts are locked in dramatic battle and the older instinct always wins against the younger one — for, as we saw, the experience of freedom only arose at a high level of consciously experienced balance between impulse and inhibition. Thus each Promethean attempt ends in defeat, punishment or humiliation; the Augean stable is never cleaned, the Danaïd's vessel never filled, Sisyphus' labours are eternally in vain: the desire for protection is stronger than the self-confidence of making the right choice. On a planet with a friendlier climate populated with a biologically less vulnerable race, mythology might take an opposite course: each battle would end with a Promethean victory over the gods and the race would grow up free, self-confident, without priests, leaders and kings — an attractive subject for dreams on a rainy day.

The conflict reaches its conscious peak in the type of myth immortalized by Oedipus Rex. Oedipus apparently retains his freedom of volition and nevertheless fulfils the pattern of his destiny. The fates know that of his free choice he would never slay his father and marry his mother, so they trick him into it under false pretences. His 'freedom' is contained in their calculus and hence not worth much. But the significant fact is that destiny is forced to accord man at least the illusion of freedom.

Christianity carried the solution an important step further. Man's freedom is no longer an illusion but reality *on the human plane*; while divinity is omnipotent, omniscient and completely determines the world *on a superhuman plane*. The dilemma has been sharpened and at the same time solved by projecting the split from mind into nature. The universe itself has been divided into levels of human volition, and divine volition=destiny. The levels stand in a hierarchic order, i.e. the laws of divine logic are impenetrable by the human mind, whereas the latter is an open book to divinity. God is 'not what I think thou art but what thou knowest thyself to be'. The Primitive's world was homogeneous in the sense that the superhuman operators of destiny thought and behaved much in the same way as the humans. The Christian world is discontinuous in the sense that separate laws operate on separate levels—the divine, the human, the animal level. The logical contradiction between freedom and determinism has been solved by attributing different types of logic to different planes in the hierarchy.

It will be useful to retain the following characteristics of the Christian hierarchy of levels:

God is the explanation of everything, but this explanation cannot be formulated on the lower (human) level.

The laws of the higher level cannot be reduced to, nor predicted from, the lower level;

the phenomena of the lower level and their laws are implied in the higher order, but

phenomena of the higher order if manifested on the lower level appear as unexplainable and miraculous.

III

The final step in the perfection and de-personalization of destiny was performed when, in the beginning of the seventeenth century, God became a mathematician. The first protagonists of the new method of explanation by measurement and quantitative laws literally believed that God had created the world according to algebraical precepts, and that the planetary laws were an expression of His desire to maintain harmony in the spheres. But now that destiny had yielded the objective principles of the universal order, there was no more need for a subjective operator, and God dissolved into natural law; for a perfect law leaves no scope for the judge.

Thus, on a higher bend of the evolutionary spiral, the world became again homogeneous. The same laws governed the conduct of atoms, stars, organic matter, the brain and its highest manifestations. The only difference was, as we saw, that determinism from above became determinism from below. The Primitive had formed anthropomorphic images of the gods; the primitive physicists made three-dimensional models of the atom-nucleus. As observation and explanation progressed, the models collapsed as the idols had. The gods became de-personified and the models de-materialized. Both the upward projection of human temperament and the downward projection of human spatio-temporal experience were insufficient for perfectioned explanation; and the commandment 'Thou shalt not make unto thee any graven image' applies to God as to multi-dimensional space, electrons, wave-packets and quanta.

Thus scientific determinism was heading towards the same crisis as that of religious determinism, expressed in the Oedipus myth. Instead of being a puppet of anthropomorphic gods, man became a physico-chemical automaton; destiny from below left as little scope for the experience of free choice as destiny from above; the iron grip of heredity and environment was as inescapable as that of the weird sisters of fate. The only difference was that philosophic jargon did its best to obscure the conflict. By the beginning of this century, however, philosophers grew tired of their own jargon, arguments on 'free will' were regarded as bad form and left to the theologians. All the volumes of the British Museum are insufficient to exhaust the implications of my sweating over this essay instead of drinking my gin.

So far we have dwelt only on the logical aspect of our paradox. What about its influence on ethics?

Ethical systems are based on the implicit assumption of free choice of action. The Primitive's code of behaviour is dictated by the aim of influencing the spirits by submission or coercion, by trickery and bribery, the latter including self-mutilation and sacrifice. Primitive ethics aim at using man's free will in such a way as to pacify destiny and thus reconcile the determinant with the determined. Ritual is the bridge between freedom and destiny.

As deity progresses towards omnipotence, the gross methods of coercion are abandoned and ethics become dominated by submission and humility. The exertion of free will is subordinated to divine guidance. This guidance can only be obtained by the sacrifice of volition: the mystic uses his freedom to focus his will into the total passivity of contemplation. In ecstasy the spirit becomes one with the principle of universal order: a total Explanation is attained. But this final triumph of one of the two conflicting instincts can only be achieved by the total defeat of the other, volition. Detachment, the foundation of all mystic techniques, may be compressed into the formula: *I will not to will*.

As deity progresses a further step and becomes transformed into mathematical law, ethics again follows suit by adapting a quantitative language: 'The greatest happiness for the greatest number'. Ethics thus remains true to its aim, i.e. to reconcile man's freedom with his destiny; but its ritual code has once more to be adapted to deity's changed character. Before the change, man's relation to 'destiny from above' was one of submission; now that destiny operates 'from below' it becomes mainly one of domination. The forces of nature determine man's fate, but at the same time technics enable him to dominate those forces; and he is more conscious of his power than of his dependence. Before the change, Explanation was only obtainable by passive contemplation; now by active research — knowledge becomes externalized. Before the change, man's condition was derived from a Fall; now from an evolutionary Rise achieved by permanent violence in the struggle for survival. The Christian method of making society conform to the divine order aimed at Change from Within; the new method of achieving a mathematically perfect society aimed at Change from Without. The new codes of behaviour emphasize activity instead of passivity, domination instead of submission, ruthlessness instead of meekness, calculation instead of guidance. The saint is succeeded by the revolutionary; the Yogi by the Commissar.

A further consequence of the change was that Explanation lost its reassuring character. The urge for both knowledge and re-assurance is rooted in the same instinct — to assimilate the un-canny to the familiar. But like all instincts it had branched out as the level of mental organization rose, so that to-day it needs the analyst's perspicacity to unearth the root. Religious determin-ism had covered all branches of the instinct: God was both explanation and protection. Scientific determinism covered only one: 'destiny from below' was unable to provide protection by a paternal power. The neglected branch took its revenge by reverting to archaic myths, and the beating of the jungle tom-tom drowned the ticking of the scientific clock.

IV

The latent crisis of scientific determinism became acute about the turn of the century in practically all branches of science, from theoretical physics to experimental embryology.

Around 1900 certain atomic nuclei were found to behave each like a miniature Oedipus. They conformed to a plan but at the same time seemed to enjoy freedom in their own terms of reference. They unfailingly fulfilled their destiny which ordained that a milligram of radium had to disintegrate at a certain given rate (about 500 million atoms per second) and in doing this emit a certain given radiation (alpha and beta corpuscles and gamma rays); but at the same time it was found that each little nuclear Oedipus was completely indifferent to physical influences in his environment. The law of Rutherford and Soddy (1903) implied that the collapse of radio-active atoms was 'spontaneous', i.e.

independent of the atom's physical state, position and environment. The most complete description of the atom's present condition in physical terms allowed no conclusions as to its future. Its fate seemed determined 'from inside and not from outside' (Jeans). The individual atom seemed to experience freedom in the sense that for its behaviour no explanation was possible *in physics' own terms of explanation*. In 1917 Einstein showed that the right to 'spontaneous' collapse had to be accorded to *all* atoms. In the 'twenties Schroedinger postulated that the whereabouts of electrons travelling through empty space can only be expressed in terms of probabilities, not in certainties; and Heisenberg that with regard to electrons inside the atom a similar uncertainty reigns; while Dirac assumed that all phenomena in space and time arise from a sub-stratum which is not in space and time and entirely beyond measurable grasp.

These findings revolutionized physics and lent themselves to wild metaphysical speculation which ranged from theological seminaries to the detective stories of Miss Dorothy Sayers. The only disappointing thing was that the apparent anarchy disappeared and determinism re-entered into its rights, as soon as we left the realm of the infinitesimal for the macroscopic world. However Oedipus-like the individual atom behaved, fair-sized atom-crowds behaved in a strictly predictable way.

Thus the significance of modern physics is not the discovery of some divine agent working inside the atom, but merely a limitation of the scope of physical explanation. It all boils down to this: microscopic events cannot be adequately described or explained in the terms of our macroscopic experience of space, time and causation. The framework of experience on the human level is inapplicable beneath that level. Modern cosmology with its curved space-time showed that it is equally inapplicable *above* that level.

The antinomy of freedom and determinism can now be translated into the realm of the atom as follows.

The 'freedom' of individual electrons, nuclei, etc., means, not arbitrariness or divine inspiration, but merely freedom from such determinants as are experienced on the man-sized scale. Their behaviour cannot be defined or explained in terms of quantitative measurement nor by thought-processes based on the elements of human experience. It is 'not of this world' if by world we mean our spatio-temporal experience. It exists on a different level of organization, whose relations and relata cannot be reduced to, nor predicted from, the macrocosmic level.

Each of the sentences in the paragraph above contains the word 'not'. All our statements about the sub-atomic level are negative statements, denoting the limitations of physical explanation. But there is no reason why the discovery of these limitations should be regarded as a tragedy, or as a proof of the immaculate conception. It only means that the hope for a complete explanation of the world by quantitative measurements proved as fallacious as deistic explanations in the past. After all it is only three centuries since God became a mathematician and we have plenty of time before us for other transformations. The monopoly of quantitative measurements is drawing to its close, but already new principles of explanation begin to emerge. Meanwhile we have to note that Science is reverting to the same expedient for solving its paradoxes as religious explanation once did: it renounces the idea of a homogeneous universe ruled by one comprehensive law, and replaces it by a hierarchy of 'levels of organization'. This is not, as many frightened scientists believe, a regression into religious thought; it is merely an analogy *in method* to solve the paradox of freedom and determinism which remains hidden and latent as long as a type of explanation is still incomplete, but explodes in a crisis as it becomes perfected.

v

In modern biology the stratification of the world into hierarchic 'levels of organization' is an even more necessary expedient than in physics. The transition from the old to the new outlook is reflected, *inter alia*, in the writings of J. Needham, the Cambridge biologist; his example is particularly interesting because Needham belongs to a school of scientists with a strong Marxist and even

Stalinist tendency and hence is most unwilling to move into a direction which smacks, if ever so faintly, of 'metaphysics' or 'vitalism'. Yet the findings in their own laboratories and intellectual honesty compel the Commissars of Science to travel, however reluctantly, with the stream. Needham's progress may be characterized by two quotations.

In 1928 he wrote: 'At the present day zoology has become comparative biochemistry and physiology biophysics'; in 1941 he wrote: 'Biological organization . . . cannot be "reduced" to physico-chemical organization, because nothing can ever be reduced to anything. As Samuel Butler once remarked: "Nothing is ever *merely* anything" . . .'[1]

The crisis in biology opened at the end of the last century with the development of experimental embryology. In 1895 Driesch showed that, against the expectations of science, all kinds of things could be done to the embryos of certain species without changing the outcome. If after the first division of the frog-egg one of the two resulting cells (which normally would have become half of the future frog) was amputated, the result was not half a frog, but a complete frog of a smaller size. If one repeated the operation in a later blastular stage, the result remained still the same; a whole crowd of cells of the blastular foetus could be removed or reshuffled, without changing the result. If the future tail of a newt was grafted into a position where the leg should be it grew not into a tail but into a leg. The matter caused great consternation. For if the cells and cell-tissues in the blastula were by physico-chemical laws 'determined' to become half-newts or newt-tails, how could they change their mind as it were, and

---

[1] In one passage Needham fights a rearguard action by saying:
'It would be correct to say that the living differs from the dead in degree and not in kind because it is on a higher plane of complexity of organization, but it would also be correct to say that it differs in kind since the laws of this higher organization only operate here.' (*Time, the Refreshing River.*)
Now according to the elementary rules of logic the statements 'differs not in kind' and 'differs in kind' cannot both be 'correct'. We are in the presence of a striking example of what ravages the infatuation with Marxian dialectics may cause in an otherwise clear brain. The fallacy in this case lies obviously in the silent assumption smuggled into the first part of the sentence that living differs from dead *only in numerical and not functional* complexity – which is contradicted in the second part of the sentence.

grow into whole-newts or legs? It was obviously absurd to assume that the physico-chemical regulative devices inside the cells *implied* the possibility of meeting Dr. Driesch's knife and the proper reactions to this event.

The consternation became even greater when it was discovered that from a certain point onwards in the development of the embryo the position becomes reversed. Embryonic parts which have reached the gastrular stage lose their flexible future and seem so strongly 'determined' to persist on their path that, if cut off and then grafted to other parts of the foetal body, they not only go on growing as if they were still in their normal position, but also force the host-tissue to adapt its own development to the function of the guest (provided, of course, that the host is still in the flexible stage). The results obtained by Speeman and Mangold (1924) by their new grafting technique were fantastic. Thus when the eye-placode of a tadpole is removed from the head and grafted under the surface of the belly, the surface-skin becomes transparent and develops a correct lens and cornea for this abdominal eye. Finally it was found by Paul Weiss that these phenomena were not confined to the embryonic stage but also occurred in the regenerative tissues of grown-ups. Thus young tissue from the stump of an amputated newt-tail grew into a leg if transplanted into a 'leggy' position, but older tail-stump tissue grew into a tail wherever grafted on.

The mechanistic idea that the laws governing life were mere extrapolations of physico-chemical laws was utterly defeated. And the findings of experimental embryology were merely the crassest examples of analogous developments in other branches of biology. The conflict between freedom and determinism became even more acute in the realm of the cell than in the realm of the atom; but here too 'freedom' should only be interpreted in the sense that the potentialities of the living are not exhausted by explanations in terms of the anorganic level. The freedom of a blastomere to develop into a quarter-frog or a whole frog is obviously the opposite of arbitrariness; but its behaviour can only be 'explained' by collecting and relating experimental facts on its proper level and not by predictions based on physico-chemical laws.

The first attempt to solve the problem was abortive. Driesch's 'entelechies' were a purely terminological sham-solution, similar to. the nineteenth-century physicist's Ether, and based on the old procedure of baptizing an X with a Greek name. One might as well introduce an entelechy into each atomic nucleus; or, to quote Dr. Broad, 'the hypothesis of an entelechy can explain the facts only if it supposes the entelechy to be so exalted a mind as to deserve the name of "god"'.[1]

During the 'thirties, after the quarrel between Vitalists and Mechanists had come to a deadlock, the expedient of splitting up the world into a hierarchy of 'levels of organization' became more or less generally accepted among biologists, though each seems to interpret the philosophical implications in his own way.[2]

The laws or 'organizing relations' which operate on each level of the hierarchy are of two kinds. (a) Non-specific laws (e.g. inertia) which are shared by all levels but which have little explanatory value; the law according to which an egg will not move from my plate unless it is pushed does not enrich my knowledge of the egg. (b) Specific laws, which contain practically all that is worth knowing about a thing. These cannot be reduced to or deduced from lower levels of the hierarchy, and can only be formulated by studying the phenomena on their proper level. Where this is impossible without completely destroying the specific order which is to be studied as, e.g., on the sub-atomic level, no laws can be formulated.

It follows that a thing will display different characteristics on different levels, according to the specific 'organizing relations' to which it is exposed. Thus a crowd of carbon molecules will display different properties as an element, in an anorganic compound, in an organic compound, on the crystalline, colloidal and bio-chemical level; and the components of a spermatozon will display

[1] C. D. Broad: *The Mind and its Place in Nature.*
[2] Such a solution had been foreshadowed by Henry Drummond, Herbert Spencer, Lloyd-Morgan, Wilson, Alexander, C. D. Broad and others, but only received its precise formulation in Woodger's fundamental work *Biological Principles* (1929).

different properties in vitro, in the scrotum, in the ovum, in the blastular state, in the gastrular state, and inside the grown-up organism. None of these specific properties can be predicted from a lower level; not even the chemical qualities of compounds from the physical data of their components; these new qualities emerge suddenly, in a jump as it were, on their appropriate level; hence the name 'Theory of Emergency'.[1]

Just as processes cannot be predicted 'upward' from a lower level, they can also never be completely analysed 'downward' into their components. To analyse means to isolate parts from the whole, and the functioning of a part in isolation is not the same as its functioning in the whole. When the physiologist studies a tissue culture he may reconstruct *to a certain extent* the conditions prevailing in the body by an artificial organic environment, but he can never succeed completely. 'The environment of a part is the whole organism' (Woodger). Thus a cell isolated from the convoluted tube of the kidney will in tissue culture exhibit the basic metabolic changes common to all cells, but its specific characteristics as a *kidney*-cell will be lost. The same applies, of course, if the analysis is pushed further down to the chemical components; for the chemist in order to reach them has usually to destroy all the intervening levels. Thus the *specific* behaviour of wholes can only be properly studied and described in terms of the relations of wholes to each other, and the specific behaviour of parts only in their relations to other parts; isolation destroys their very character of 'part-ness'; and so down to parts of parts.

Analysis reveals only the common factors contained in a process, but the process cannot be reconstructed by putting these factors together again; their law of integration is different on each level. Thus if I analyse a square into dots I have to put them together according to the laws of multiplication; if the dots belong to an ellipse I have to apply the laws of integral calculus; if they are parts of a portrait, new relations emerge. The levels do not differ from each other by the things they contain, but by the way these

---

[1] Or 'emergent vitalism'. It has, however, nothing in common with vitalism of the Driesch brand, and the sooner the discredited term is dropped the better.

things associate on each level, and the new properties and values which emerge by this specific type of association. The 'freedom' of a level consists in these new values and relations which were not present among the determinants of the lower level; the 'destiny' of a level is its dependence on the laws of the next-higher level — laws which it cannot predict nor reduce.

In other words: the freedom of the whole is the destiny of the part; the only way to comprehend destiny is to comprehend one's part-ness. That is precisely what the mystics said. But that does not mean a victory of mysticism over science; only the recognition of the limitations of science within its own terms of reference.

VI

It is fascinating to watch how the concept of a hierarchy of levels and of their irreducibility by uniform quantitative laws arose independently in various branches of science.

In psychology, quantitative measurements began to fade into the background at the beginning of the century; Gestalt-Psychology, developed by Koehler, Koffka and Wertheimer in the late 'twenties is entirely dominated by the concept of 'wholeness' and the specific laws which integrate elementary sense-data into perceptional wholes.

Let the whole be a triangle; then, by analysing it into its parts I get three straight lines of given length which I can measure. But obviously a black line of two inches in length is *as a sense perception* something quite different from the hypotenuse of a triangle. Its specific character can only be perceived if it is in its proper place in the whole. *As a sense perception* 'black line' is as different from 'hypotenuse' as a kidney-cell in isolation from a kidney-cell in the kidney. I have twice underlined the words 'as a sense perception' because *on the drawing-board* the black line remains unchanged whether it is part of a triangle or not. I may cover the other two sides and the line remains the same — in its physical existence on the paper. But it does not remain the same as a *percept*. On the perceptual level the black line changes its character when exposed to the influence of the other two parts. This inter-action of perceptual elements in the mental field is as real as the inter-action of kidney cells. Accordingly it must have some physiological equivalent in the brain, and Koehler assumes that there are self-distributing electromagnetic currents between the cortical projections of retinal points. Other physiological hypotheses are equally possible; the essential point is not the nature of the physiological process but the fact that on the level of the drawing-board the three lines are a static mosaic which leave each other alone, whereas on the brain-mind level they automatically enter into dynamical relations with each other and emerge as wholes. All this may appear as fairly obvious to the layman who does not realize how hopelessly bogged the old atomistic psychology had become in its ambiguous distinctions of 'sensation', 'perception', 'meaning', etc. In atomistic psychology the brain served as a kind of screen on to which the retina projected its static mosaic; this implied the necessity of a second observer or brain who transformed the 'sensation' into 'perception' and invested it with the 'meaning' of triangularity. Gestalt-Psychology does not explain the emergence of the mental level, just as biology does not explain the emergence of life; but once that level is given, the things which are lifted on to it become integrated by specific organizing relations, and the mystery of the mind is reduced to the already familiar principle of a hierarchy of qualitatively different levels.

VII

We may imagine our hierarchy of levels as a series of terraces on an ascending slope, or as a broad ascending staircase. Then the horizontal surfaces of the steps will represent the field in which the laws of a given level operate, and the vertical surfaces the 'jumps' which lead to the emergence of the higher levels. The succession of steps will be roughly this: Space-time, sub-atomic phenomena, physics, chemistry, crystals (para-crystals), (viruses), non-dividing organic constituents (proteins, enzymes, hormones, etc.), dividing organic constituents (cell-parts and some cells), higher (non-dividing) cells and organs; and so on up to the higher mental functions. Some of these steps will have to be divided into sub-steps and in the higher regions the staircase will branch out; but this can be neglected from the point of view of our argument. There will also be 'mezoforms' — hybrids like the para-crystals and probably the viruses; some Mechanists argued that these are a proof of continuity between the levels. But this position is practically abandoned by modern biology — just as nobody will try to deduce from the existence of hermaphrodites that the male and female functions differ only in degree, not in kind. 'If we look carefully at the steps between the successive levels of organization', says Needham, 'we find that the sharp lines of distinction are only made all the more sharp by the mezoforms which occur between them . . These forms of existence, the more clearly we understand them, will all the more clearly serve to bring out the essentially new elements of higher order which characterize the form of organization we call life.'[1]

If we now represent our staircase diagrammatically, we find that there are two ways of looking at it:

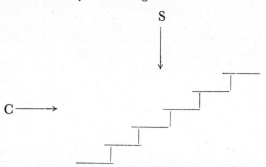

The perpendicular arrow marked 'S' indicates the Scientific observer; to him the levels of the staircase appear projected on one horizontal plane, spread out as a kind of continuous spectrum from physics to psychology, and the jumps between the levels appear

[1] J. Needham: *Time, the Refreshing River.*

merely as thin dividing lines. Within each area everything is 'explainable' or shortly will be; law and order reigns and there is no mystery — apart from those irritating divisions.

But if we contemplate the staircase as indicated by the horizontal arrow 'C', everything becomes unexplained mystery. The surfaces of the steps disappear, and we only see the vertical jumps between them. S sees the phenomena as given; C is faced with the secret of their *being given* in unpredictable lifts; not in one act of creation but in a rhythmic creatio continua.

'What has not yet been done, however, is to elucidate the way in which each of the new great levels of organization has arisen', Needham writes with unconscious irony — for that which 'has not yet been done' was the primary aim of scientific explanation. 'It must always be remembered that though we can chart out quite fully the laws existing at a given high organizational level, we can never hope to understand how they fit into the picture of nature as a whole, i.e. how they join with the next higher and next lower levels. About this there is nothing obscurantist, nothing animistic. . . .'[1]

There is indeed nothing obscurantist in the admission of an obscurity. This obscurity consists, as we saw, in the fact that specific organizing relations only operate on 'horizontal' planes and that we cannot predict or reduce them; in other words, *we have no laws which operate in the vertical direction.*[2]

A 'vertical' law would be a law enabling us to explain or predict how and when and why higher forms of existence are generated. But though we cannot formulate such laws in scientific terms, we have an inkling of the general tendencies involved in the generation of higher levels. Such 'transordinal' tendencies of 'building up' are, e.g., the duality of aggregation and segregation which manifests itself on various levels as attraction and repulsion, integration and specialization, growth and division, sex-instincts and death-instincts, etc. Other tendencies involved are symmetry, and adaptation or harmony. Once more I quote Needham, the

[1] Needham, *op. cit.*

[2] Except non-specific laws like the conservation of energy, etc., which do not explain anything about the emergence of new specific properties.

ex-Mechanist and neophyte of Marxism, who is so anxious to avoid obscurantism:

> ... Still, we can say with Drummond that there may be something analogous between the bonds appropriate to each of the different levels of organization in the world. And we remember that great book in which Siegmund Freud described what he called 'the task of Eros' ... From this point of view, the bonds of love and comradeship are analogous to the various forces which hold particles together at the colloidal, crystalline, molecular, and even sub-atomics levels. ...

Symmetry, harmony, love as the common organizing tendencies on all levels of existence — the ring of this is rather familiar to us. But if this is mysticism, it is mysticism with a difference. The *'ignoramus'* is pronounced at the end, not at the beginning of the journey.

VIII

Religious explanation, caught in the paradox of destiny and freedom, had to give up the homogeneous conception of the world and stratify it into a hierarchy of levels. To-day science has to adopt the same expedient. A comparison between the Christian and Scientific hierarchies will show the basic sameness of method. We said (p. 231) about the Christian hierarchy that:

> the laws of the higher level cannot be reduced to, nor predicted from, the lower level;
> the phenomena of the lower level and their laws are implied in the higher order, but
> phenomena of the higher order when manifested on the lower level appear as unexplainable and miraculous.

All this holds equally good for the relation between, say, biochemistry and embryology.

Religion further taught that there are two ways of knowing: *exploration* of the horizontal, worldly planes, and *contemplation* of the vertical or transcendental order. The second way means trespassing across the boundaries of all separate levels; hence the mystic is viewed with equal distrust by the Churches and Sciences, by scholars and scholastics. And yet both clergy and schoolmasters have had to recognize their own limits and the validity of the 'other' method of grasping the ultimate and intimate problems of existence.

The staircase of religion has only a few steep steps between inanimate matter and divinity, roughly corresponding to the six days of creation. The staircase of science has a great number of more delicate steps. The difference in height between the levels is often hardly visible, and more and finer sub-divisions are likely to emerge. But nature knows no continuity, only jumps, and a staircase never becomes a slope, even if the steps are made infinitely small. For we can always choose a correspondingly small particle which will remain at rest on the staircase but roll down the slope; and in a perpendicular light the whole staircase will always remain in shadow for him who contemplates it from the front.

The two ways of knowing do not invalidate, but complete each other. We have lost an illusion and regained the right to deepen our understanding of reality — by methods which a generation ago nobody dared to mention without blushing. Newton once saw a thing fall from a tree and calculated its mass, energy and acceleration. To-day we are going back to the fact that the thing which fell was an apple.

I X

Once the principle of Levels of Organization becomes as firmly established in our mental habits as was the idea of the homogeneousness and reducibility of all things in the nineteenth century, much confusion will be avoided in aesthetics, ethics, and the theory of knowledge. This confusion arises from the application of the specific laws of one level to another, and by our ingrained habit of 'reducing' — e.g. reducing ethical values to biological relata.

Freud's essay on 'A Childhood Memory of Leonardo da Vinci' is a masterpiece of applied psychology; its ingenuity equals

Champollion's deciphering of the Hieroglyphs. The analysis of the Gioconda's smile is more exciting reading than any detective story — about the artistic values of the portrait it explains nothing. Leonardo becomes an open book for us — except for the fact that he was a good painter. 'It is not the aim of pathography', says Freud, 'to explain the achievement [of Leonardo]; one should not reproach me for having broken a promise which I never made ... We would be glad to retrace artistic activity to its instinctual origins — but that is just the point where our means let us down ...' Freud knew the limits of his method — so did Marx. But Freudians and Marxists don't; they raise totalitarian claims to explain all phenomena by a method which is for them a magic panacea. This attitude is not always intellectually conscious; the analyst when cornered will admit that the specific values of a canvas can neither be reduced to the chemistry of the paint nor to the case-history of the painter; and the Marxist will indignantly deny that he ever claimed Economic factors could explain everything. But their unconscious tendency expresses itself by an obsessional over-emphasis; and thus in practice the Marxist *will* 'explain' fascism in purely economic terms and the Adlerian *will* 'explain' Napoleon by his shortness — without, however, telling us why all short people do not become Napoleons. Whence follows, *inter alia*, that creative people should avoid being psycho-analysed as long as their intimate miseries do not impair their creativeness. In theory analysis should help the artist to sublimate his complexes; but mostly this externally induced sublimation does not express itself in artistic creation but in rationalizations and in diminishing or destroying the generating tension. I have never heard of a neurotic becoming an artist by learning to sublimate on the analyst's sofa. The paintings which Jung's patients produce as a substitute for throwing a fit are always lamentable, whereas the drawings of schizophrenes are mostly admirable.

It also follows that the so-called 'better understanding' of an artist's work gained by reading his biography, historical introductions, etc. is a non-specific, reductive understanding which interferes with the perception of the specific order of values on their own level. Prefaces should be read after, not before the work. *Julius Caesar* has been for ever spoiled for me by the information that the treatment of Brutus by Shakespeare was biased by the trial of Essex; since I read Freud's Leonardo I can't help seeing the Gioconda as a pathological exhibit; and young X.'s admirable love-lyric is tainted with bathos since I saw his Beatrice getting tight on mild-and-bitter at the 'George'. The debunking of values is not a symptom of decadence, but on the contrary a hangover of the optimistic tendency to reduce heterogeneous levels to homogeneous laws.

x

The tendency to 'reduce' and the ensuing confusion of levels lead to particularly tragic results in the realm of ethics.

We may distinguish five main types of degenerated ethical systems in our time, which result from (a) the reduction of ethical values to the zero level, and/or the application of (b) biological, (c) psychological, (d) quantitative, and (e) mystical concepts to the ethical sphere. Usually we find a mixture of several of these, but it is more convenient to treat them separately.

(a) The obsession for analysing and reducing ethical values leads, if unchecked, to explicit or implicit nihilism. Reduction becomes reductio *ad infinitum* and *ad absurdum*. 'When he believes he does not believe that he believes, and when he does not believe, he does not believe that he does not believe', says Kirillov in *The Possessed*. '. . . All the planet is a lie and rests on a lie and on mockery. So then, the very laws of the planet are a lie and the vaudeville of devils.'

Nihilism seldom assumes the explicit forms of a political movement as among the Russian intelligentsia of the eighteen-sixties, or crystallizes into such monstrous figures as Bakunin's friend Nechaev and his group. But elements of it can be traced everywhere in materialist philosophy. It also permeates the 'private philosophies' of corrupt politicians, prostitutes, big business, criminals and cads. Everybody with some experience in social welfare work knows that most asocials have some such sort of jealously-guarded private philosophy which they believe to be their unique discovery. Once we accept the principle of reduction as legitimate, there is no means of refuting it. If the world is assumed as completely homogeneous, its laws must be traceable either upward to God or downward to chaos; nihilism takes the second course.

An inverted kind of nihilism is expressed in the phrase 'tout comprendre c'est tout pardonner'. It is one of the woolliest phrases ever uttered. 'Pardonner' implies an ethical judgment, based on the assumption of free choice which, as a datum of experience, is a specific property of the ethical level *only*. This judgment should now be 'pardoned', that is invalidated, by understanding. Now either this understanding is *specific*, then it must lead to a judgment identical to that which it is supposed to invalidate. Or the understanding is derived from *reduction* to psychological, biological, etc. levels, then it leaves out the really significant factors on which the judgment is based and can never invalidate it.

Thus my condemnation of Nazism is based on the observation of the social disturbances which it produces and on the implicit assumption that each individual has, within certain limits, the choice of becoming a Nazi or not; hence I fight those who are Nazis and try to prevent others from becoming Nazis. This judgment is based on my understanding of what I observed and therefore cannot be invalidated by it. If, however, I concentrate *merely* on the historical, racial and environmental factors in the make-up of my Nazi then I may pardon him by saying 'the poor chap couldn't help it'. But my pardon was obtained at the price of reducing him to the level of an animal or automaton and thus excluding him from the level on which my judgment was pronounced. And if he is merely an animal or machine, irresponsible for his acts, I shall be entitled to fight him the more mercilessly under the cover of my understanding. I pardon my rusty razor, but I throw it on the rubbish-heap.

Thus 'tout comprendre c'est tout pardonner' either produces an effect directly contrary to its intentions — or it simply boils down to the platitude that judgment should be based on observation not on emotion. In which case it would be less misleading to say simply: 'Bien observé c'est bien jugé'.

(b) The projection of *biological* laws on to the level of human ethics leads to Darwinistic conceptions of sociology — survival of the fittest, the 'natural rights of the Superman', etc. — of which the ethics of Fascism is the most consequential expression. Biology is the sociology of the jungle, and its application to a higher level must lead to the appropriate results. One of the most fascinating treatises on the application of 'Natural Law' to ethics was, by the way, written by the Marquis de Sade.

(c) The reduction or debunking of ethical values to the level of psychology and psycho-pathology is a trend of little political but great cultural significance, especially amongst the intelligentsia. What we said about the reduction of aesthetical values also applies here — with this difference, that while Freud himself was fully conscious of the limitations of his method in the first case, in the second he was not; his attitude to the question of the autonomy of ethical values was, to put it mildly, ambiguous. Geniuses are panzer-spearheads; their lightning advance into no-mind's-land necessarily leaves their flanks unprotected. It would be the task of the infantry which follows to broaden the base and secure the lost contact with other advancing faculties; instead they behave as if each of them were a little tank. The Freudian infantry (like the Marxist battalions) has conquered hardly any new ground; but they have played havoc in the philosophical hinterland. The 'reduction' of *social* values like courage and self-sacrifice, to the *psychological* level of masochism, the death-instinct, etc., is a process analogous to the reduction of live organisms to their chemical components. For on the sociological level the individual emerges as part of a new whole, and the integrative relations on this level are once more specific and irreducible.

Take, for example, the ethical concept of 'conscience'. In Freud's writings this concept appears frequently in ironical inverted commas — we might just as well do the same to 'carbon' or 'fish'. In the Freudian system the origin of conscience is traced to the super-ego which in turn is traced to partial identification with the parental authority. But this reductive account leaves out the essential and specific feature of the thing analysed: namely, that a good or bad conscience is based on the conviction that the act in question was committed by free choice. Freedom as a datum of experience hardly plays any role in the Freudian system. But it is just this new and specific factor which functions as an organizing relation on the ethical level, and distinguishes the new social whole from the herd, flock or swarm.

The new factor emerges, as we saw, by the focusing of a precarious balance between impulse and inhibition. But this merely describes the conditions which must be fulfilled for its emergence, not the process of emergence itself; the latter is the vertical jump. Thus we may describe the chemical, thermal, etc. conditions which must be present at the generation of life matter; and yet the process of generation remains unexplained and its result is on a new level. Incidentally, the state of 'precarious balance' which characterizes the emergence of experienced freedom is also characteristic for the original instability of organic molecules and other emergent biological levels. New forms of existence are narrow victories of the tendency towards integration over its opponent.

Freud's famous question 'Why should I love my neighbour?' (*Civilization and Its Discontents*) cannot be answered by neurological formulations of the libido; it can only be answered by considering myself and my neighbour in the integrative relation of parts to the whole. And if we agree, for convenience's sake, to use the term 'libido' as a name for the integrative tendencies on *all* levels, then we have to bear in mind that this 'libido' assumes different specific forms in the force of gravitation, on the molecular level, in the growth of a crystal, the growth of the gastrula, the syngamy of organ-parts, the reproduction of organic wholes and the integration of the social whole.

(*d*) The transfer from the physical to the ethical level of the principles of quantitative measurement has probably produced the most disastrous results. The implied paradoxa of this kind of 'Commissar-Ethics' are less obvious to us than those of the biological ethics of Fascism because we have been so thoroughly trained to think in quantitative terms that the application of mathematical criteria to ethical method appears to us simply as an act of common sense. Thus we accept as quite logical that a given number of people should be sacrificed in the interest of a greater number of people. *Ergo*, as Mr. Chamberlain said in the days of Munich, one cannot reasonably expect a great nation to take risks for the sake of a small one. But at the same time we do expect a front-line ambulance to risk the lives of their crew of five to save one wounded man. We accept the argument of Soviet apologists that it is better to keep a thousand innocents in jail than to let one spy go free whose activity might endanger the lives of tens of thousands. And we do not notice the hitch in the argument — namely, that we have no physical instruments to measure the exact amount of harm caused by the detention of the thousand innocents and to compare it with the amount of harm to be expected from the hypothetical spy. We have mistaken a system of empirical rules of thumb, applicable only where conditions are fairly obvious, for a scientific method of ethics. Our quantitative criteria let us down each time just at the point where the pro's and con's are balanced and ethical guidance is most needed. In a revolution traitors and fools have to be shot: but at what precise point does a man who disagrees with me on points of tactics become a traitor or a fool? At what precise point does the healer's lancet change into the butcher's hatchet? At what point does the Dictatorship of the Proletariat change into the Dictatorship of a Bureaucracy? 'Dialectics' tells us that quantity changes into quality; unfortunately we are not told at what point. A system of ethics based on quantitative criteria is a slope on which there is no halt because all is a matter of degrees and not of (qualitative) values.

A related fallacy of Commissar-ethics lies in the tenet that the End justifies the Means. Again, as a rule of thumb the tenet is valid in obvious situations; as a system of philosophy, however, it implies that social developments are as rigidly predictable as only certain isolated mechanical processes are. To proclaim such a crassly fallacious system a supreme law must lead to moral disaster. Three hundred years ago Gallileo already knew that the rules of computation cannot be applied to the symbols 0 and ∞; Commissar-ethics has still to learn that the individual stands in the social equation both for Zero and the Infinite.

(e) 'Yogi-ethics' is the attempt to transfer the values derived from passive contemplation into practical action. This is not an impossible undertaking, but extremely difficult. The Contemplative focuses his attention on the vertical aspect of the staircase and is apt to neglect the intricate factual relations on the horizontal planes. This leads to a naive, amateurish, and often crankish approach to social problems. Such dilettantism is fraught with dangers: the most obvious among them is the danger of quietism, escapism, of sinning by omission. 'So at length, gentlemen, we have reached the conclusion that the best thing for us to do is to do nothing at all, but to sink into a state of contemplative inertia', says another hero of Dostoievsky's.

Closely connected with this is the optimistic reliance on the contemplative faculty in others and the recommendation to listen to the 'inner voice of conscience'. But the 'inner voice' of people inexperienced in the technique of contemplation is simply the echo of unconscious conditioning by convention and tradition. I saw a striking example of this in a little girl of seven, our housekeeper's daughter, who had grown up at a time when to show a light through one's window was a crime and a sin. On the day when the blackout was relaxed in London she came to my room, whose window shone as a bright square in the dark street. She had never seen such a sight before and was horrified. I tried to calm her by appropriate explanations, but the horror did not leave her eyes and I felt that no rational arguments could convince her; and indeed her mother told me the next morning that the child had complained to her with bitter sobs that 'Uncle Arthur does not believe in God'.

Our 'inner voice' regarding social, sexual behaviour, etc., does not differ much from that child's, and to accept it as sole guide before we have mastered the technique of contemplation means simply to vote Tory at the next election. Contemplation should help to free us from the fetters of our conditioning; it is the opposite of dogmatism, scientific or religious. C. S. Lewis in his *Screwtape Letters* makes the devil write to his nephew, whose job is to tempt a Christian convert: 'Above all do not attempt to use science (I mean the real sciences) as a defence against Christianity. They will positively encourage him to think about realities he can't touch and see. There have been sad cases among the modern physicists.' Thus to imply that the only alternative to mechanism is the Church of England, and that the only approach to what we can't touch and see is through Christian dogma, is indeed disarmingly naive coming from a Fellow of Magdalen College in 1944. There is something repulsive in the way the scholastic gloats over the difficulties of science — like a lecherous dotard wooing a girl disappointed by her young lover.

And finally there is the danger, opposite to quietism, of fanatic enthusiasm. The Church Militant, in trying to enforce Change from Within by a radical Change from Without, is caught in the paradox of Ends and Means. Huxley's *Grey Eminence* is a masterly exposition of the Mystic who acts as an inverted Commissar.

XI

These, then, are the pitfalls of yogi-ethics. And yet when all is said, contemplation still remains the only source of guidance in ethical dilemmas where the rule-of-thumb criteria of social utility fail. But the method of contemplation has to be learned just like the methods of scientific observation; and for modern man this is an incomparably more difficult task. The will not to will is a faculty lost on the long, arduous trek. And those who rediscover it become so absorbed into their new world that they lose touch with the old one and their grip on reality; the vertical view of the staircase is as one-sided as the horizontal one. Thus the pendulum goes on swinging from infra red to ultra-violet and back.

EXPLORATIONS

The significance of our era is that science has been forced by its own development to recognize its limitations, and thus to make room again for the other way of knowing, whose place it usurped for almost three centuries. The quantitative method is approaching perfection and with it saturation; its aggressiveness is beginning to change into the modesty of achievement. The flat, two-dimensional plane of nineteenth-century mechanism is gaining depth and height by the erection of the new hierarchy of levels, and the validity of the 'vertical' approach is beginning to be recognized again. This creates an historic opportunity to achieve the synthesis. The basic paradox of man's condition, the conflict between freedom and determinism, ethics and logics, or in whatever symbols we like to express it, can only be resolved if, while thinking and acting on the horizontal plane of our existence, we yet remain constantly aware of the vertical dimension. To attain this awareness without losing the other is perhaps the most necessary and most difficult task that our race ever faced.

But pious exhortations are not enough. To recover the lost half of our personalities, man's wholeness and holiness, the art and science of contemplation has to be learned; and in order to be learned, it has to be taught. But this teaching should not be left to the hacks of yogi-journalese, nor to crank-philosophers who dispense a minimum of information about breathing-technique wrapped in a maximum of obscurantist bombast. I still have to meet the bus-driver who after his nine-hour shift will derive any profit from Heard's *Training for the Life of the Spirit* — though it is meant 'for the people' and only costs eightpence. Contemplation survives only in the East and to learn it we have to turn to the East; but we need qualified interpreters and above all a reinterpretation in the terms and symbols of Western thought. Mere translations are useless, except to those able to devote their whole lives to the task, and to snobs. The Vedanta bores me to death and Tao doesn't mean a thing to me. 'The practiser of Hathayoga', Swatmaram Sami informs me, 'should live alone in a small hermitage or monastery situated in a place free from rocks, water and fire; of the extent of a bow's length and in a fertile country ruled over by a virtuous king where he will not be disturbed.' Think of the bus-driver.

If we are in earnest about the recovery of our lost halves, we have to find new ways of teaching and learning; if we are in earnest, we should not be frightened of aiming at a stage when contemplation is taught in schools side by side with Science and P.T. — and instead of religious dogma. Not to produce cranks: but to re-form man's integrity.

And we have every reason to be in earnest about it. The crisis in Explanation has found its most violent expression in the ethical crisis and its political projection. Its root is the paradox of the individual whole which has to function as a social part; and again of social wholes — classes and nations — which have to be integrated into a whole of a higher order. This integration can never be achieved by Wellsian exhortations addressed to the intellect alone. It has to emerge, facilitated by a 'vertical' approach which brings to the dry concepts of part-ness, love and all-oneness the igniting spark of experienced reality. Neither the saint nor the revolutionary can save us; only the synthesis of the two. Whether we are capable of achieving it I do not know. But if the answer is in the negative, there seems to be no reasonable hope of preventing the destruction of European civilization, either by total war's successor Absolute War, or by Byzantine conquest — within the next few decades.

It needs no great intellectual acumen to see this, and only the inertia of our imagination prevents us from believing it — just as in peace we never believe that there will be a war, and in war that there will ever be peace again. For beneath the Cassandra-voice of reason there is another smug and smiling voice in us, which whispers into our ear the gentle lie that we shall never die, and that to-morrow will be like yesterday.

It is time we learnt to distrust that voice.

October 1944

JONATHAN CAPE PAPERBACKS

Prices obtain in UK only

J. E. NEALE

THE AGE OF CATHERINE DE MEDICI and Essays in Elizabethan History

JCP1   10s. 6d. *net*

Professor Neale gives a clear and concise survey of the period of the French wars of religion, describing the religious and social conditions which provoked them. THE AGE OF CATHERINE DE MEDICI provides the continental background to Elizabethan history, many aspects of which are discussed in ESSAYS IN ELIZABETHAN HISTORY. Professor Neale shows how the past throws light upon the present, as well as the present on the past.

GARRETT MATTINGLY

CATHERINE OF ARAGON

JCP2   10s. 6d. *net*

For twenty-four years Catherine of Aragon was the wife of Henry VIII. England loved her; Henry loved, respected and finally feared her. Wolsey hated her. Twice she saved England, once from invasion, once from civil war. Garrett Mattingly has clothed the story of her life—uncovered in years of painstaking research—in rich and vivid prose.

'There is no doubt that he has written what is now the standard work on Catherine.'—*Observer*

A. L. ROWSE

SIR RICHARD GRENVILLE OF THE *REVENGE*

JCP3   10s. 6d. *net*

'Herein lies one of the notable features of Mr. Rowse's biography. He knows his sixteenth-century Cornishmen as few or no others do … Mr. Rowse has found an unpublished document in the Spanish archives, describing the battle and written apparently by someone aboard the Spanish flagship. It is an important discovery, both for the intrinsic merits of the description and because the existing evidence about this famous battle is slight and extremely confusing … The picture of Grenville which we now have is the traditional story, a mixture of heroism and heroics; the story of a man who scorned to fly from the enemy or surrender. It is truly Elizabethan … There is no doubt that Mr. Rowse's book will establish itself as the standard biography of Grenville, and he deserves our unstinted thanks for the patient research that he has put into it.'

J. E. NEALE in the *Sunday Times*

GEORGE BURTON ADAMS

CONSTITUTIONAL HISTORY OF ENGLAND

JCP4   15s. *net*

This standard work first appeared in 1921, since when it has gone through fourteen impressions and has been in steady demand. In his original introduction the author wrote: 'I have endeavoured in writing this book to keep constantly in view the needs of the general reader and of the college student.' There is by now ample evidence that he has succeeded.

GAETANO SALVEMINI

THE FRENCH REVOLUTION 1788–1792

JCP5   10s. 6d. *net*

This book is a study of the break-up of the feudal regime in France, of the early years of the Revolution and of the leading personalities who took part in it. The author makes clear the underlying causes of the Revolution and the political and intellectual forces which sprang from these causes and have, in fact, led to all the great movements of our time.

'His book is evidence that history ... can be exciting as well as scholarly.'—*Sunday Times*.

Translated from the Italian by I. M. Rawson.

JOHN BOWLE

POLITICS AND OPINION IN THE NINETEENTH CENTURY

JCP6   12s. 6d. *net*

The theme of this book is the development of liberal-social-democratic political thought from the Romantic Age to the early twentieth century, the attacks made upon it by doctrines of class war, nationalism and nihilism, and its later reinforcement by the beginnings of modern sociology.

'This is a good book, comprehensive, vigorous and easy to read ... The book is a monument to the industry, impartiality and talent for lively exposition of its author.'—*Manchester Guardian*

DAVID HARRIS WILLSON

KING JAMES VI & I

JCP7   12s. 6d. *net*

Professor Willson has written a biography of James the Sixth of Scotland and First of England which is at the same time a contribution to scholarship and a fascinating, witty story for the general reader. King James was a baffling combination of learning and pedantry, shrewdness and folly, lofty aspirations and contemptible practice, whose interests included theology, natural history, poetry and witchcraft, not to mention hunting. The Scottish part of his life, so dramatic, but so complicated and baffling to the student of English history, here finds its proper treatment.

'A brilliant and fair-minded book.' — *The Times*

PHYLLIS DOYLE

A HISTORY OF POLITICAL THOUGHT

JCP8   10s. 6d. *net*

'This is an able and interesting account of the chief theories of government from Plato to T. H. Green ... In Miss Doyle's book the analysis of the most famous works on political theory is very well done and the sketch of the political conditions which were the occasions for each theory is vivid and vigorous.' — *Spectator*

PHILIP WOODRUFF

THE MEN WHO RULED INDIA

Vol. I: The Founders   JCP9   10s. 6d. *net*

This is the story of the men who ruled India for over three centuries. It is a story about men, not about tendencies or policies, an attempt to show what these men were like, what they thought and felt, how they came to rule so many people with so little use of force. And yet, because they were responsible for running the country, an account of what they did must touch at point after point on the whole history of India. The author's method is biographical; he chooses one man who seems representative and gives some account of his life and opinions, leaving out a hundred and passing on ruthlessly to the next, including in his gallery obscure as well as famous men.

'It will take its place as a standard work.' — *Economist*

THE MEN WHO RULED INDIA

Vol. II: The Guardians   JCP10   10s. 6d. *net*

In his second volume, THE GUARDIANS, Mr. Woodruff carries the tale of THE MEN WHO RULED INDIA from the Mutiny to the end of British rule on August 15th, 1947.

'As in the first volume, against the background of high policy and administrative problems, its author deftly weaves a glowing tapestry of the lives, personalities, eccentricities and intimate thoughts of some of the handful of men who composed that "impartial and immovable civil service"—the Indian Civil Service.' — *Daily Telegraph*

DUFF COOPER

TALLEYRAND
JCP11   13s. 6d. *net*

'Mr. Duff Cooper has a perfect gift of selection. He has woven his tangled material into a tissue of silken smoothness. If biography is to be defined as "the history of an individual conceived as a work of art", then Mr. Duff Cooper's book should serve as an exhibit. It is historical in that it conveys the proportions of events; it describes an individual, since it concentrates on character; and it is, without question, a deliberate work of art.'—HAROLD NICOLSON

'A brilliant portrait painted upon a background of sound judgment and historical knowledge.'—DESMOND McCARTHY

C. V. WEDGWOOD

THE THIRTY YEARS WAR
JCP12   15s. *net*

'A book which is, and will long remain, the standard authority on the subject ... I doubt if there is anything in any European language which covers the ground so comprehensively and so satisfactorily.'
A. L. ROWSE in the Spectator

'This is one of the best pieces of historical work that I have encountered for a long while, and I most heartily wish it an audience worthy of its merits.'—G. M. YOUNG in the *Sunday Times*

C. V. WEDGWOOD

THOMAS WENTWORTH First Earl of Strafford 1593–1641
A Revaluation
JCP13   13s. 6d. *net*

'A quarter of a century ago Miss Wedgwood delighted us with a biography of Strafford and she has now entirely rewritten this with the help of new materials not then available. The result is superb ... She is wonderfully fair and leaves the tragic and vigorous story to speak for itself. In her pages we seem to live Strafford's life till that last day.'—ROGER FULFORD, *Evening Standard*

'No more satisfactory history of Strafford and his age is likely to supersede this brilliant book. The scholarship is first class, the character-drawing excellent, the style most distinguished.'
CONSTANTIA MAXWELL in the Sunday Times

'The result is an enthralling and dramatic book, written with Miss Wedgwood's wonted craftsmanship ... Miss Wedgwood's book will be read with pleasure by specialist and non-specialist alike. No one could fail to admire her artistry and persuasiveness, or the honesty of her attempt to rethink her subject.'
CHRISTOPHER HILL in the Spectator

THE DRAWINGS OF LEONARDO DA VINCI

JCP 14   320 pages of illustrations   18s. *net*

This book was originally planned and about two-thirds of the photographs collected by Sir Kenneth Clark. With his approval this collection of Leonardo da Vinci's drawings, the most comprehensive ever to be published, has been completed by Mr A. E. Popham, formerly Keeper of Prints and Drawings, British Museum.

'The editor in this outstanding instance has performed his task with the finest judgment and scholarship.'—*The Times Literary Supplement*

'This is a book which will rightly take its place as an important contribution to the proper understanding of the stature of Leonardo as an artist and draughtsman, essential to the student and both enlightening and interesting to the general reader.'—*Studio*

W. H. DAVIES

THE AUTOBIOGRAPHY OF A SUPER-TRAMP

JCP 15   10s. 6d. *net*

The first edition, in 1908, of this now famous book was prefaced by Bernard Shaw, to whom the author had sent his manuscript. This preface is retained in the present edition, not only because it contains interesting biographical information but also because it describes the impact made by the book upon readers at that time and still makes upon readers of the present day.

'I have read it through from beginning to end,' says Shaw, 'and would have read more of it had there been any more to read.' He praised the book for its 'very curious quality'. So many readers have agreed with him and the book has been in such constant demand for over half a century now that it can rightly be described as a minor classic.

PETER FLEMING

BRAZILIAN ADVENTURE   JCP 16   12s. 6d. *net*

'Peter Fleming's BRAZILIAN ADVENTURE is the best travel book I have read for a long time. It is crammed with sound observation, good writing, humour, and a unique blend of disillusion, foolhardiness and high spirits.'—J. B. PRIESTLEY

'This account of the expedition has that essential double interest which is characteristic of all really great books of adventure. Mr. Fleming has the most delightful sense of humour and he writes brilliantly.'—DAVID GARNETT in the *New Statesman*

C. A. R. CROSLAND
THE FUTURE OF SOCIALISM   JCP 17   15s. *net*

Mr Crosland, in preparing this new edition, has found it unnecessary to revise the substance of the argument and has concentrated on shortening the book; this he has succeeded in doing without losing anything of importance.

'THE FUTURE OF SOCIALISM is very good indeed. It is within its chosen field exhaustive, written with a professional economic, political and sociological equipment, and illuminated by touches of wit; the product of a cultivated and humane intelligence. It is a major work and no one must in future take part in the current and, I trust, growing and continuing controversy on Socialism, without having read it.'—JOHN STRACHEY, *New Statesman*

'He eschews expediency and proclaims ethical principles for his politics, like the first fine Christian Socialists in the last century, or the late-lamented Evan Durbin in this. Secondly he has, accordingly, the courage of his convictions, and scant respect for the wan, worn, weak dogmas of British Socialism. And lastly, he is an economic realist who loves our humane, urbane, West European culture, who wishes to generalize it for modern masses, and who is inspired to write trenchantly and well. Tories, Liberals and men of no political abode should read a book into which he has put so much thought and courage ... his fellow-Socialists need to read it even more.'
GRAHAM HUTTON, Spectator

ARTHUR KOESTLER
THE YOGI AND THE COMMISSAR
JCP 18   10s. 6d. net

Arthur Koestler has divided this volume into three parts: 'Meanderings', 'Exhortations', 'Explanations'. The first two parts consist of important essays on literature, politics and the problems of our time. The third part, 'Explorations', contains a well-documented survey of the Soviet experiment with the conclusions to be derived from it. As Harold Laski wrote on its first appearance, 'nobody needs to be told that whatever Mr Koestler writes will be full of insight and written with an imaginative brilliance that cannot fail to stimulate'.

CHARLES M. DOUGHTY
TRAVELS IN ARABIA DESERTA

Introduction by T. E. Lawrence
Illustrated

Vol. I   JCP 19   25s. *net*
Vol. II   JCP 20   25s. *net*

'Were I to be asked to choose a single modern book in which the virtues which I most admire are exemplified, I should, I think, pick Doughty from the shelf.'—SIR ARNOLD WILSON, *Observer*

'He conveys the whole character of a land and a people and a way of life. A parched fiery wind blows across his pages. They evoke with almost painful vividness dry air and a remorseless sun beating down on interminable sand.'—MALCOLM MUGGERIDGE, *Time and Tide*

KAREN BLIXEN
OUT OF AFRICA JCP 21   13s. 6d. *net*

'Karen Blixen's second book—her masterpiece—first appeared in 1937. She translated it from her own Danish. Sometimes she reversed this process, which was always a painful one. It is one of those works that appeal particularly to writers. It is not surprising that Hemingway, Laurens van der Post, Gerald Hanley and Thomas Hinde should have revered OUT OF AFRICA. They knew and know Kenya. But Malcolm Lowry, a very different sort of writer, who had never set foot on the ground she made so much her own, was never without a copy of it, wherever he found himself. The very simplicity of the book makes it difficult to describe. It is at once intensely personal and supremely objective. She identified herself with the green hills and blue horizons of Kenya. Her patrician spirit enabled her to evoke that magic landscape, its people and its animals, without sentimentality or proprietariness. She was there from 1913 to 1931 and missed the subsequent confusions, but this marvellous book—it is full of marvels—can never lose its validity.'—JOHN DAVENPORT

KILVERT'S DIARY

Selections from the Diary of the Rev. Francis Kilvert, 1870-9

Chosen, Edited and Introduced by William Plomer

With decorations by John Piper JCP 22   13s. 6d. *net*

This Diary, which paints a unique picture of country life in mid-Victorian times, has come to be recognized as a classic: its author has been compared to Dorothy Wordsworth, whom he admired, and even to Pepys. It was kept from January 1870 until March 1879, and was closely written in 22 notebooks.

'The discovery of the extensive diary of the Reverend Francis Kilvert some years ago added a new classic to English diary literature. The original selections, in three volumes, appeared under the careful and sympathetic editorship of William Plomer between 1938 and 1940. The present abridged one-volume edition with decorations by John Piper has been admirably prepared and selected by the same hand.

For Kilvert fans it may serve as a travelling companion or bedside book; for the uninitiated it is the perfect introduction.'

C. V. WEDGWOOD, *Time and Tide*

'The best picture of quiet vicarage life in Victorian England that has yet been given us.'—JOHN BETJEMAN, *Daily Herald*

FELIX GREENE

THE WALL HAS TWO SIDES JCP 23 13s. 6d. *net*

'No one can travel in China without feeling enchanted, angry, over-whelmed, frustrated, touched, saddened, optimistic, puzzled—everything but bored. There is a prevailing opinion in the West that the Chinese are being threatened, brainwashed, or bludgeoned into work of national industrialization; that a small group of power-hungry Communist leaders have fastened themselves on to an unwilling and resentful population and are driving them fiercely forward against their will. I believe this picture is the very opposite of the truth.'

So writes journalist Felix Greene of the 10,000-mile journey he made through China to take a close look at her social and economic awakening. Visiting communes, factories, schools, hospitals, prisons and law courts, he talked to peasants, workers, intellectuals and civil servants without restraint.

'The most valuable account since Edgar Snow exploded his Red Star over China twenty-five years ago.'

NICHOLAS WOLLASTON, *Spectator*

THEODORE H. WHITE

THE MAKING OF THE PRESIDENT, 1960

JCP 24 13s. 6d. *net*

'Theodore H. White's THE MAKING OF THE PRESIDENT, 1960 describes the first two parts of his campaign. It is a triumph of political reporting. In organisation and sweep, in the selection of telling detail and social comment, it exceeds journalism and approaches literature. It is even superior to Mencken's classic of 1952, MAKING A PRESIDENT.'—ANDREW SINCLAIR, *The Guardian*

'His account of the final struggle is outshone by his brilliant and exhaustive narrative of how the two candidates won their parties' nomination ... he reports the course of events fully and fairly and he analyses the complexities of the American political scene with assured skill.'—DAVID BUTLER, *Sunday Telegraph*